Re-citing Marlowe

To my parents, Jean and Peter,
whose love and support made my doctoral thesis and this book possible.

To my darling Simon,
for his love and support.

Re-citing Marlowe

Approaches to the Drama

CLARE HARRAWAY

Routledge
Taylor & Francis Group

LONDON AND NEW YORK

First published 2000 by Ashgate Publishing

Reissued 2018 by Routledge
2 Park Square, Milton Park, Abingdon, Oxon OX14 4RN
711 Third Avenue, New York, NY 10017, USA

Routledge is an imprint of the Taylor & Francis Group, an informa business

Publisher's Note
The publisher has gone to great lengths to ensure the quality of this reprint but points out that some imperfections in the original copies may be apparent.

Disclaimer
The publisher has made every effort to trace copyright holders and welcomes correspondence from those they have been unable to contact.

A Library of Congress record exists under LC control number: 99068870

ISBN 13: 978-1-138-70104-5 (hbk)
ISBN 13: 978-1-138-70103-8 (pbk)
ISBN 13: 978-1-315-20428-4 (ebk)

Contents

Introduction

Words Are What Remain

In an effort to find a beginning for the present work on Christopher Marlowe, I will first rehearse a selection of introductions to Marlovian studies written over the last fifty years or so.

Is this a true story?

Yes, in the sense that it is fact rather than fiction. The people in it are real people, the events I describe really happened, the quotations are taken verbatim from documents or books of the period. Where there is dialogue I have reconstructed it from reported speech. I have not invented anything.

C. Nicholl, *The Reckoning: The Murder of Christopher Marlowe*, 1992, p. 3.

The following chapters are an imperfect attempt to trace the dominant psychological themes in Christopher Marlowe's plays. They began with a conviction that our tendency to ignore or minimize Marlowe's homosexuality was effectively limiting our understanding of his work, and they evolved over a considerable period of time, part of which was spent assimilating psychoanalytic theory which I quickly recognized as the type of psychological speculation most likely to prove helpful in analyzing Marlowe's work.

C. B. Kuriyama, *Hammer or Anvil: Psychological Patterns in Christopher Marlowe's Plays*, 1980, p. ix.

It used to be thought that, because Christopher Marlowe was a University man and William Shakespeare was not, that Marlowe was socially the superior. We now know that the exact opposite was the case. Shakespeare's family background at Stratford was solid and respectable, with an Alderman for father, and his mother, an Arden, connected with gentlefolk. His life and career were in keeping.

Everything about Marlowe was unrespectable, except his genius; and that was so original and striking that we have to deplore his death – which he brought upon himself – as the greatest loss to our literature.

A. L. Rowse, *Christopher Marlowe: A Biography*, 1964, p. vii.

The first obligation of a study of the mind of Marlowe is to interpret all the available biographical evidence of his thought. This basic material, the Rosetta stone for all that follows, is here treated at the head of the section on religion, since it falls almost exclusively within that field. The extant plays and poems are next to be interpreted, only secondarily as separate works of art, and primarily as mirrors of the thought, learning, and character of their creator.

P. H. Kocher, *Christopher Marlowe: A Study of his Thought, Learning and Character*, 1946, p. 3.

The problem about the title of this book is the 'and'. The relationship between Marlowe and the Elizabethan theatre is concealed from focus for the greater part of the book. There are general arguments about Elizabethan theatre and specific studies of plays of Marlowe, but the connection is not explicitly theorised.

The problem is to know what is being connected with what. For a start, the name 'Marlowe' may be taken in several different senses.

S. Shepherd, *Marlowe and the Politics of the Elizabethan Theatre*, 1986, p. xi.

These passages bring together a variety of twentieth-century critical approaches to Marlowe which include biography, psychoanalysis and cultural materialism. However, despite their apparent methodological distinctiveness, these extracts betray a common concern with the figure of the author: a concern, moreover, which I will argue characterizes Marlovian scholarship to its detriment. Deploying the man as the marker of authenticity, each of the critics cited above recovers their own personal Marlowe: for A. L. Rowse he is the Renaissance dramatist who is not Shakespeare; for Constance Brown Kuriyama he is the poet obsessed by his homosexuality; for Paul H. Kocher he is the sombre religious reformer; while for Simon Shepherd and Charles Nicholl respectively he is the figure who draws together the plays and political factions of the period. The conspicuous proteanism of the character conjured by the word 'Marlowe' is, nevertheless, strikingly ignored by most of these critics. Shepherd alone goes on to explain the multiple significances which surround the dramatist's name.[1] More insidious than the revivification of the author to fight the critic's battles in the first four of these extracts is the repeatedly-conveyed impression that Marlowe is in some sense an effortlessly recuperable character. Implying the essential knowability of the author in their assertions of truth and reality and their cajoling phrases, such as 'We now know',[2] most of these critics seem to consider the recovery of Marlowe to be a relatively easy task. As simple as putting back together the scattered pieces of a jigsaw puzzle, the process of refiguring Marlowe, described above, discloses a belief in the essentially static and accessible nature of the dramatist.

This sense of the dramatist's accessibility and recuperability has prevailed in Marlovian scholarship for centuries. It depends on the assumption, which has remained largely unchallenged, that Marlowe could not help putting his personality into his plays. The dramatist is consequently made available to scholarship by a process of textual excavation which uncovers the plays to reveal the man, and vice versa. Illustrating the extent to which Marlowe studies is obsessed by the figure of the dramatist, Thomas Dabbs employs the canon of nineteenth-century Marlovian criticism as a model or exemplum of the Romantic rehabilitation of the author. In *Reforming Marlowe* Dabbs concludes that studies of Marlowe have 'never recovered from the various and disparate turns that his biography took during the Victorian era'.[3]   He maintains, moreover, that modern critics still return to the circumstances of Marlowe's life 'as if they were recent issues brought up by more scientifically expansive investigations'.[4] In a similar vein, Kenneth Friedenreich introduces his annotated bibliography of Marlowe criticism with eight propositions about the author which he argues have blighted twentieth-century scholarship. Friedenreich lists the following assumptions about the dramatist:

> 1) that Marlowe wrote about passions rather than people; 2) that his plays frequently degenerate into nonsense or excess; 3) perhaps most important, his characters invariably mouth his own held opinions; 4) that his characters were mere puppets, vessels containing his ideals and opinions so that, 5) Marlowe lacks sympathy or compassion for ordinary people; 6) he has no sense of humor; 7) he cannot fully realize a plot and is disinterested in dramatic structure; 8) he is a great poet but not a great playwright.[5]

The figure of the author is clearly identified here by Friedenreich as the locus of critical myopia.   The compulsion to return to Marlowe's life for explanations of his work is, according to Friedenreich, not a consequence of the author's peculiar subjectivity but rather a result of the obsessive way in which criticism has constructed Marlowe in relation to Shakespeare.[6]

The astonishing availability of Marlowe to the processes of biographical archaeology is dependent upon viewing his career in relation to the life of another supposedly more elusive and certainly more celebrated artist – Shakespeare. As A. L. Rowse makes clear in the extract cited above, Marlowe is the exact opposite of Shakespeare; he is not gentle, not solid and not respectable. It is this nonconformity, however, which seems to make Marlowe's personality impossible to conceal. The logic of this argument is tantalizingly inescapable as resistance is clearly more conspicuous than consent. However, the characterization of Marlowe's and Shakespeare's lives in binary opposition importantly fails to disguise the insinuation that Shakespeare is the greater artist because his personality is less available from his works. Marlovian criticism consequently boasts its ability to rehabilitate Marlowe, only to reveal that the man thereby recovered is artistically and personally inferior to Shakespeare. Scholarship's rationalization is obvious here; if Marlowe can be comprehended with such ease he cannot be worthy of great critical appreciation. As A. L. Rowse maintains in his biography of Marlowe, 'No writer was ever more autobiographical than he was – it was a serious limitation upon him'.[7] Moreover, Rowse goes on to marshal Shakespeare as the yardstick of creative genius against which Marlowe fails to measure up. He claims Marlowe 'tells us a great deal about himself – where Shakespeare, the true dramatist, holds himself behind his creations, is so elusive: we can only track him indirectly in his affinities, his sympathies and preferences'.[8] The Marlowe Rowse refigures is a pale imitation of an inexplicable and therefore more accomplished artist. The fraudulent nature of Rowse's claim is, however, exposed by Richard Wilson in his recent examination of the modernist recuperation of Shakespeare in *Will Power*. Wilson notes that the 'popular misconception of Shakespeare's transcendental anonymity has been perpetuated in defiance of ... massive documentation'.[9] Wilson goes on to explain that the critical blindspot which characterizes the scholarly perception of Shakespeare's life is because 'we actually know *too much* about the Stratford man ... one cannot yet tolerate so much reality'.[10]

The refiguring of Marlowe the man falters factually and theoretically here; Marlowe is not only as knowable as Shakespeare in terms of how much historical information we have about him, he is also as impossible to know as Shakespeare because selfhood is not considered to be a stable and recoverable entity in the postmodern age.[11] Apparently unmindful of both these points, Marlovian criticism remains premised on the availability of the author to scholarly scrutiny. This assumption informs critical studies as well as ostensibly biographical studies of Marlowe. In their recent collection of Marlovian sources, Vivien Thomas and William Tydeman bring together a number of extracts from texts which are meant to be relevant to Marlowe's canon. An admirably scholarly and undoubtedly useful work, Thomas's and Tydeman's collection is nevertheless constructed on the notion that all the information concerning the life and work of the author is easily accessible to the reader; it implies that knowledge of Marlowe can somehow be finite and containable. More than fifty years prior to this work, John Bakeless performed a similar polymathic project in the two volumes of his *Tragicall History* which were meant 'to bring together everything that can now be known about Christopher Marlowe'.[12] Manufacturing myths of authorial and artistic availability, such studies shackle critical responses to Marlowe with 'truths' which are actually no more than theories.

The apparently compulsive recourse of Marlowe criticism to the figure of the author, whether for biographical, psychoanalytical or historical studies, belies a paranoid anxiety about interpretative proliferation. For by circumscribing all investigations of Marlowe's work with the figure of the man who wrote them, scholarship effectively reveals an attempt to confine the variety and extent of possible readings. The practice of critical containment at play in Marlovian scholarship operates as the perfect example of what has come to be known as 'the author function'. In Michel Foucault's influential article 'What is an author?', the critic proposes that an author is 'the ideological figure by which one marks the manner in which we fear the proliferation of meaning'.[13] An indication of critical anxiety, according to Foucault, the notion of the author provides scholarship with a means to limit signification. Thus when a text can be tied to a writer whose opinions, prejudices and period of existence are thought to be knowable, a whole variety of meanings can be dismissed as inapplicable, ahistorical or just plain wrong. Conceding this circumstance in terms which ironically echo Foucault's own assertion, Andrew Butcher notes in his introduction to William Urry's *Christopher Marlowe and Canterbury* that an understanding of the social construction of the author achieves 'a significant limitation of the possibilities in the interpretation of the works'.[14] The author is therefore the concept which polices meaning in all areas of textual criticism. What I am arguing here, however, is that the construction of the author functions in Marlowe criticism in a more pronounced way than in almost any other branch of literary scholarship. The reasons for this circumstance are twofold and have been touched on in part already.

The impulse to refigure Marlowe is motivated by two critical desires. Firstly, the desire to canonize Shakespeare as a greater poet and a greater man than his rival Marlowe. Secondly, the understandable critical longing to make sense of the mysterious events surrounding Marlowe's death. Obviously, both these points disclose a common need to render Marlowe intelligible by painting his character with very bold brush strokes. For if Marlowe is sexually, religiously and politically unorthodox, he is not simply a more exciting figure to conjure, he is also a more useful one. Indeed, it is only by categorizing Marlowe as a rebel that scholarship can describe Shakespeare as a liberal humanist. However, what criticism often fails to notice is the flimsiness of the evidence which refigures a militant Marlowe. Apart from the highly ambiguous information contained in his plays, the only official documentation which proves Marlowe's heterodoxy is contained in the depositions of a tortured man and the note of a known government informer.[15]

Contrary to conventional responses to debates about the nature of Marlowe's character, I would like to argue that the significance of the evidence claiming to describe his opinions does not depend on its authenticity but rather upon its very textuality. Baines's famous assertion that Marlowe believed 'all they that loue not Tobacco & Boies were fooles',[16] consequently need not be viewed as a statement either of fact or of fiction but rather as one of a series of documents which are open to textual interpretation. The potential to resurrect a fixed and stable self for the dramatist remains impossible whether or not Baines was telling the truth, as language cannot convey either character or intention in an unproblematic and easily recuperable way. It is, therefore, as irresponsible to assert that Marlowe was a homosexual because he wrote a play about the reign of Edward II, as it is to take Baines's comments as a statement of fact; both these notions are evidenced by language which does not offer uncomplicated access to a singular, unitary meaning. The fact that all writing is open to multiple interpretations simply underlines this point. I have therefore set myself the task of redirecting the movement of Marlovian criticism from its preoccupation with the man, to the texts written by and about him. My analysis consequently refuses to posit evidence and instead turns to exegesis. Indeed in *The Reckoning*, Charles Nicholl explains that 'Words are what remain of Christopher Marlowe'.[17] Probably the only indisputable fact which criticism has brought to light thus far, the very textuality of what scholars call 'Marlowe' is central to a reappraisal of the canon the name denotes. Importantly implicated in this flurry of paper which surrounds the modern construction of Marlowe are the words of his critics. I shall therefore consider in more detail the prominent branches of twentieth-century author-based Marlovian criticism, before explaining how my own method of analysis differs. Marlowe scholarship can generally be divided into four separate approaches: factual and fictional biography, comparison with Shakespeare, psychoanalysis and historicism. I will consider the most significant contributions to each of these genres, beginning with factual and fictional biography.

Factual and Fictional Biography

The most recent and certainly most fascinating Marlowe biography to date must surely be Charles Nicholl's *The Reckoning*. Through an exhaustive process of documentary investigation, Nicholl reconstructs the events leading up to Marlowe's murder in Deptford. Providing a series of compelling descriptions of Marlowe's accomplices and ultimately assailants, Nicholl illuminates the murky world of Elizabethan espionage. However, setting to one side Nicholl's many remarkable accomplishments in *The Reckoning*, his suspenseful 'whodunnit' is framed by an awkward appeal to the reader on a personal, almost emotional, level. It is in this vein that Nicholl introduces his work:

> It all happened a long time ago, but I believe it was a case of murder and an unsolved murder does not really age. It continues to require our attention, our questions, our unease. We owe the dead man something, and these are what we have to offer. We may never find the truth, but we can dig away some of the lies, and perhaps find beneath them a faint preserved outline where the truth once lay.[18]

Instilling his project with a dramatic sense of urgency, Nicholl seeks to persuade the reader that he has a responsibility to the murdered author. It is this sort of highly subjective engagement with the dramatist which characterizes the majority of Marlowe biographies and which encourages the inappropriate critical obsession with the life of the man.

What are, for the most part, isolated moments of subjectivity in Nicholl's biography, are transformed by other biographers into the dominant tone of their works. Dedicated Marlowe biographers, such as Della Hilton, A. D. Wraight and Virginia F. Stern, do not restrict their emotional outbursts to the opening pages and instead pepper their studies with personal comments about the author. Epitomizing this approach is the biographers' unembarrassed use of either the dramatist's Christian name or a diminutive of it. For instance, in the flamboyantly titled *Who was Kit Marlowe?: The Story of the Poet and Playwright*, Della Hilton constantly refers to the dramatist by a nickname. Similarly in *In Search of Christopher Marlowe*, A. D. Wraight and Virginia F. Stern conclude their description of the dramatist's murder by bemoaning 'poor Christopher lying there'.[19] Having personally invested so much in their work, it is not surprising that these biographers are reluctant finally to make an end of their hero. In *Who was Kit Marlowe?*, Della Hilton claims that the dramatist did not die at Deptford. She explains that the man actually murdered was a fourth person, one Morley, who had accompanied Poley in the Netherlands.[20] As the victim's facial wound made him unidentifiable, Morley's name was switched with Marlowe's.[21] Forced into hiding at Scadbury, according to Hilton, Marlowe busied himself with a draft of *Macbeth* which another playwright was later to finish.[22] Hilton then argues that, having made a start on an eighth play, Marlowe took his own life 'because of the desolation of anonymity spreading out before him'.[23] If correct, these events would certainly prove the old adage about fact being stranger than fiction. However, supported by no historical evidence, Hilton's twist in the tale reveals more about criticism's desperation than Marlowe's. Such fanciful stories disclose scholarship's willingness to contort the available information in order to construct its preferred Marlowe.

In spite of the avowedly historical nature of *Who was Kit Marlowe?*, Hilton's work usefully functions as a marker of the blurring of fact and fiction which most biographies of Marlowe perform. This process of fictionalization was, however, already under way long before the twentieth century. Indeed it would seem that from the very moment of Marlowe's death the man became myth. Even the earliest accounts of his murder colourfully describe the crime as an event of more than earthly significance. William Vaughan maintains in the second edition of *The Golden-Grove* (1608) that the manner of the author's death shows the divine justice which God executes upon 'impious atheists'.[24] In a similar vein Thomas Beard famously recalls the murder in his *Theatre of God's Judgments* (1597), explaining that the dying Marlowe 'euen cursed and blasphemed to his last gaspe, and togither with his breath an oath flew out of his mouth ... that is not only a manifest signe of God's iudgement, but also an horrible and fearefull terrour to all that beheld him.'[25] Commentators determinedly make Marlowe's demise meaningful, then, by endowing his murder with multiple layers of significance. What is more, reading his death through the presumed circumstances of his life, scholarship's mythologizing turns upon a matter of moral judgement – God's, history's and ultimately criticism's.

Exerting a powerful hold on a writer's imagination, the myth of Marlowe has spawned numerous fictional works. Authors have transformed the words which remain into yet more words by exploiting the interpretative possibilities inherent in the details of the dramatist's life and death. Fictionalized by such notables as the writer Anthony Burgess and even the actor Herbert Lom, the story of Marlowe has proved fertile ground for speculation. In *Enter a Spy: The Double Life of Christopher Marlowe*, Herbert Lom presents a potential film version of the tale in which Marlowe is depicted as a heterosexual involved in a romantic affair with Frances Walsingham. Describing his project in the introduction, Lom explains: 'It is history as it *might* have been'.[26] Testimony to the very textuality of what is known about Marlowe, these accounts manipulate the opportunities which the vagaries of history present. Thus the doubts and uncertainties of the dramatist's documented life become the coincidences and significances of fiction.

Typifying this circumstance, Liam Maguire's novel *Icarus Flying: The Tragical Story of Christopher Marlowe* (1993) depicts Marlowe murdered not by Frizer but by Richard Baines, the reporter of his alleged unorthodoxies. When another secret agent named Morley or Marley is slain at Deptford, Thomas Walsingham takes advantage of the situation to swap the identity of the dead man with Marlowe's. The dramatist refuses, however, to comply with this plan to avoid his interrogation on charges of heresy, and flees from his erstwhile friends at Scadbury to London, where Richard Baines kills him, throwing his corpse into the Thames. Maguire's retelling of events is obviously indebted to Della Hilton's research. Yet another example of the confusion of fact and fiction which the genre of biography cannot help initiating, Maguire's novel makes explicit the ambiguity of its relationship with reality on its cover. Decorated with a sketch which substitutes Marlowe's face for that of the magician's on the title page of the 1624 *Doctor Faustus* quarto, Maguire's novel openly represents its mixing of the genres of biography, drama, fiction and history.

Perhaps the most fitting fictional metamorphosis Marlowe has undergone thus far is Peter Whelan's translation of the dramatist's life into drama. First performed in 1992 by the Royal Shakespeare Company at The Other Place, Whelan's *The School of Night* stages Marlowe's final months. Significantly, however, Whelan's play fails to focus solely on Marlowe. Instead, *The School of Night* is an artistic parable describing the inevitable destruction of a lesser writer by a truly great one. Depicting the Bloomian struggle to overcome influence, the drama shows how Marlowe loses the will to live when he meets an actor going by the name of Stone who is actually William Shakespeare.[27] Whelan shamelessly presents Shakespeare as the transcendent genius who marks the dawning of the individual talent. Unlike Marlowe, Stone/Shakespeare composes verse flawlessly and at such a rate that his rival suggests he must have 'a mechanism in his brain that transfers his thoughts to paper, fair copied and corrected'.[28] Not only a poetic superman, Stone/Shakespeare is also an amateur philosopher who propounds a series of theories about art. Disagreeing with the other characters about ensemble creativity, Stone/Shakespeare maintains that a play is a 'unique vision of the mind ... Unique is one. I. Me. Singular. Not the many ... My mind's purpose'.[29] Stone/Shakespeare dismisses both audience and actors alike to claim that drama is the unmediated outpouring of Romantic genius. Not surprisingly, Marlowe is more than a little shaken by Stone's/Shakespeare's assertions so that when he is offered the opportunity to switch identities with a corpse and escape to Venice, he refuses. Apparently reading the death of his identity as an augury of Stone's/Shakespeare's artistic ascendance, Marlowe turns on his accomplices complaining, 'You're not killing me off. (*Thinks of* STONE.) And nor is he'.[30] In the ensuing struggle Marlowe is stabbed. He instructs Frizer 'Not in the heart! In the head!'[31] Provoking the very details of his own murder, Marlowe is portrayed as an author who surrenders to the inevitable victory of a greater artist. In keeping with this interpretation, the final scene of the play shows Stone/Shakespeare standing over Marlowe's unmarked grave: indebted yet ultimately triumphant. Leaving a powerful impression on the imagination, it is this image of Shakespeare as Marlowe's inheritor which recurs in many accounts of the dramatist, and which I will examine next.

Comparison with Shakespeare

The keynote in an impressive collection of essays on Marlowe, Kenneth Muir's 'Marlowe and Shakespeare' claims that Shakespeare's career was contingent upon Marlowe's death:

> A few months before Leslie Hotson discovered that Marlowe had been killed by a future churchwarden, Clemence Dane, better known as a novelist, wrote a verse play entitled *Will Shakespeare* in which Marlowe is killed by his great rival. Although literally untrue, the act has a certain symbolic value: it could be said that the most important event in Shakespeare's career took place in Eleanor Bull's tavern at Deptford. For the next few years Shakespeare was without a serious rival.[32]

Muir's article characteristically introduces a study of Marlowe's work with a description of his contribution to another playwright's career. Lashing together the lives of Marlowe and Shakespeare, Muir typically redirects critical attention from Marlowe's own achievements to those of Shakespeare. In this way, Marlowe is made significant only by comparison; he is the inferior precursor of a great poetic genius. Moreover, constructing Marlowe as Shakespeare's second-rate father, Muir fails to recognize the dramatists as exact contemporaries; they were both born in 1564. In similar chronologically-confused depictions, some critics place Marlowe artistically after Shakespeare as the imitator of a more important talent. In his *Theatrum Poetarum* of 1675, Edward Phillips calls Marlowe 'a kind of second Shakespeare',[33] while Harry Levin suggests 'Marlowe's name is the one that comes after Shakespeare's in any discussion of English tragedy'.[34] Thus there is an innate inequality, either artistic or personal, implied by such comparisons.

Comparison between writers of the same period who work in the same genre is probably inevitable; the degree to which Marlowe and Shakespeare are compared is, however, unprecedented. Arguably contrasted with one purpose in mind, the juxtaposition of the two dramatists means Shakespeare's character and work can be glorified at the expense of Marlowe's. Central to such analogies is the assumption, mentioned earlier, that Marlowe is somehow a more knowable figure than Shakespeare because he was more nonconformist. The reinforcement of this misconception of Marlowe as an essentially knowable character, which biographers like A. L. Rowse initiated, continues to this day. Indeed, in 'Marlowe and Shakespeare: Censorship and Construction' (1993), Richard Dutton claims: 'While Shakespeare, as a personality, remains enigmatically elusive, the opposite might be said to be true of his exact contemporary, Marlowe.'[35] Employing Marlowe as a foil for Shakespeare, even in the present decade, criticism has largely refused to recognize that the circumstances of Shakespeare's life are not more elusive than those of Marlowe's but, rather, less exciting. We know when and where Shakespeare was born, whom he married, how many children he had, the success of his business and property interests and the date of his death; the details of Marlowe's life are not more numerous, they are simply different. The scandalous allegations and secretive operations which characterize what we know of Marlowe's life, actually render his character less available to research than Shakespeare's. Ultimately, perhaps, it is this fact which inspires critics, perversely, to endeavour to bring coherence and certainty to the image of Marlowe. I shall now examine those psychoanalytic studies of Marlowe which seek to clarify our perception of the playwright even further.

Psychoanalysis

Concertedly psychoanalytic studies of Marlowe are surprisingly few and far between. This circumstance can in part be accounted for by the inclusion of assumptions about the playwright's psychology under the guise of other critical approaches, such as biography and comparison with Shakespeare. However, by taking for granted the dramatist's personality as a sexual, political and religious subversive, Marlovian criticism largely manages to avoid more complex, and potentially more interesting, psychoanalytic investigations. Indeed, even those studies which seek to redress the pyschoanalytic imbalance in Marlowe scholarship, often fail to theorize fully the dramatist's works and instead remain fixated on the man's supposed sexuality. Illustrating this point, Constance Brown Kuriyama's study, *Hammer or Anvil*, concentrates solely on the way Marlowe's homosexuality informs his plays. Explaining that her enterprise 'began with a conviction that our tendency to ignore or minimize Marlowe's homosexuality was effectively limiting our understanding of his work',[36] Kuriyama's project takes for granted Marlowe's sexual identity. Rather than reading Marlowe's sexuality from his plays, Kuriyama explicitly reads Marlowe's sexuality into his work. This process would be problematic in relation to the work of a known homosexual writer, such as Joe Orton, but in relation to the canon of a dramatist whose sexuality remains a mystery, it is reductive in the extreme. Raising further questions about the usefulness of her study, Kuriyama's tone barely disguises her distaste for the subject with which she has chosen to deal. In her introductory remarks, Kuriyama explains her surprise and discomfort at some of her findings:

> I did not, for example, expect to find fantasies of anal rape in Marlowe's work, although the ending of *Edward II* should certainly have forewarned me. Psychoanalytic critics fortunately or unfortunately, are just as apt to overlook unpleasant facts as anyone else. Once I recognized the prominence of this fantasy in *Tamburlaine*, I seriously considered remaining silent on the subject, but finally concluded that if I were trying to demonstrate the psychological coherence of Marlowe's work I couldn't very well ignore it.[37]

A generally well-meaning work, Kuryiama's study is disabled by both its theoretical amateurism and its unwitting sexual prejudices. According to Simon Shepherd, Kuriyama's attitude towards the dramatist is typical. He argues that 'Most people who write about Marlowe don't like homosexuality in writers, if at all'.[38] Furthermore, he maintains that most Marlovian critics believe Marlowe's homosexuality leads to 'a failure in artistic discipline' as he feels compelled 'to drag it into his works'.[39] Ridiculing the assumption that homosexual writers can only write about homosexuality, Shepherd exclaims: 'why heterosexuality, stamp collecting or wine tasting don't have similar effects I'm not sure'.[40]

Shepherd's argument is amply born out by Wilbur Sanders's *The Dramatist and the Received Idea*, which deploys Marlowe's homosexuality as simultaneously the focus of and the flaw in his work. Sanders's most extreme reaction to Marlowe's sexuality may be found in his chapter on *Edward II*, in which he proposes that the dramatist 'was attracted to the reign of Edward by the opportunity it offered him to treat a forbidden sexual deviation'.[41] As a consequence of Marlowe's personal engagement with Edward's life, Sanders contends, the dramatist loses a grip on his material: 'Does he, in short, *use* the homosexual motif, or does it use him?'[42] Adopting yet more hyperbolic terms, Sanders goes on to argue that in *Edward II* Marlowe falls victim to an unhealthy obsession with homosexuality, or what he prefers to call a 'fascination with disease'.[43] Sanders concludes:

> When we succumb to the fascination, we confuse the deep satisfactions of great imaginative literature with the idle pleasure of indulging our curiosity about the fringes of human sanity. Delirium is, so to speak, mistaken for the authentic poetic 'frenzy', and neurotic intensity is confounded with imaginative power.[44]

Sanders warns against reading Marlowe's play as an expression of real imaginative talent. Instead, he argues that the intensity of Marlowe's verse depends on the dramatist's inability to keep his 'sickness' out of his work. Describing homosexuality as a form of mental neurosis, Sanders represents the very worst excesses of homophobic Marlovian criticism.

A welcome departure from this sort of ill-informed and sometimes bigoted psychoanalytic criticism is Sara Munson Deats's *Sex, Gender, and Desire in the Plays of Christopher Marlowe*. Making a genuine contribution to both pyscho-analytic theory and Marlovian scholarship, Deats's study reads Marlowe's work through post-structuralist ideas about gender and sexuality. The methodological rigour of Deats's approach is underlined by her provision of two introductory chapters summarizing modern and early modern theories respectively. Unlike Kuriyama and Sanders, who use the drama to confirm their assumptions about the dramatist's sexuality, Deats restricts her theorizing to the texts themselves. She consequently provides fascinating readings of the plays which redirect attention from the author to notions of sexual authority. For instance, in her interpretation of the two parts of *Tamburlaine*, Deats considers the way in which Calyphas and Olympia diminish the protagonist's might by offering different forms of feminine resistance. A psychoanalytic consideration of the plays and not the playwright, Deats's work is an exemplar of contemporary Marlovian scholarship.[45]

In 'Homophobia and the Depoliticizing of *Edward II*' Stephen Guy-Bray sums up the problems which author-centred psychoanalytic studies of Marlowe inevitably encounter, and which I have been gesturing towards above. Using interpretations of the murder of Edward II to demonstrate his thesis, Guy-Bray explains that: 'The belief that the scene shows a sick mind in conflict with itself denies the possibility that the scene is a critique of the political and social situations that applied in Edward's time and, indeed, in Marlowe's.'[46] Guy-Bray makes the point that reading Marlowe's sexuality into his plays simultaneously provides a platform for unwelcome homophobic comments, as well as precluding more important social and political readings of the dramatist's work. It is to these alternative interpretations of Marlowe's canon that I shall now turn, under the category of historicism.

Historicism

Early efforts this century to historicize Marlowe have largely fallen victim to the same debilitating preoccupation which characterizes other branches of Marlovian scholarship: an unjustifiable concentration on the figure of the man. Primarily focusing on whether or not the attitudes expressed by the author in his works are representative of the dominant beliefs of his society, these studies limit themselves to either affirming or denying Marlowe's supposedly militant character. Typical of those critics who consider the dramatist a rebel, Harry Levin notes at the start of *The Overreacher* that 'no other poet has been, so fully as Marlowe, a fellow-traveller with the subversive currents of his age'.[47] By contrast, in *Marlowe's 'Tamburlaine'*, Roy Battenhouse regards the author's work as the glue which holds together all the most influential branches of Renaissance philosophy. Wholeheartedly embracing the beliefs of his contemporaries, Marlowe is, according to Battenhouse, the most historically conventional of writers. The oppositional characterization of the dramatist, which offers the reader the choice between a militant or a conformist Marlowe, remains the prevalent mode of criticism even in more recent historical studies.

In Stephen Greenblatt's seminal collection of essays, *Renaissance Self-Fashioning*, Marlowe's dramatic canon fails to get the full New Historicist treatment and is instead considered in traditional Romantic terms as an expression of the artist's personality. Opening with an extract from an Elizabethan merchant's account of the conquest of Sierra Leone, 'Marlowe and the Will to Absolute Play' concentrates on the dramatist's depiction of imperial conquest in *Tamburlaine*. Despite framing his study with an anecdote from the margins of history, Greenblatt ultimately places Marlowe the man at the centre of his analysis. Indeed having taken a circuitous route through all the plays, Greenblatt refigures an orthodox Marlowe who stages subversive opinion only in order to neutralize it. Greenblatt argues that Marlowe's protagonists rebel in ways which unwittingly accept the system of Renaissance orthodoxy: 'Marlowe's protagonists rebel against orthodoxy, but they do not do so just as they please; their acts of negation not only conjure up the order they would destroy but seem at times to be conjured up by that very order.'[48] By rebelling in ways which society anticipates and acknowledges, Marlowe's characters are firmly contained inside the parameters of their cultures. In Greenblatt's reading of the plays Marlowe stages the very impossibility of revolution.

Taking his thesis a step further, Greenblatt relates this mechanism of containment to the conditions of the Elizabethan theatre. The audience, according to Greenblatt, is made complicit in the Marlovian rehearsal of subversion because they are reminded that they can only watch acts of rebellion which they can never perform. Relating the audience's political and theatrical inactivity to a moment in his own life, Greenblatt recalls how he once observed a pickpocket steal a camera from a tourist's shoulder-bag and replace it with a rock. He notes: 'The thief spotted me watching but did not run away – instead he winked, and I was frozen in mute complicity'.[49] Greenblatt concludes, therefore, that Marlovian heterodoxy is constantly emasculated by the delights of theatre as the audience learns that dramatic enjoyment entails submission to, not transgression of, spectacle. Drawing his chapter to a close, Greenblatt traces this method of theatrical playfulness back to the personality of the author in a movement which reaffirms the most Romantic strains of Marlovian criticism:

> In his turbulent life and, more important, in his writing, Marlowe is deeply implicated in his heroes, though he is far more intelligent and self-aware than any of them. Cutting himself off from the comforting doctrine of repetition, he writes plays that spurn and subvert his culture's metaphysical and ethical certainties.[50]

Greenblatt constructs a subversive Marlowe who cannot help writing about himself; this figure bears a startling resemblance to both Levin's Overreacher and Rowse's passionate rebel.

It has therefore, paradoxically, been left to critics other than Stephen Greenblatt to conduct more conventional New Historicist readings of Marlowe's works. These include Roger Sales's study of the dramatist, William Zunder's *Elizabethan Marlowe* (1994), Thomas Healy's *Christopher Marlowe* (1994) and Darryll Grantley and Peter Roberts's excellent collection of essays, *Christopher Marlowe and English Renaissance Culture* (1996), which contains noteworthy articles by Richard Wilson and Gareth Roberts. Although Greenblatt's account of Marlowe seems to reinforce rather than challenge the author-centred bias of Marlovian scholarship, other recent studies do not. This new departure in Marlowe studies was arguably initiated in 1986 by the publication of Simon Shepherd's *Marlowe and the Politics of Elizabethan Theatre*. Shepherd's work made the important gesture of prising the Marlovian canon free from the clutches of traditional biographical criticism. Indeed, in his introduction, Shepherd examines the various Marlowes scholarship has conjured and decides that for his study the author's name will simply signify 'certain playtexts'.[51] Consequently concentrating on the plays themselves, Shepherd discusses Marlowe's works in relation to the theatrical and political trends of the dramatist's day. A remarkable and painstakingly-researched work, Shepherd's study reads Marlowe's plays alongside other less well-known texts which criticism has previously forgotten or dismissed. It is this act of literary conservation which makes Shepherd's book so valuable. His study demands that scholarship re-examine previously marginalized dramas to recognize what actually constituted the Elizabethan theatre.

A timely decentring of the author, Shepherd's study serves as an important reminder to critics that the critical and dramatic Marlovian canons offer an excellent embarkation point for the consideration of pressing theoretical and historical issues. In 'Textual Indeterminacy and Ideological Difference: The Case of *Doctor Faustus*' (1989), Leah Marcus deploys Marlowe's drama as an opportunity to demand that when a play is extant in substantially different versions, each edition should be examined individually. Explaining the folly which surrounds the traditional quest for a copy text, Marcus argues that the impulse to construct a 'pristine Marlovian "original"' depends on a desire to 'remove Marlowe from history and from the contingency of meaning that historicism almost inevitably carries with it'.[52] Marcus claims further that the notion of the copy text also belies an attempt to render the Marlovian text with 'a fixity and permanence it certainly did not have in the Elizabethan theater'.[53] Utilizing the mistakes of Marlovian scholarship to establish important assertions about how Renaissance drama should be edited and studied, Marcus represents a new wave of critics ready to fill the theoretical gaps bequeathed by their predecessors. Similarly, Emily Bartels turns the myopia of previous critics to insight in her study *Spectacles of Strangeness* (1993). Looking at the notion of the Other in Marlowe's canon, Bartels supports her modern theoretical perspective with Elizabethan historical and political evidence.

Few though they are, these studies may mark a turn in the tide of Marlowe criticism. Marlovian scholarship may at last be learning to survive without the author, or at least, with a radically revised conception of his uses. Having identified the preoccupations of Marlovian scholarship it is now time to respond to them in new ways. It is to this next stage which we must now turn.

A New Method: Opening Up

Taking my cue from the work of Shepherd, Marcus and Bartels, I also recognize the unique opportunity which Marlowe's critical and dramatic canons present for the investigation of theoretical issues otherwise ignored by early modern criticism. This opportunity depends on two factors: firstly, the state of Marlovian scholarship which until a decade ago was characterized by the worst excesses of author-centred criticism; and secondly, the unusually contentious nature of the documents employed to refigure Marlowe, which overtly direct attention to the very textuality of all knowledge and thereby to post-structuralist theories of language. The combination of these circumstances renders the work by and about Marlowe particularly ripe for a method of investigation which incorporates an analysis of traditional scholarship with an understanding of twentieth-century philosophies of textuality. For by reading how Marlowe has been constructed in the past, it will be possible to ascertain how he should be considered in the future.

The Janus-faced method of analysis which this study adopts is reliant upon theories of textuality indebted to the insights of deconstruction. In *Of Grammatology*, Jacques Derrida considers what he calls 'The Exorbitant. Question of Method'. He maintains that traditional critical readings, such as Rowse's, Battenhouse's and Kuriyama's described above, do little more than double the text.[54] They simply reiterate and thereby reproduce what is already explicit in the text itself. In opposition to this method, Derrida argues that the proper 'task of reading' is not to double but rather to open up the text.[55] Importantly, the achievement of a reading which opens up the text to new approaches does not entail the disposal of traditional tools of criticism. Derrida describes these tools as the 'indispensable guardrail' which prevents readings from taking 'any direction at all'.[56] It is consequently only after having doubled the text that the critic can open it up. For by doubling the text, criticism exposes those inconsistencies of argument which deconstructive readings make productive.

My own methodology, therefore, places Marlovian scholarship under the spotlight to reveal textual moments which are marked by either criticism's obsessive concern or its unaccountable neglect. These moments will then become the lens for my own investigations or openings up of the texts. Hence, I have chosen to call this study, *Re-citing Marlowe*. I have placed a hyphen in the term recitation to underline both the reiterative nature of my method and the way in which it throws the term quoted into relief. In *Citation and Modernity*, Claudette Sartiliot remarks upon the dual uses of quotation. She argues that according to its legal usage, the term citation suggests simultaneously a 'means of proof' and 'a call, a summons'.[57] Quotation consequently always involves an assertion and a question; it is at once a piece of evidence and a witness for interrogation. In this way, the process of extraction and relocation which citation involves provides an ideal opportunity for my own method of textual exhibition and examination.

Despite the undeniable usefulness of my methodology, it finds no precedent in current early modern studies. Deconstructive readings of early modern works are generally discouraged. This circumstance is summarized by Thomas Healy's chapter on deconstruction in his guide to early modern theoretical practice. In *New Latitudes*, Healy reserves for deconstruction the distinction of the most unhelpful method available to the Renaissance scholar. He observes:

> If there is little unfettered deconstructive activity operating within Renaissance studies currently, it is largely because the questions critics wish to ask of texts are premised on ideas opposed to accepting that a text cannot speak about anything but itself.[58]

Healy's assertion discloses an apparently wilful, although common, misapprehension about the nature of deconstruction. Dismissing the method for being unable to consider anything beyond the text itself, Healy radically misreads the practice of deconstruction. Jacques Derrida's claim in *Of Grammatology* that 'There is nothing outside of the text' seems to be partly responsible for the critical disregard for deconstruction.[59] Although, on a superficial level, Derrida seems to be confirming Healy's reading, within the context of his argument about the doubling and opening up of texts, he is actually describing the way in which all avenues of criticism are mediated through language and are therefore textual, or inside the text. Historical, political and psychoanalytic readings are as accessible to the deconstructionist as they are to any other early modern scholar. For the deconstructionist, however, they are simply more overtly derived from the linguistic limitations of the text.

The historical and political sensitivity of deconstruction fails to be denied by even its harshest critics. For instance, in *Literary Theory: An Introduction*, Terry Eagleton grudgingly concedes that deconstruction is 'an ultimately *political* practice' which does not 'deny the existence of relatively determinate truths, meanings, identities, intentions, historical continuities' and which seeks to consider 'the effects of a wider and deeper history – of language, of the unconscious, of social institutions and practices'.[60] Eagleton concludes:

> The widespread opinion that deconstruction denies the existence of anything but discourse, or affirms a realm of pure difference in which all meaning and identity dissolves, is a travesty of Derrida's own work and of the most productive work which has followed from it.[61]

It seems, therefore, that a Marxist can be more accepting of Derrida's practice than a New Historicist or a Cultural Materialist, despite the fact that the methodology of the latter two critics is overtly indebted to ideas derived from deconstruction. Indeed, the materialist theories which have dominated early modern studies since the late 1970s are ironically informed by the notion of history as text which deconstruction formulates and promotes. In 'Demanding History', Geoff Bennington remarks that deconstruction is 'the most historical of discourses imaginable'.[62] For by foregrounding textual issues, deconstruction initiates those debates about discourse, power and historiography which have made early modern scholarship of the last two decades the most vibrant and exciting area of study. It is therefore with an awareness of early modern criticism's distrust of deconstruction that I embark undeterred upon my present study of the textuality of Marlowe's drama. Having explained why and with what method this study is to be conducted, I shall conclude with a description of how it is to be organized.

Chronology

Because my methodology demands detailed textual examinations, *Re-citing Marlowe* devotes a separate chapter to each of Marlowe's plays, with the exception of the two parts of *Tamburlaine* which are considered in unison.

While these chapters offer self-contained analyses of the individual plays, they also develop a network of theoretical issues which overflow and circulate between the readings. It would probably be more usual in a study which examines the plays separately to organize their related chapters according to a tentative chronology either of composition or of performance; the chapters would thereby be ordered according to where in the Marlovian canon their plays belong. The present study, however, avoids such structures for two reasons. Firstly, as Marlowe's writing career and indeed his life were so short, it is difficult to be precise about dating seven plays which must have all been composed within the space of less than a decade. Secondly, efforts to date the plays tend to rely upon assumptions about either the circumstances of Marlowe's life or the development of his artistic talent which are inappropriate for a study which decentres the author. My examinations of the plays are consequently organized thematically rather than biographically. Thus, although each of the chapters is informed by the same theories of textuality and language, they are, for convenience's sake, divided into sections which contain chapters with broadly similar concerns. Hence the first section in the study, 'Reading and Writing', examines the staging of reception and of inscription in *Doctor Faustus* and *Edward II* respectively. The second section, 'Repetition', analyses anxieties about the possibility of fathering an original work which the two parts of *Tamburlaine* and *Dido, Queene of Carthage* both disclose. The third and final section of my study, 'Re-formation', brings together *The Jew of Malta* and *The Massacre at Paris*, both of which are plays informed by subversive revisions of conventional structures.

Having navigated a passage for my own study between and around other studies of the plays, it is only left for me to make explicit what I mean by the term 'Marlowe'. In this study the word 'Marlowe' primarily signifies a group of seven plays from the Elizabethan era. Secondarily, it connects a school of criticism whose idiosyncrasies initiated this study. 'Marlowe' is one word among many which remain.

Notes

1.   Shepherd, S. (1986), p. xii.
2.   Rowse, A. L. (1964), p. vii.
3.   Dabbs, T. (1991), p. 138.
4.   Dabbs, T. (1991), p. 138.
5.   Friedenreich, K. (1979), p. 6.
6.   Friedenreich, K. (1979), p. 6.

7. Rowse, A. L. (1964), p. 32.
8. Rowse, A. L. (1964), p. 32.
9. Wilson, R. (1993), p. 19.
10. Wilson, R. (1993), p. 19.
11. For a fuller exposition of the recuperability of the author see Roland Barthes's influential essay 'The Death of the Author', in Lodge, D., ed. (1988), pp. 167–72, in which Barthes argues that because all we can know about an author is his words, and these are protean and imprecise, we cannot recover the artist and describe his artistic intentions. Furthermore, postmodernism defies the notion of singular, unitary selfhood; we are all unknowable whether from our writing or from personal interaction with us because there is no essential human self. See the entry entitled 'The person divided?' in Barthes's critical guide to his own writings, *Roland Barthes by Roland Barthes* (Macmillan, 1977), pp. 143–4, where Barthes wittily explores current concepts of the ever-shifting nature of identity. Barthes writes that 'when we speak today of a divided subject, it is never to acknowledge his simple contradictions, his double postulations, etc.; it is a *diffraction* which is intended, a dispersion of energy in which there remains neither a central core nor a structure of meaning: I am not contradictory, I am dispersed.'

    For an early modern realization of the problems of the non-essential, continually changing self and the problems of capturing this in writing, see Michel de Montaigne's essay 'On Repenting': 'I am not portraying being but becoming: not the passage from one age to another (or, as the folk put it, from one seven-year period to the next) but from day to day, from minute to minute. I must adapt this account of myself to the passing hour. I shall perhaps change soon, not accidentally but intentionally. This is a register of varied and changing occurrences of ideas which are unresolved and, when needs be, contradictory, either because I myself have become different or because I grasp hold of different attitudes or aspects of my subject.' See the translation of *Montaigne's Essays* in Penguin, by Michael A. Screech (1991), pp. 907–8.
12. Bakeless, J. (1942), vol. 1., p. vii.
13. Foucault, M. (1980), p. 159.
14. Urry, W. (1988), p. xix.
15. See Thomas Kyd's confession, extracted under torture in the spring of 1593, in Maclure, M. (1979), pp. 32–6. See also Richard Baines's note about Marlowe's unorthodox opinions, cited in Maclure, M. (1979), pp. 36–8.
16. Maclure, M. (1979), p. 37.
17. Nicholl, C. (1992), p. 4.
18. Nicholl, C. (1992), p. 3.
19. Wraight, A. D. and Stern, V. F. (1965), p. 291.
20. Hilton, D. (1977), p. 144.
21. Hilton, D. (1977), p. 144.
22. Hilton, D. (1977), p. 146.
23. Hilton, D. (1977), p. 148.
24. O'Neill, J., ed. (1969), p. 12.
25. Maclure, M. (1979), p. 42.
26. Lom, H. (1978), p. 23.
27. See Harold Bloom, *The Anxiety of Influence: A Theory of Poetry* (1973). New York, Oxford University Press.

28.   Whelan, P. (1992), p. 41.
29.   Whelan, P. (1992), p. 59.
30.   Whelan, P. (1992), p. 96.
31.   Whelan, P. (1992), p. 97.
32.   Muir, K. (1988), p. 1. In K. Friedenreich, R. Gill and C. B. Kuriyama, *'A Poet and a filthy Play-maker': New Essays on Christopher Marlowe* (1988). New York, AMS Press.
33.   O'Neill, J. (1969), p. 13.
34.   Levin, H. (1961), p. 11.
35.   Dutton, R. (1993), p. 1.
36.   Kuriyama, C. B. (1980), p. ix.
37.   Kuriyama, C. B. (1980), p. xi.
38.   Shepherd, S. (1986), p. xii.
39.   Shepherd, S. (1986), p. xii.
40.   Shepherd, S. (1986), p. xii.
41.   Sanders, W. (1968), p. 123.
42.   Sanders, W. (1968), p. 125.
43.   Sanders, W. (1968), p. 141.
44.   Sanders, W. (1968), p. 141.
45.   See Deats, S. M. (1996).
46.   Guy-Bray, S. (1991), p. 129.
47.   Levin, H. (1961), p. 18.
48.   Greenblatt, S. (1980), p. 210.
49.   Greenblatt, S. (1980), p. 216.
50.   Greenblatt, S. (1980), p. 220.
51.   Shepherd, S. (1986), p. xiv.
52.   Marcus, L. (1989), p. 4.
53.   Marcus, L. (1989), p. 4.
54.   Derrida, J. (1974), p. 158.
55.   Derrida, J. (1974), p. 158.
56.   Derrida, J. (1974), p. 158.
57.   Sartiliot, C. (1993), p. 22.
58.   Healy, T. (1992), p. 35.
59.   Derrida, J. (1974), p. 158.
60.   Eagleton, T. (1983), p. 148.
61.   Eagleton, T. (1983), p. 148.
62.   Bennington, G. (1987), p. 17.

Reading and Writing

Chapter 1

Rewriting *Doctor Faustus*

In the final moments of both texts of Marlowe's *Doctor Faustus*, the plays' protagonist reaffirms his commitment to the diabolical contract he composed at the start of the action. As Faustus waits for death at last to make an end of him and of his plays, the Old Man visits for the final time, offering him hope of redemption. Telling Faustus that he sees an angel hovering over his head 'with a vial full of precious grace' (A: V.i.55/B: V.i.58), the Old Man entreats the scholar to 'call for mercy' (A: V.i.57/B: V.i.60).¹ Left alone with Mephistopheles, however, Faustus determines not to repent of the unholy contract, but rather, to repeat it. Offering to rewrite the document which earlier promised his soul to the Devil, Faustus says:

> Sweet Mephistopheles, entreat thy lord
> To pardon my unjust presumption,
> And with my blood again I will confirm
> The former vow I made to Lucifer.
> (A: V.i.70–73/B: V.i.73–6)

This speech is a textually telling one as it seems to imply that either the exigencies of time or the vacillations of Faustus's faith have somehow rendered the bond less secure than when it was first composed in act two. For indeed, the contract cannot be as certain as it was at the instant of its creation or it would neither require, nor permit, rewriting. It is almost as if the meaning of the deed of gift evaporated while its bloody script was still drying on the parchment. The irony of this scene seems to be wasted on Faustus, however, for the scholar seeks to confirm his commitment to the Devil in the same medium which he has already employed and found wanting – writing. The very moment when Faustus might question the veracity of his earlier contract and thereby confound his apparently diabolical destiny, is paradoxically the same moment when he determines to verify it by repetition.

Besides Mephistopheles's immediate response to the proposal – 'Do it, then' (A: V.i.74/B: V.i.77) – the plays do not offer enough evidence either to confirm or to deny the literal re-enactment of Faustus's contract. With no further internal stage directions in the texts, it falls upon a director to decide how these lines should be realized. Placing the problem of presentation to one side, however, this moment of anticipated rewriting, whether or not it is actually staged, remains central to plays which raise questions about the nature of reading and writing in an age of mechanical reproduction. While suggesting the necessity of rewriting the bond of blood which he first inscribed some twenty-four narrative years previously in the action, Faustus discloses a fear which is arguably incumbent upon the freedoms of textual interpretation: the anxiety that writing may not be able to remember itself. Importantly, this concern with the recuperability of writing is central, not only to the texts of *Doctor Faustus*, but also to their critical and editorial contexts. For the state in which the plays exist explicitly complicates the belief that writing can be unproblematically repeated, reproduced and remembered. It is to the critical and editorial responses to the challenge of the two texts of *Doctor Faustus* which I shall now turn.

The Fantasy of an Unproblematic Copy Text

In 'Textual Indeterminacy and Ideological Difference', Leah Marcus aptly summarizes the anxiety caused by the two texts of *Doctor Faustus*. Describing what she calls 'a wish-fulfillment scenario for Marlovian editors and biographers', Marcus imagines the delights of discovering a parcel of old manuscripts in a bricked-off attic of suburban London which includes not only papers 'elucidating such mysteries as the nature of his [Marlowe's] religious belief' but also 'an autograph copy' of *Doctor Faustus*.[2] She concludes:

> The *Faustus* manuscript – perhaps the most sensational find of all – allows scholars to settle once and for all the vexing textual problems surrounding the play by establishing a definitive authorial version that is polished and close to flawless, far superior to either the quarto of 1604 or the quarto of 1616 over which modern editors of Marlowe have puzzled and wrangled for over a century.[3]

Marcus's fantasy importantly discloses three textual issues which are central to the modern perception of Marlowe's *Doctor Faustus*. Firstly, the belief that knowledge of the dramatist's religious sympathies will enhance readings of the plays. Secondly, the editorial preference for a copy text derived from the author's own papers. Finally, the critical longing for a single text of *Doctor Faustus* which it is thought will provide uncomplicated and unitary meaning.

Marcus's daydream consequently identifies both the central position of the figure of Marlowe in the critical and editorial reception of the plays, and the scholarly misapprehension that a single text will produce a single reading, or at least a more limited number of readings. Testimony to the anxiety caused by the two texts of *Doctor Faustus*, Marcus's article rehearses scholarly desires in an effort to redirect the critical gaze to the different ideological contexts which produced the plays. She thereby makes a persuasive case both for editing and reading the two texts according to their different historical moments. Marcus's equitable agenda is, however, the exception rather than the rule in Marlowe studies. The aim of most editors and critics remains the quest for a single, authorized text despite the state in which the plays of *Doctor Faustus* actually exist.

Extant in two versions, both of which were printed more than a decade after Marlowe's death, the plays of *Doctor Faustus* have paradoxically inspired editorial confusion and critical certainty in equal measure. Entered in the Stationers' Register by Thomas Bushell in 1601, the first surviving text of the plays did not appear until 1604.[4] The edition published at this time has come to be known as the A-text. This version of the dramas runs to some 1,517 lines of print.[5] Fourteen years later, in 1616, a second version of the plays was published for John Wright,[6] which has since been named the B-text. This edition is 2,121 lines long,[7] and therefore enlarges the text of the A-quarto by over a third. Included in the elaborated B-text are not only single line alterations, but more importantly narrative events unmentioned in the edition of 1604, such as the Saxon Bruno episode and the plan to humiliate Faustus by the duped Horse-Courser and his tavern accomplices.

Attempts to determine a single, authorized version of the play have been further complicated by a 1602 entry in Henslowe's *Diary* commissioning a revision of *Doctor Faustus* by William Birde and Samuel Rowley.[8] Although none of the extant versions are attributed to these playwrights, the 1619 reissue of the B-text bears the phrase 'With new Additions' on its title page.[9] Aside from the obvious confusion contingent upon unauthorized rewriting, the editions of *Doctor Faustus* remain implicated in general and specific debates which point to a hand other than Marlowe's in the initial moments of the plays' compositions. In his 1991 edition of the A-text, Michael Keefer claims that collaboration would have been normal practice in the Elizabethan theatre.[10] Supporting this view, Marlovian criticism has repeatedly drawn attention to stylistic variations in the texts of *Doctor Faustus* which indicate that more than one author worked on the manuscripts. Thus the most recent edition of the plays by David Bevington and Eric Rasmussen for the Revels series takes for granted that the A-quarto of *Doctor Faustus* was the product of a collaborative effort, possibly with the dramatist Henry Porter.[11] Further proliferating the problem of identifying a single author of a single text, Marlowe's *Doctor Faustus* relies on source material by other authors. The plays are overtly indebted to the 1592 English translation of the German *Faustbuch* by P. F. However, the title page of P. F.'s translation bears the phrase 'Newly imprinted, and in convenient places imperfect matter amended',[12] implying the existence of an earlier version of the Faust story, presumably by yet another writer. Thus the A- and B-texts rest at the centre of a network of contributors and collaborators, at whom scholarship can only wonder with awe and not a little frustration.

The reiterated actual and virtual versions of the Faustus story literalize the theme of textual uncertainty caused by repetition, on which the plays' narratives dwell. Ignoring the opportunity this coincidence of text and context offers, however, editors have busied themselves with the unrewarding and irresolvable task of trying to distinguish Marlowe's intended drama. For instance, in their 1985 edition of the A-text, David Ormerod and Christopher Wortham triumphantly claim to have rehabilitated

> a version which will be arguably closer to the play as it was probably envisaged by Marlowe, and which will hence provide the first real opportunity for Marlowe's twentieth century audience to come to grips with whatever it is we invoke when we allude to such logically vexed issues as the 'meaning' of the play or the nature of the playwright's 'intentions'.[13]

In a similar vein, Michael Keefer defends his subsequent edition of the A-text (1991) with sophisticated historical arguments which are finally reduced to an acknowledgement of authorial intent as the decisive editorial factor:

> For while the meaning of a text is indeed interactively reconstituted within the contexts of its reception, it remains the case that any attempt at a properly historical understanding requires us to distinguish the various reinscriptions of the textual palimpsest. Moreover, any adequate sense of a text's 'effective-history' must include some awareness of its prehistory and of what one might call its originary intentional horizon – and the most obvious name for what connects these with its subsequent history is 'author'.[14]

Such justifications are, to a certain degree, understandable in editions which are obviously designed to promote one version of the plays over the other; they are, however, incongruous in collections of both texts which, typographically at least, pretend to treat the dual dramas with critical equity. Despite the apparently even-handed treatment of the two texts in W. W. Greg's monumental parallel edition, the introduction reveals a partiality for the B-text as the Marlovian original. Greg explains that 'none of the passages peculiar to B represent the addition paid for by Henslowe in 1602 ... the B-text preserves the more original and the A-text a maimed and debased version of the play.'[15] Determined to exclude any possibility of revision from the B-text, Greg constructs an intricate explanation for traces of Rowley's hand in the quarto. He argues that Rowley was the collaborator on the first, authorially-sanctioned, version of the play,[16] thereby disregarding chronological logic in order to make Marlowe's text coincide with his own favoured version.

More than forty years after Greg's edition, Bevington and Rasmussen's Revels text assumes the burden of printing both plays, this time consecutively rather than on facing pages. Gesturing towards critical neutrality in its presentation of the texts, the introduction of the dual edition nevertheless promotes the A-text as Marlowe's originary drama. Bevington and Rasmussen maintain that the B-quarto is a historical parody of an Ur-*Faustus*, stating: 'critical differences ... between the two texts offer confirming evidence that the A-text is close to the Marlovian original and that the B-text trivialises the very nature of Faustus's tragic experience by its endless appetite for stage contrivance'.[17] Deference for the importance of both quartos on the pages of these publications is consistently undermined by a desire to recover the text which uniquely embodies the author's singular intentions: the text whose authenticity depends, therefore, on its timeless ability to reproduce, repeat and re-present Marlowe's drama.

The search for a single text of *Doctor Faustus*, which all the editions described above belie, depends largely on the Romantic belief that a text can unproblematically communicate its author's intentions to its reader. According to this theory, were Marlowe's intentions for *Doctor Faustus* only to be known, the reading public could be given an accurate edition of the play. However, what the editorial history of the two plays of *Doctor Faustus* actually communicates is the impossibility of this desire for textual wholeness. It is not simply that we do not have access to Marlowe's intentions for *Doctor Faustus*, it is that they can never be made un-problematically available to us. Moreover, the unavailability of Marlowe's intentions is not simply premised on the indeterminate processes of signification, but also upon the problem of revision. Were Marlowe to be undecided about his intentions for the play, or worse, to have revised his intentions after composing the play, which text would be authorially sanctioned? The complications involved in the promotion of one text as fully and completely meaningful are consequently various and insoluble. In *A Critique of Modern Textual Criticism*, Jerome J. McGann reviews conventional principles of editing. Explaining that neither author nor manuscript can be rehabilitated and placed in a direct relationship with the reader, McGann writes:

> Having learned the lesson that authors who wish to make contact with an audience are fated by laws of information theory, to have their messages more or less seriously garbled in the process, textual critics proposed to place the reader in an unmediated contact with the author. This project is of course manifestly impossible ... though everyone today recognizes this inherent limitation on all acts of communication the idea persists in textual studies that a regression to authorial manuscripts will by itself serve to reduce textual contamination.[18]

By clinging to the idea of intentionality, editors wilfully ignore the way that texts are reinterpreted by every age which produces or reads them. When we invoke the author's intention, what we actually mean is the reading which cultural consensus has determined at the moment of transmission or reception. For, as McGann explains, the textual authority derived from the notion of the author 'is a social nexus not a personal possession'.[19] Hence the textual multiplicity which the A- and B-quartos literally express is in fact the state in which all texts exist whether or not there is actually more than one version of them.

In this way the editorial history of the plays of *Doctor Faustus* is rendered doubly useful; the almost obsessive quest by generations of editors to locate a single text of the plays offers an obvious point of interrogation and engagement with issues of textuality, while the multiple versions of the quartos coincidentally mirror the theme of textual reiteration upon which their narratives dwell. Grappling with issues of textual and interpretative plurality, then, the plays of *Doctor Faustus* are inscribed by the exegetical confusion contingent upon a century of unprecedented book production. Indeed, becoming the site of anxiety within the dramas, reading is, as Simon Shepherd remarks, 'a problem'.[20] Like the story of the Emperor's new clothes, the *Doctor Faustus* plays enact the moment when the underling raises his finger to point out the ideological myth which maintains the power of his ruler – the flimsiness of authority. Unlike the little boy in the folk-tale, however, Faustus comes to learn the price of his textual rebellion; he can only gain interpretative emancipation by at the same time assuming responsibility for his readings. Faustus's challenge to the notion of textual authority must, therefore, ultimately beg the question: how can one read well or be well-read?

Learning to Read

Ample support for the importance of this query may be found in the first scene of the plays of *Doctor Faustus*, which discovers the protagonist reading and interpreting aloud. *Edward II* begins with a similar moment of reading as Gaveston recites and comments upon a letter from his lover, the new king. Gaveston's exegetical process is, however, less sophisticated than Faustus's. Unlike the scholar whose textual interpretations are dramatic because they are so partial, Gaveston's reading is noteworthy because it is ironic; the news of Edward I's death becomes a source of celebration in Gaveston's reading. The phrase 'My father is deceased' (I.i.1) elicits Gaveston's response 'Ah words that make me surfeit with delight' (I.i.3). The first in a series of staged moments of reading and writing, Gaveston's letter initiates a debate about language in *Edward II* which also finds expression and elaboration in the two texts of *Doctor Faustus*. The handwritten letters and signed documents which dominate *Edward II* are, however, significantly replaced by printed books in the plays of *Doctor Faustus*. Consequently, while *Edward II* is concerned with missives meant for a coterie audience, the A- and B-texts of *Doctor Faustus* dwell on the nature of material published for the reading public at large.

Visually presenting Faustus as a voracious consumer of print, the first scene finds the scholar in his study surrounded by books. Moreover, working from one text to another, Faustus employs a reading strategy which considers and then confutes every branch of accepted learning. Citing, translating and confounding the thoughts of revered authors, Faustus's methodology is, however, not as logical as it may at first appear. The scholar opens the plays with an encomium to the author of the *Analytics*, Aristotle, exclaiming:

> Sweet *Analytics*, 'tis thou hast ravished me!
> [*He reads.*] *Bene disserere est finis logices.*
> Is to dispute well logic's chiefest end?
> Affords this art no greater miracle?
> Then read no more; thou hast attained the end.
> (A: I.i.6–10/B: I.i.6–10)

Implied textually, by Faustus's resolution to read no more, and editorially, by the modern stage direction '[*He reads.*]', this scene should probably be performed with the scholar referring to a book he has just opened. It is as the very image of learning that Faustus delivers his analysis of logic. Focusing on the goal of Aristotle's art, Faustus uses the quotation and translation of a supposedly authoritative source to argue that the ability to dispute well is unrewarding. This visually and verbally learned performance is, however, not all it seems. Enacting the moment of reception and ostensibly reasonable interpretation, the plays invite the audience to scrutinize Faustus's reading strategy.

In *The Renaissance Drama of Knowledge*, Hilary Gatti points out that the phrase which Faustus cites in Latin and renders into English is not to be found in the *Analytics*, but instead in the opening sentence of Peter Ramus's *First Book of Dialectic*.[21] Although Faustus does not explicitly connect the quotation with his reference to the seductions of the *Analytics*, there can be little doubt that their ordering within his argument is designed to encourage the impression that the title and the text are linked. Furthermore, Faustus is not only guilty either of misquoting or of misattributing his thesis; he is also responsible for lashing together the work of two philosophers who Renaissance thinkers would have considered diametrically opposed. Widely held to be the rewriter and reviser of Aristotle, Ramus was the inventor of a more 'simplified method of reasoning',[22] which was acclaimed by Protestant cultures. In Marlowe's *Massacre at Paris*, the Catholic Guise taunts Ramus with his denunciation of Aristotle before killing him. By treating the theories of Aristotle and Ramus interchangeably, Faustus is able to perform what Gatti calls 'a double act of deliberate cultural provocation',[23] and dismiss them both in one fell swoop. In a display of scholarly arrogance, Faustus creates a text laminated with the writings of revered classical and modern thinkers, which significantly invalidates the boundaries of intellectual property and therefore the related notions of textual and authorial authority. In other words, Faustus shows no respect for the interpretative limitations of his reading material nor for the individuality of its authors.

Reckoned an irrelevance by some critics,[24] or an illustration of the scholar's academic shortcomings,[25] these instances of unorthodox reading may be more easily disregarded than Faustus's consequent erratic exegesis of the Bible, which a churchgoing Elizabethan audience would surely be expected to recognize. Reading aloud once more, this time from the Vulgate, Faustus ironically notes:

> Jerome's Bible, Faustus, view it well.
> [*He reads.*] *Stipendium peccati mors est.* Ha!
> *Stipendium*, etc.
> The reward of sin is death. That's hard.
> [*He reads.*] *Si peccasse negamus, fallimur*

Et nulla est in nobis veritas.
If we say that we have no sin,
We deceive ourselves, and there's no truth in us.
Why then belike we must sin,
And so consequently die.
Ay, we must die an everlasting death.
(A: I.i.38–48/B: I.i.36–46)

Consulting the Bible in the same way that he has already referred to Aristotle and Ramus, Faustus misattributes and partially cites his source. He first quotes from Romans, stating: 'The reward of sin is death'. Although Faustus accurately cites this line from the Vulgate, he does not finish it. Amputating the start of the line from its optimistic conclusion, he conceals the full meaning of the text, which should read: 'For the wages of sin is death, but the gift of God is eternal life through Jesus Christ our Lord'.[26] He performs a similar act of truncation to the line beginning 'If we say that we have no sin' and also misascribes this source to the Jerome Bible he is holding. Nowhere to be found in the Vulgate, the Latin phrase is correctly translated into English by imitating its entry in the 1559 *Book of Common Prayer*. Part of the Order for Morning Prayer in this edition, the line should continue: 'If we confess our sins, he is faithful and just to forgive us our sins, and to cleanse us from all unrighteousness'.[27] Thus Faustus twice removes the message of redemption with which these lines conclude.

The boldness of this reading strategy is, moreover, only emphasized when it is recognized that 'any moderately knowledgeable Christian in Marlowe's audience would have known that Faustus has rigged his syllogism by neglecting to quote in full the source of its two premises'.[28] Flaunting his spiritual and textual defiance, Faustus audaciously draws attention to the act of interpretation and interpolation. This act offers the scholar's audience a revolutionary thesis: the proposition that the reading of an individual is as valid as the reading which convention has conferred upon a text. Faustus's interpretative strategy consequently threatens the notion that a text can only ever mean one eternally repeatable thing. Proving by his performance in the first scene the obvious impossibility of this notion, the scholar's rereading offers meanings which radically refuse to conform to traditional exegesis. Rehearsing the emancipation of the critical reader, the texts of *Doctor Faustus* mark the moment when the principle of authorial and textual authority lost its time-honoured respect. Thus Faustus's approach to reading promotes the right of the reader to read according to his desires.

How to Make Reading Active

Preoccupied with the exercise of this right, the Renaissance witnessed a thorough review of its reading habits. In 'Studied for Action', Lisa Jardine and Anthony Grafton claim 'that some Elizabethan great houses supported a recognizable class of scholar ... acting less as advisers in the modern sense than as facilitators easing the difficult negotiations between modern needs and ancient texts'.[29] Operating as a conduit for interpretation, scholars would convey readings to their masters who were either unwilling or unavailable to read themselves. In their article, Jardine and Grafton maintain that Gabriel Harvey was just such a professional reader. Employed in the Earl of Leicester's household, Harvey's duties involved the dissemination of readings of classical and modern texts to an informed and interested audience. Humanists thereby showed that history and literature were to be prized as sources of political exemplar and consequent advice. Thus the professional reader, much like Faustus, revivified texts by making their meanings of moment. Asked to make apparently unrelated modes and eras of thought relevant to contemporary contexts, the scholar was involved in a system of exchange founded upon the use-value of reading. Emphasis was placed not upon the act of reading in and of itself, but rather upon the subsequent act of interpretation which rendered the texts useful or usable. For as Jardine and Grafton explain, Renaissance readers 'persistently envisage action as the *outcome* of reading – not simply reading as active, but reading as trigger for action'.[30] Reinventing what it meant to read, the Renaissance transformed the study into a workshop and the book into a tool of employment, indistinguishable from a hammer or an axe.

This industrialization of reception was, however, not only metaphorical. The Renaissance responded to the new methods of reading with actual mechanization, with Agostino Ramelli's book-wheel. Designed to enable 'its user to lay out on flat surfaces as many books as he might choose, to move them as he needed them without losing his places, and to stop at any selected text',[31] the book-wheel resembled the structure of a watermill with a book laid open at the end of every spoke. Creating a constant stream of information, the wheel could be rotated allowing a reader to consult one text after another without having to waste time finding and laying open different volumes. By enabling the simultaneous manipulation of multiple texts, Ramelli's innovation uncannily realizes the receptive strategy Faustus stages in the first scene. In their construction of readings from parallel, apparently incompatible quotations, Faustus's interpretations unfix the book as surely as Ramelli's machine which actually turned it on its head and through 360 degrees. An invention whose utility was directly proportional to its reserve of reading material, the book-wheel needed the printing press to keep its machinery in motion, its spokes well stocked. Ramelli's wheel may be imaged therefore as the inevitable climax in a sequence of events which the printing press initiated; by increasing book production, the presses enlarged the availability of texts for comparison and interpretation thereby complicating or revising theories of reception and ultimately necessitating the invention of the book-wheel.

Making the importance of the printing press yet more explicit, Francis Bacon famously asserts in his 'New Organon':

> it is well to observe the force and virtue and consequences of discoveries, and these are to be seen nowhere more conspicuously than in those three which were unknown to the ancients, and of which the origin, though recent, is obscure and inglorious; namely, printing, gunpowder, and the magnet. For these three have changed the whole face and state of things throughout the world.[32]

Bacon's aphorism categorizes the invention of print alongside those of gunpowder and the compass in a movement which implicates book production in an economy of destruction and redefinition. An unwittingly revealing comparison, Bacon's list involves the printing press in the same conquest of space to which gunpowder and the compass contribute. Thus, while Renaissance Europe was achieving geographic mastery with its military and cartographic knowledge, it was also expanding its intellectual territories with the help of the printing press. However, as with the other inventions Bacon mentions, the achievements of the printing press were double-edged; for at the same time the printing press increased the availability of reading material, it also challenged the singularity of interpretation by producing the book again and again.

Bringing in its wake a tide of unforeseen complications, the printing press re-invented the idea of the text by reproducing it. Indeed, not only increasing the number of texts available to the Renaissance reading public, the presses also diminished the confidence invested in the book by displaying signs of its emendation. In *The Printing Press as an Agent of Change*, Elizabeth Eisenstein explains that the ability to publish errata 'demonstrated a new capacity to locate textual errors with precision and to transmit this information simultaneously to scattered readers'.[33] However, in the very act of communicating error, the printing press simultaneously bore witness to the unattainability of the repeatable definitive or definite text. In this way the processes of textual improvement ironically betrayed the inevitability of mistakes and hence misreadings, or at least rereadings. Ramelli's book-wheel and the printing press therefore return us to the figure of Faustus reading and rereading in his study; a figure implicated in the myths of early book production by his namesake Johann Fust.

Diabolical Books

Obscured behind the contradictory masks of the entrepreneur, the inventor, the thief and the witch, the figure of Johann Fust defies satisfactory historical rehabilitation. Nevertheless, the printer's biography, whether mythic or real, does provide an important connection between the science of book production and the art of magic. The only incontestable facts concerning Fust's life are concisely related by J. W. Smeed, who explains:

> Johann Fust was born in Mainz and died in Paris in or about 1466. Around 1450 he advanced money to Gutenberg, who set up a printing-shop in an attempt to exploit his invention. But Gutenberg was no businessman, and he failed to meet Fust's financial conditions. Fust sued him for repayment and, after a lawsuit, gained possession of the equipment and stock. Fust then continued to run the press on his own account, aided by Gutenberg's onetime foreman, Peter Schöffer, who later married Fust's daughter.[34]

The details of Fust's career offer the ingredients for Marlowe's story: an unexplained death, a contract which costs a man his livelihood, while the life-imitating power of reproduction remains at stake. Concealed in the gaps which punctuate the Fust biography are alternative narrative elements which more immediately relate to the construction of the *Doctor Faustus* plot. Considering these less obvious versions of the printer's life, Douglas McMurtrie cites a tale which was reputedly handed down 'from aged and trustworthy men'[35] to one Junius, who states:

> This Johann, after he had learned the art of casting types and combining them – in fact, the whole trade – took the first favorable opportunity, on Christmas Eve, when everyone was at the church, to steal the whole type supply, with the tools and all the equipment of his master. He went first to Amsterdam, then to Cologne, and finally to Mainz, which was out of striking distance and there opened a printing establishment and reaped the fruits of his theft.[36]

In direct opposition to the legality of Gutenberg's foreclosed contract, the Junius anecdote depicts Fust as a criminal. He is a robber and a traitor: a man capable of exploiting the eve of Christ's birthday in order to commit a crime against an employer who is at prayer. The Fust apocrypha begin to make more explicit the connection between the printer and the damned scholar; both men are guilty of spiritual as well as professional transgression.

Armed, whether by stealth or business acumen, with Gutenberg's expertise and equipment, Fust printed an edition of Jerome's Bible whose decorative quality awarded it legendary bibliographical status. In search of a market for this special edition, Fust travelled to Paris where his books were initially well received. However, when it was found that Fust was selling one Bible after another, the Guild of Bookmakers called in the authorities, claiming that 'such a store of valuable books could only be in one man's possession through the devil himself'.[37] Apparently fearful of being charged with necromancy, the printer fled Paris, taking his remarkable editions with him. In J. W. Smeed's telling of the story, the charge of diabolism levelled at Fust depends not upon the limitless supply of his Bibles, but instead upon their fraudulent sale as manuscript copies.[38] Arguing that Fust took advantage of the superlative quality of his editions to market them as expensive handwritten books, Smeed notes: 'when his [Fust's] customers came to compare their copies they found them so alike in all particulars they concluded that they had been swindled and demanded compensation'.[39]

Whatever the precise cause of the charge brought against Fust, one thing remains certain. It was the unnatural reproductivity of his Bibles which initiated it, Bibles which were, coincidentally, of the same type as the one Faustus refers to in the first scenes of the plays. Indeed as Elizabeth Eisenstein concedes:

> Whether the new art [of printing] was considered a blessing or a curse; whether it was consigned to the Devil or attributed to God; the fact remains that the initial increase in output did strike contemporary observers as sufficiently remarkable to suggest supernatural intervention.[40]

The silhouette of Fust retreating from Paris, his Bibles under his arm, connects the witch-hunts that swept Europe with Renaissance suspicions about the necromantic ability of the printed book to reproduce itself. What is more, these suspicions provide two important links between the figure of Fust the printer and Faustus the scholar. Firstly, they connect the idea of increased book production with Faustus's interpretative performance in the first scenes of the plays. Secondly, they connect writing with conjuring in a way which questions

the possibility of language to force events, of magic to make things happen. It
is the latter connection which preoccupies the middle and final sections of the
plays of *Doctor Faustus*, as the scholar is repeatedly faced with the limitations
of necromantic texts.

Witch Manual?

In spite of, or perhaps in response to, the charges of magic imputed against
printing, the Renaissance conducted its witch discourse in print. The
unprecedented extent of the witch craze at this time has largely been attributed
to the intervention of religious and political authorities, who inscribed the
irrational anxieties of the masses and printed them for all to read.[41] Kindled by
the witch manuals whose popularity prompted numerous reissues, the Parisian
bonfire Fust evaded soon spread throughout Europe.   James Sprenger and
Henry Kramer's papally-commissioned *Malleus Maleficarum* or 'hammer
against witches' of 1484 was one of the most famous in a series of editions
designed to explain how to identify and deal with witches. The importance of
these manuals to the plays of *Doctor Faustus* does not depend, however, on
their descriptions of witchcraft, but rather on their misrepresentation of opinion
as fact. For as Sydney Anglo explains in 'Evident authority and authoritative
evidence: The *Malleus Maleficarum*', the manuals presented partial readings of
the Scriptures as 'time-honoured evidence'.[42] Like Fust's apparently self-
generating editions of the Vulgate, the arguments on which the manuals were
based largely relied on the repetition of theories which rapidly assumed the
status of truth. Wayne Schumaker makes this point in *The Occult Sciences in
the Renaissance*:

> The basic weakness of reasoning, obviously, is the reliance placed upon
> 'authorities' ... The oftener the traditional stories were repeated the stronger
> the 'proof' became. If Sprenger and Kramer, for example, picked up a tale
> from the life of one of the early Saints and Guazzo borrowed it from them, it
> acquired the support of a fourth author. The next user became a fifth, a still
> later writer a sixth, and so on indefinitely, until the list acquired an apparent
> solidity that made disbelief next to impossible.[43]

Creating a network of self-sustaining authorities, the witch manuals required
sophisticated techniques of reception to be challenged effectively.

Reginald Scot was one of the first writers to apply a process of sceptical rereading to the witch manuals. He discredited the scriptural certainties on which the manuals were based by investigating the etymology of the words employed to prove the existence of witches. Most importantly, Scot argues in *The Discoverie of Witchcraft* (1584) that the biblical Latin terms *veneficos* and *maleficos*, usually translated as 'witches', could be more accurately, although less supernaturally, rendered as 'poisoners'.[44] It is ironic, then, that Faustus is led to diabolism by the same reading strategy which Renaissance sceptics were using to defy the European witch craze: the revelation of interpretative multiplicity. When Faustus determines to 'Resolve me of all ambiguities' (A: I.i.82/B: I.i.79) it is consequently in direct opposition to the technique of reception with which he began both the plays. Faustus rejects the freedom of textual emancipation for the counterfeit delights of diabolical servitude. The wrongness of this decision is, moreover, foregrounded by the plays' repeated scenes of reading and writing which culminate in the re-signed contract. Like the man who locks the stable door after the horse has bolted, Faustus's attempts after his first soliloquies to make texts singularly meaningful actually only succeed in showing the scholar's fearfulness and folly.

Conjuring Language

Apparently disregarding the reading strategy of the initial scene which opened writing to interpretation, Faustus summons the Devil by trying to make language immediately and unproblematically significant. He writes the name of God in anagrams with the abbreviated names of saints in the belief that 'the spirits are enforced to rise' (A: I.iii.13/B: I.iii.13). However, when Mephistopheles does appear to the scholar, it is not as a victim of linguistic coercion, but rather as an independent investigator of the heresies which have reached his ears. Faustus even quizzes Mephistopheles about his misapprehension, asking 'Did not my conjuring raise thee?' (B: I.iii.43).[45] Mephistopheles explains that Faustus has not made him appear; he has come because he heard a soul in danger of damnation. Faustus has therefore failed to make language singularly meaningful; he has failed to make his words command one outcome. The very presence of Mephistopheles contradicts the capacity of magic to force events. Lacking the power to compel, language is revealed to Faustus as an unstable and amorphous entity. It is surprising then, that when Faustus decides to regulate his diabolical dealings, he complies with

Mephistopheles's suggestion, and turns once more to that which has already defied fixity – writing.

Describing the significance of the contract in the source text for Marlowe's plays, the narrator of the *English Faust Book* states that 'even as CAINE he [Faust] also said his sinnes were greater than God was able to forgive; for all his thought was on his writing, he meant he had made it too filthy in writing it with his own blood'.[46] The scholar of the *English Faust Book* underlines the inexorability of his diabolical text by locating the impossibility of his repentance in the bloodiness of his writing. In stark contrast, the plays of *Doctor Faustus* dramatize the blood contract as a document which is ironically in imminent danger of becoming insubstantial, inconsequential and hence unbinding. Introduced by Mephistopheles, the bond is supposedly designed to satisfy the Devil's need for reassurance: 'For that security craves [Lucifer]' (A: II.i.36/B: II.i.36). The contract is therefore repeatedly imaged by Mephistopheles as a compelling document; a deed which will 'bind thy [Faustus's] soul' (A: II.i.50/B: II.i.50). However, in spite of these diabolical testimonies to the document's surety, the bond persistently reveals the instability of its own writing. Unlike the contract of the *English Faust Book*, then, Marlowe's bond is thwarted time and again by the possibility of its extinction.

Having already had the flow of his writing interrupted by the temporary coagulation of his blood, Faustus completes the deed of gift only to witness yet another indication of the difficulties contingent upon inscription. Faustus exclaims as he seals the deed:

> *Consummatum est.* This bill is ended,
> And Faustus hath bequeathed his soul to Lucifer.
> But what is this inscription on mine arm?
> '*Homo, fuge!*' Whither should I fly?
> If unto God, he'll throw me down to hell.–
> My senses are deceived; here's nothing writ.–
> I see it plain. Here in this place is writ
> '*Homo, fuge!*' Yet shall not Faustus fly.
> (A: II.i.74–81)[47]

In the very moment when writing is meant to have decided the present and determined the future, Faustus experiences a display which suggests that inscription is unable to prevent its own erasure. As the bloody words mark, unmark and re-mark his arm, Faustus must recognize that the ink with which he penned his destiny may also vanish and thereby obliterate the conditions of his engagement. The scholar's eagerness to reinscribe the contract at the end of the plays only serves to support this thesis. Re-enacting the scene of inscription, the plays of *Faustus* return to the fear with which this chapter began: the anxiety that writing may not be able to remember itself.

Writing and Remembering

Both texts of *Doctor Faustus* are inscribed with the anxiety that writing may not be able to retain a fixed and repeatable meaning over time. This anxiety is, however, extremely ironic because the very usefulness of inscription depends on its ability to persist, to be repeated long after the moment of composition. Able to sustain speech beyond the temporality of its own existence, nevertheless writing fails to resuscitate the tone or intention of an articulation. The value of writing consequently depends on a repeatability which can never return the same message. As the textual remains of the plays of *Doctor Faustus* demonstrate, inscription can only ever supply the ghost of an idea, the phantom of a thought; it lies with the reader to surmise or to interpret the rest. Like Faustus presenting a spirit in the shape of Alexander because the Emperor's body defies revivification, writing tantalizingly promises to put the past on stage, while actually keeping it waiting in the wings, just out of sight.

The paradoxical nature of writing which can recite words without being able to repeat their meaning has been the subject of post-structuralist theories. Bridging the gap between the early modern reading and writing machines of Ramelli and Fust, Freud's Mystic Writing Pad engages with the same inscriptional anxieties about repetition. In 'Freud and the Scene of Writing', Jacques Derrida outlines Freud's search for a metaphor to encapsulate the mind's 'potential for indefinite preservation and … unlimited … reception'.[48] Eventually happening upon a child's toy, which realized both these characteristics, Freud deployed the Mystic Writing Pad as a model for his consideration of memory. Freud's machine makes explicit the fraught connection between writing and remembering; the processes of inscription resemble the mind's capacity to remember, and the mind's capacity to remember resembles the processes of inscription. Similarly, Ramelli's book-wheel and Fust's printing press also express, through their staging of the book either in production or reception, the desire for writing to be infinitely repeatable by being able to remember itself. All three reading and writing machines are therefore implicated to varying degrees in an examination of inscription's ability to persist over time: to be remembered. Unlike Ramelli's and Fust's inventions, the Mystic Writing Pad returns to the initial moment of composition and the act of inscription. Freud's Pad is, moreover, a children's toy whose novelty relies on its mysterious ability to obliterate the words written on its surface. A slab of resin with a sheet consisting of an upper layer of celluloid and a lower layer of wax paper attached to one end, the Mystic Writing Pad enables its user to write and then erase that writing by simply lifting the covering free from the base. Separating the transparency from the resin, the marks disappear; they remain, nevertheless, just perceptible, as indentations on the pitted surface of the slab. Freud claims that by imagining the Pad's operator involved in a process of constantly writing and erasing, 'we shall have a concrete representation of the way in which I [Freud] tried to picture the functioning of the perceptual apparatus of our mind'.[49]

Contrary to Freud's use of the Mystic Writing Pad as a metaphor for memory retrieval, Derrida deploys the machine as a metaphor for inscriptional instability. Consequently, he does not ponder why memory is like a text, but rather what the nature of a text must be to render it analogous to memory. Derrida extrapolates from Freud's 'Note on the Mystic Writing Pad' a theory of writing, and more generally, of language which underlines the inability of writing's meaning to persist. Claiming that inscription, like the marks on the surface of the Mystic Writing Pad, is only made possible by its promise of subsequent removal, Derrida maintains that traces 'produce the space of their inscription only by acceding to the period of their erasure'.[50] Traces are therefore 'constituted by the double force of repetition and erasure, legibility and illegibility'.[51] According to this argument, inscription inscribes its own temporariness because it must always be ready to erase itself and so make room for new marks. The Mystic Writing Pad's game of writing and unwriting may therefore be considered as the most extreme literalization of the instability inherent in all acts of inscription. Freud's machine expresses the paradoxical nature of writing which is repeatable because it is not permanent; writing cannot fix its meaning and convey it consistently over time. The processes of inscription and erasure which Freud's Pad describes connect twentieth-century theories of textuality with the bloody writing which marks and unmarks Faustus's arm; both machine and theatrical moment stage the impossibility of permanent, repeatable meaning.

Revealing the anxiety that writing may not be able to remember itself, Marlowe's plays of *Doctor Faustus* dramatize a concern with inscriptional erasure which also preoccupied other Renaissance writers. In his *De Laude Scriptorum*, Johannes Trithemius compares the written word on parchment which will last a 1,000 years with the printed word on paper which he does not expect to survive for more than 200 years.[52] Concluding from this hypothesis that the scribe is paradoxically even more important in an age of mechanical reproduction, Trithemius instructs copyists to write out useful printed books which will otherwise 'not last long'.[53] Trithemius therefore equates the quality of endurance with the least reproductive medium: with writing, not print. It is almost as though the fecundity of print somehow increases the instability of textuality by multiplying the number of pages with erasable marks on them. What is more, Trithemius characterizes the copying of printed books as an act not only of conservation but also of improvement. By converting print into writing, Trithemius claims a scribe 'will render mediocre books better, worthless ones more valuable, and perishable ones more lasting'.[54] Returning elsewhere to this fear of textual breakdown, Trithemius recounts an anecdote which significantly involves the notorious figure of Faust. He claims:

> Certain priests in the same town told me that he [Faust] had said, in the presence of many people, that he had acquired such knowledge of all wisdom and such a memory, that if all the books of Plato and Aristotle, together with their whole philosophy, had totally passed from the memory of man, he himself, through his own genius, like another Hebrew Ezra, would be able to restore them all with increased beauty.[55]

Trithemius interestingly characterizes Faust as the antidote to complete inscriptional erasure by showing our protagonist's antecedent in the process of reiterating texts. Replacing a vanishing corpus with his own corpse, Faust implies not only the likelihood of writing's eventual disappearance, but more importantly, the impossibility of its repetition without alteration; the texts which Faust promises to restore are not identical to their predecessors, but rather of 'increased beauty'.

Unlike the Faust of Trithemius's anecdote, however, Marlowe's protagonist denies writing's instability. In direct opposition to his reading strategy in the opening scenes of the plays, Faustus subsequently adheres to a belief in the absolute permanence and authority of writing. This belief is expressed not only in Faustus's attempt to conjure up the Devil with words, but also in his misapprehension that the bloody contract will convey his intentions despite the passing of time and the exigencies of textuality. Faustus's tragedy is consequently tinged with irony; he determines his diabolical enslavement in the medium which has taught him how to flout its authority. The folly of Faustus's position is, moreover, foregrounded by the plays' staging of the inconsequentiality of language.

Lies Damned Lies

Having signed his soul to the Devil, Faustus understandably expects to see the benefits of his bargain. His hope that the Devil will supply all his intellectual, social and sexual needs is, however, short-lived. Requesting a wife, Faustus is instead delivered a devil dressed as a woman, with fireworks. In both texts of *Doctor Faustus* Mephistopheles attempts to distract the scholar from his conjugal disappointment by giving him a book. Mephistopheles explains:

> Hold, take this book. Peruse it thoroughly.
> The iterating of these lines brings gold;
> The framing of this circle on the ground
> Brings whirlwinds, tempests, thunder, and lightning.
> Pronounce this thrice devoutly to thyself,
> And men in armour shall appear to thee,
> Ready to execute what thou desir'st.
> (A: II.i.161–8)[56]

Offering Faustus a book containing spells to achieve economic, environmental and military mastery, Mephistopheles attempts to make amends for denying the scholar a wife. In the B-text the scene ends at this point; however, in the A-text, Faustus is less easily appeased and demands yet more knowledge from Mephistopheles. Faustus requests firstly 'a book wherein I might behold all spells and incantations, that might raise up spirits when I please' (A: II.i.169–71), secondly, 'a book where I might see all characters and planets of the heavens' (A: II.i.173–4), and finally, 'one book more' with 'all plants, herbs, and trees that grow upon the earth' (A: II.i.177–9). In response to each of Faustus's demands, Mephistopheles makes the same reply; he directs the scholar back to the book already in his hands. Renouncing the possibility that any information could exist outside the volume Faustus already possesses, Mephistopheles frustrates the protagonist's desires. In the A-text the scene concludes with Faustus's exclamation of disbelief that the knowledge for which he sold his soul can be confined in a single volume, 'O, thou art deceived' (A: II.i.181), to which Mephistopheles replies, 'Tut, I warrant thee' (A: II.i.182).

It is a commonplace of *Doctor Faustus* criticism that Mephistopheles is an unusually honest devil; he does not appear to deceive the scholar and even warns him about the torments of hell. However, Mephistopheles's attempt to convince Faustus that all knowledge can be contained in the book he has already been given stands out as an obvious moment in the plays when the devil may be living up to his reputation and lying to the scholar. The A-text's extended version of the scene repeats Faustus's denied request for more books until the scholar voices his fear of deception. It should be noted here that Faustus's 'O, thou art deceived' (A: II.i.181) may refer either to Mephistopheles's mistaken belief in the completeness of the knowledge contained in the book, or to Faustus's realization that the devil has been lying to him. The importance of this moment in the A-text does not rely, however, upon the identification of the deceiver and the deceived, but rather upon the staging of the scholar's disbelief. By questioning the possibility of an omniscient book, Faustus foregrounds the textual anxiety with which the plays began: the anxiety that language and therefore writing cannot make knowledge unproblematically communicable.[57] The bargain Faustus strikes with the Devil, selling his soul in return for all that is knowable, is revealed by the plays to be founded on a fundamental misapprehension about the nature of meaning.

Despite mounting evidence to the contrary, Faustus continues throughout both the A- and B-texts to cling to a notion of singular, direct linguistic meaning. Indeed ignoring the implications of Mephistopheles's diabolical book which attempts to deceive its reader into believing in the possibility of absolute knowledge, Faustus foolishly returns to language to determine his salvation. In one of the most memorable moments from the plays, Faustus tries to repent by calling on Christ. Angered by Mephistopheles's refusal to respond to his inquiry 'Tell me who made the world' (A: II.iii.66/B: II.iii.66), Faustus seeks redemption, wondering: 'Is't not too late?' (A: II.iii.77/B: II.iii.78). However, exclaiming: 'Ah, Christ, my Saviour,/ Seek to save distressèd Faustus' soul!' (A: II.iii.82–3),[58] the scholar is answered not by the arrival of the Messiah, but instead by the entrance of Lucifer. This most famous of moments from the plays is conventionally interpreted by critics as evidence either of the absence of God from the world of the play, or of the reluctance of Faustus to believe in the possibility of his own redemption.[59] Alternatively, the scene can be read as another instance of Faustus mistaking the power of language. Having attempted to seal his fidelity to the Devil in words which disappear and distort themselves, Faustus should know better than to seek his salvation in yet more words. For just as Faustus's conjuring does not make Mephistopheles come to him, nor can his verbal appeal to Christ force God to save him. Apparently wilfully refusing to appreciate the unstable nature of textuality which the plays repeatedly present, Faustus is instead distracted by the illusory delights of shows and tricks. When Lucifer appears in place of Christ, the Devil deflects Faustus's attention away from his thwarted salvation towards the pageant of the Seven Deadly Sins. This process of theatrical distraction continues throughout the plays as Faustus becomes increasingly forgetful of why he sold his soul. The concern with the memory of writing which preoccupies the first two acts of the plays is therefore displaced by the dramas' middle scenes which depict Faustus's failure to remember the terms of his diabolical contract.

Remembering and Re-Membering

Faustus's amnesia is ultimately only cured by the striking of the clock which punctuates his final soliloquy. Until this point, the scholar has been distracted by a series of shows which each underline the problematic nature of remembrance. For instance, when Faustus conjures Alexander and his Paramour for the Emperor of Germany, he makes clear that he can only present 'shadows' (B: IV.i.104); the 'true substantial bodies' of the dead have been 'consumed to dust' (A: IV.i.49–50) and cannot be revivified. Faustus's power over the past is consequently deceptive; he can only remember, or indeed re-member, by employing spirits to play the characters of the dead. Similarly, at the end of the plays when Mephistopheles offers Faustus Helen of Troy, the ancient beauty is nothing more than a spirit in drag. This is a significant departure from the plays' source text. In P. F.'s translation of the German story, Faust lives with Helen and she bears him a child.[60] Unlike his namesake, the Faustus of the plays is neither permitted a relationship with Helen, nor a child by her. The unproductivity of Faustus's encounter with Helen is only emphasized as his sexual desires for the woman are replaced with images of consumption; instead of giving the scholar a child, Helen sucks out his soul (A: V.i.94/B: V.i.96). The inconsequentiality of Faustus's magic tricks repeatedly foregrounds the plays' concern with the possibility that writing, like conjuring, will prove unable to put the past on stage.

The plays' anxieties about writing and remembering culminate in the scene when Faustus offers to reiterate his bloody contract. In response to Mephistopheles's threat to tear Faustus's flesh 'in piecemeal' (A: V.i.69/B: V.i.71) if he does not stop thinking about redemption, the scholar promises to confirm his vow to Lucifer by rewriting his contract in blood. Cutting his arm and rewriting his deed of gift, however, Faustus draws attention to the very impermanence of his initial contract with the Devil. The necessity of Faustus's reinscription of the bond does not confirm the scholar's allegiance to Lucifer, but rather the suggestion which has haunted the plays, that writing cannot remember itself. The contract which initiated the action of the plays would neither permit nor require rewriting were inscription able to convey a singular, fixed and repeatable meaning. The scene is, of course, heavy with irony; Faustus seeks to evade Mephistopheles's immediate threat of violence by contracting himself to an eternity of torment. More ironic yet is the fact that Faustus's rewriting of the bond implies that the contract he believed sold his soul to the Devil has always lacked the force to compel his damnation; Faustus has always been free to be saved. The drama of the scene consequently rests upon the tantalizing potential for the scholar to realize that his diabolical destiny has not been sealed by his writing. Faustus is eventually damned not because he has signed away his soul but because he believes he cannot be saved.

Ultimately deceived both by the instability of his initial readings and the impermanence of his eventual writings, Faustus is appropriately preoccupied with the issue of perpetuity in his final soliloquy. As the clock strikes out his last hour, Faustus remains unable to remember what it was he once knew about the proteanism of words, that which initially empowered him to seek knowledge from the Devil. Dwelling upon the idea of eternity as simultaneously damnation and evasion, Faustus ponders the possibility of a 'Perpetual day' (A: V.ii.71/B: V.ii.144) to thwart being 'damned perpetually' (A: V.ii.67/B: V.ii.140). Faustus's hope of delay is, however, futile. He cannot stop the onset of time. Indeed, the one force which has proved constant within the plays is the power of time to conquer the present. It is, significantly, this power which the human endeavours of writing and remembering seek to overcome. The possibility of reiterating the past in the present, of resurrecting an intention in an inscription, or of re-presenting the dead in a theatrical show, is radically dismissed by the plays' endings. Instead, the audience is offered a world in which only God can allow man to cheat death, and He will not be summoned by words.

Leaving the stage promising: 'I'll burn my books' (A: V.ii.123/B: V.ii.191), Faustus fails to identify the source of his damnation. It is not the books which have damned him but rather his belief in the ability of language to force events.[61] Faustus's refusal to appreciate the failure of words, be they written or spoken, to conjure either his damnation or his salvation, means that he fails to seal his redemption outside language. It is for this reason that Faustus is damned. The scholar's dilemma, would he could remember it, is ultimately not how to escape his diabolical contract, but rather, how to sue for God's redemption without words.[62] The resolution of this dilemma is, of course, unimaginable in the fallen world of language. It is nevertheless to the negotiation of this problem which the plays finally direct us.

Notes

1. All references are to the Revels Plays edition, of both the A- and B-texts, ed. David Bevington and Eric Rasmussen (1993). Manchester: Manchester University Press.
2. Marcus, L. (1989), p. 1.
3. Marcus, L. (1989), p. 2.
4. Bevington, D. and Rasmussen, E. (1993), p. 62.
5. Jump, J. D. (1962), p. xxvi.
6. Bevington, D. and Rasmussen, E. (1993), p. 62.
7. Jump, J. D. (1962), p. xxvi.
8. Gill, R. (1990), p. xv.
9. Bevington, D. and Rasmussen, E. (1993), p. 62.
10. Keefer, M. (1991), p. xix.
11. Bevington, D. and Rasmussen, E. (1993), p. 72.
12. Logeman, H., ed. (1900), p. xvi.
13. Ormerod, D. and Wortham, C. (1985), preface.
14. Keefer, M. (1991), p. xxi.
15. Greg, W. W. (1950), p. 29.
16. Greg, W. W. (1950), p. 99.
17. Bevington, D. and Rasmussen, E. (1993), p. 47.
18. McGann, J. J. (1983), p. 41.
19. McGann, J. J. (1983), p. 48.
20. Shepherd, S. (1986), p. 96.
21. Gatti, H. (1989), p. 89.
22. Gatti, H. (1989), p. 89.
23. Gatti, H. (1989), p. 89.
24. Gill, R. (1990), p. xxiv.
25. Hattaway, M. (1970), p. 56.
26. Bevington, D. and Rasmussen, E. (1993), p. 16.
27. Gill, R. (1990), p. xxv.
28. Bevington, D. and Rasmussen, E. (1993), p. 16.
29. Jardine, L. and Grafton, A. (1990), p. 35.
30. Jardine, L. and Grafton, A. (1990), p. 40.
31. Jardine, L. and Grafton, A. (1990), p. 46.
32. Bacon, F. (1965), p. 31.
33. Eisenstein, E. (1979), vol. 1, p. 80.
34. Smeed, J. W. (1975), p. 99.
35. McMurtrie, D. C. (1943), p. 170.
36. McMurtrie, D. C. (1943), p. 170.
37. Goldschmidt, E. P. (1928), p. 44.
38. Smeed, J. W. (1975), p. 100.
39. Smeed, J. W. (1975), p. 100.
40. Eisenstein, E. (1979), vol.1, p. 50.
41. Larner, C. (1984), p. 4.
42. Anglo, S. (1977), p. 18.
43. Schumaker, W. (1972), p. 100.

44. Scot, R. (1930), p. 64.

45. Compare the A-text, 'Did not my conjuring speeches raise thee?', I.iii.46.

46. Logeman, H., ed. (1900), p. 126.

47. See also the version from the B-text, II.i.74–81:

> *Consummatum est.* This bill is ended,
> And Faustus hath bequeathed his soul to Lucifer.
> But what is this inscription on mine arm?
> '*Homo, fuge!*' Whither should I fly?
> If unto heaven, he'll throw me down to hell.–
> My senses are deceived; here's nothing writ.–
> O, yes, I see it plain. Even here is writ
> '*Homo, fuge!*' Yet shall not Faustus fly.

48. Derrida, J. (1978), p. 222.

49. Derrida, J. (1978), p. 226.

50. Derrida, J. (1978), p. 226.

51. Derrida, J. (1978), p. 226.

52. Palmer, P. M and More, R. P (1936), p. 63.

53. Palmer, P. M and More, R. P (1936), p. 65.

54. Palmer, P. M and More, R. P (1936), p. 65.

55. Palmer, P. M and More, R. P (1936), p. 85.

56. See also the version of this speech from the B-text:

> Here, take this book and peruse it well.
> The iterating of these lines brings gold;
> The framing of this circle on the ground
> Brings thunder, whirlwinds, storm, and lightning.
> Pronounce this thrice devoutly to thyself,
> And men in harness shall appear to thee,
> Ready to execute what thou command'st.
> (B:II.i.158–64)

57. This scene can also be read as a satire on the Protestant notion of the Bible as an autonomous authority.

58. The B-text version, at II.iii.83–4, is as follows: 'O, Christ, my Saviour, my Saviour,/Help to save distressèd Faustus' soul!'

59. For traditional discussions of the motives behind Faustus's refusal to repent, see Bevington and Rasmussen's (1993) introduction, p. 30; Warren, M. J. (1981), p. 124; and Keefer, M. H. (1991), pp. lxiv–lxv.

60. Logeman, H., ed. (1900), p. 115.

61. In the B-text Mephistopheles claims to have guided Faustus's eye over his books and thereby created his damnation: 'When thou took'st the book/To view the Scriptures, then I turned the leaves/And led thine eye' (B: V.ii.99–101). This can be read as another diabolical misuse and misrepresentation of the power of language to make things happen. Faustus cannot be forced to read in a particular way, just as his readings cannot force

events to take a certain course. This is yet another of Mephistopheles's epistemological deceptions.

62. Compare the English metaphysical poets, John Donne and George Herbert, who are also self-consciously concerned with how to express devotion to God without the use of fallen language.

Chapter 2

Edward II: Underwriting History

If the plays of *Doctor Faustus* examine writing's ability to remember itself, then *Edward II* extrapolates from this analysis a consideration of the dramatic genre which is most explicitly concerned with inscriptional remembrance: the chronicle history play. What in the plays of *Doctor Faustus* is an exposition of the nature of writing generally, becomes in *Edward II* a specific examination of the dramatization of those texts on which knowledge of the past is based. The printed books and blood contracts which preoccupy the plays of *Doctor Faustus* are therefore replaced on stage in *Edward II* by more overtly historical documents expressing the will of the sovereign and the concerns of his citizens. Dwelling on the explicitly textually-derived genre of the chronicle play, *Edward II* elaborates and expands the *Doctor Faustus* plays' staging of the scholar's contract to consider a whole host of letters, declarations and riddles. Opening with Gaveston's reading of the king's letter, the play's narrative is diverted through the Bishop of Canterbury's letter to the Pope, the proclamation banishing Gaveston, Margaret de Clare's letters from her uncle and her lover, the ransom request from Scotland, the reports from Normandy, the roll call of the dead and the torn name of Mortimer, eventually culminating in the Latin riddle. Thus the debate about writing, which in *Doctor Faustus* revolves around the scholar's contract, is expressed in *Edward II* through more numerous dramatizations of inscription and reception. Raising the textual stakes, *Edward II* multiplies moments of reading, writing and signing until the play reaches its conclusion with the letter whose very instability, ironically, renders it the safest weapon with which to kill the king.

Afraid of Edward's power even after his abdication, Mortimer decides to have his erstwhile king murdered. In an effort to disguise his responsibility for ordering the crime, Mortimer conceals his intentions in an unpunctuated Latin phrase. Mortimer explains:

> This letter written by a friend of ours
> Contains his death yet bids them save his life.
> '*Edwardum occidere nolite timere bonum est*':
> 'Fear not to kill the king, 'tis good he die.'

But read it thus, and that's another sense:
'*Edwardum occidere nolite timere bonum est*':
'Kill not the king, 'tis good to fear the worst'.
Unpointed as it is, thus shall it go,
That being dead, if it chance to be found,
Matrevis and the rest may bear the blame,
And we be quit that caused it to be done
(V.iv.6–16)[1]

Like the plays of *Doctor Faustus*, *Edward II* has at its heart a document designed to effect a man's death. Resembling the scholar's contract in more than its intent, however, Mortimer's letter is also remarkable because it requires repetition. Like the reiterated blood contract of the *Doctor Faustus* plays, Mortimer's letter reveals its significance by being doubly recited. Read one way, the letter instructs its recipient to protect the king; read another, it orders its recipient to kill the king. The instability of inscription, which Faustus fatally ignores in his own plays, is the very source of its usefulness in *Edward II*.

In spite of Mortimer's apparent mastery of language's proteanism, the Latin riddle precipitates a rather unexpected ending. Instead of avoiding responsibility for the letter because its meaning is ambiguous, Mortimer is readily identified as the culprit of the crime. The young King Edward III produces the supposedly untraceable letter in the final moments of the play and accuses Mortimer of murdering his father. Brandishing the letter, the king maintains 'if this be the hand of Mortimer' (V.vi.44) then he is guilty of sending a murderer to kill Edward. Acknowledging the hand as his own, Mortimer is punished; his severed head is brought on stage at the end of the play as proof that justice has been done.

The identification of Mortimer's guilt from the handwriting of the letter is somewhat surprising, not because character was not thought to be conveyed in inscriptional style, but rather because Mortimer claims that the letter has been 'written by a friend' (V.iv.6). Whether the line is an oversight, an admission that the Latin is derived from the author of the play's source, or an expression of the complicated relationship between writing and writer, it indicates an anxiety about language which permeates the whole play. Although Mortimer's description of the letter is ostensibly straightforward, on closer examination it is riven with contradictory ideas about textuality and identity. Firstly, Mortimer destabilizes his own identity in the Latin letter in order to destroy what he ironically believes to be Edward's unimpeachable identity as king. At this point in the play Edward is not a king and Mortimer should not persist in calling him one, nor in fearing his power as monarch. Mortimer is ultimately undone not by Edward II but instead by his son, Edward III. Mortimer's paradoxical view of identity foregrounds one of the play's key textual questions: whether or not the will of a sovereign dies with him or persists. Peopled significantly by three kings named Edward, the play dwells upon notions of perpetuity central to textual debates about identity and naming. Secondly, in a similarly contradictory vein, Mortimer concludes that should the letter be found 'being dead' (V.iv.14) he will not be held responsible for the crime it sanctioned. Imagining the letter and not Edward deceased, Mortimer confuses notions of absence and presence which define textual identity. In this way, Mortimer characterizes the animate Edward as the possessor of an eternal identity, while describing the inanimate letter in mortal terms. The conclusion of the play's complicated consideration of the stability of identity and the persistence of intentionality, Mortimer's Latin letter may also serve as an introduction to *Edward II*'s consideration of the textuality of history. A consideration which places the drama at a historical and theatrical moment when the textual performance of the past was being opened to analysis.

A Vantage Point? Dating

The play's self-conscious staging of the textuality of history depends, to a certain extent, upon the dating and generic classification of *Edward II*; for if the drama is not written as a chronicle history play after that genre was established in the theatre, it cannot occupy the necessary vantage point from which to examine the Elizabethan dramatization of the past. Attempts to date *Edward II* are complicated by two factors: the paucity of documents mentioning performance and the lack of information known about the company which probably owned and acted the play. The title page of the earliest extant edition in 1594 claims that *Edward II* was publicly performed in London by the Earl of Pembroke's Men.[2] Theatre historians know very little about this company. In *Literary Patronage in the English Renaissance: The Pembroke Family*, Michael Brennan cursorily dismisses Pembroke's Men as 'a miscellaneous group of players' drawn from 'fragments of other companies' under the management of James Burbage.[3] The extempore nature of the company finds explanation, however, in E. K. Chambers's connection between the appearance of Pembroke's Men and the resurgence of plague in London. Chambers maintains that the company developed as a consequence of the 'special conditions of the plague-years 1592–3' from the 'division for traveling purposes of the large London company formed by the amalgamation of Strange's and the Admiral's'.[4] Pembroke's Men were therefore a pragmatic response to a natural disaster; the company was created with the express purpose of touring outside the infected city. The title page's claim that *Edward II* was publicly performed in London before 1594 is consequently hard to verify. The only recorded appearance of the players in the capital occurs at court during the Christmas revels of 1592 when they performed on 'St John's Day, at night' and 'Twelfth Day, at night'.[5] Chambers concludes from this evidence that *Edward II* was one of the plays produced before the queen on these occasions.[6] Marlowe's drama of civil unrest and regicide was therefore probably played both inside and outside the capital between 1592 and 1593, as part of the court entertainments and the touring repertoire of Pembroke's Men.

Financial difficulties seem to have forced the company to cut short its provincial tour. Henslowe notes that Pembroke's Men returned to London in September 1593, selling their costumes and properties to the highest bidder.[7] Bankruptcy also necessitated the sale of other assets; a number of playbooks thought to have been owned by Pembroke's Men were entered in the Stationers' Register between 1593 and 1594, including *Edward II*. Mentioned in the register as early as 6 July 1593,[8] the first surviving edition of Marlowe's play was not printed until 1594, entitled:

> The troublesome/raigne and lamentable death of/Edward *the second, king* of/England: with the tragicall/*fall of proud* Mortimer.[9]

The play was reissued some years later in 1598 with an addition to the title; inserted after 'Mortimer' were the words:

> And also the life and death of Peirs Gaveston, the great Earle of Cornewall, and mighty fauorite of king Edward the Second.[10]

The quarto of 1598 is preserved in one form with the first two leaves supplied in manuscript. The handwritten title page of this volume records its date of publication as 1593. This indicates that an edition of the play was produced in 1593, probably in response to the public attention surrounding Marlowe's death, which a scribe used as his copy text for the 1598 printing.[11] From this outline of the play's performance and publication history, it seems likely that *Edward II* was composed early in 1592 when the genre of the chronicle drama was already established on the stage. Therefore, by the time *Edward II* was performed in London, public audiences would have already acclaimed all three parts of *Henry VI*, *Edward III*, *King Leir*, *King John* and *Jack Straw*. Emerging from the melting-pot of such success, Marlowe's chronicle play glistens with the newness of its medium, while bearing the tarnishes of a received genre.

A Vantage Point? Genre

The categorization of *Edward II* as a chronicle history play should not be taken for granted. Criticism of *Edward II* focuses primarily on the contested generic status of the play. Often awarded a place in a transitional genus of historio-tragedy, or treated as a misshapen attempt at a novel dramatic form, *Edward II* occupies an uncomfortable position somewhere between innovation and inadequacy. Recognized by some critics as the keynote in a new theatrical mode, *Edward II* is praised for its blending of history and tragedy.[12] In *The English History Play in the Age of Shakespeare*, Irving Ribner identifies the tragic element of the drama in the characterization of the usurped king. He maintains that *Edward II* represents 'for the first time in Elizabethan drama, a tragedy of character'.[13] Elaborating Ribner's argument, critics such as Harry Levin highlight Marlowe's selection of source material for *Edward II* which, it is claimed, prioritizes the personal over the public, the domestic over the political, and the tragic over the historical. Levin even proposes that *Edward II*'s adaptation of a public form for the expression of private emotions constitutes a 'unique contribution' to the stage.[14]

Of course, the promotion of *Edward II* as a private tragedy has significant critical ramifications. Most importantly, it concentrates attention on the personal relationship between Edward and Gaveston to the exclusion of the political and historical plots of the play. Moreover, giving a relationship which occupies only two-fifths of the action centre stage, this line of criticism opens the drama to somewhat skewed and partial readings. The most alarming of these readings must surely be Wilbur Sanders's consideration of *Edward II* in his study of Marlowe and Shakespeare. Claiming that the 'problem' with the play is 'Marlowe's mind', Sanders maintains that in *Edward II* the dramatist's imagination is 'a compulsively driven one, delivered up to deep internal drives'.[15] Removing the play from its historical context, Sanders relocates the drama in what he considers to be Marlowe's obsessively homosexual unconscious.

More recently, scholarship has recognized the importance of the play's political narrative. In 'Bedfellows Make Strange Politics', Sharon Tyler goes some way to redressing the critical imbalance when she argues: '*Edward II* is more than the tragedy of a man who happens to be a king, more than domestic tragedy on a large stage. It is a demonstration of the fact that, however personally unsuitable, a king is inescapably a king.'[16] In a similar critical volte-face, Michael Hattaway attempts to confound the categorization of the play as tragedy, claiming: 'It is arguable in fact that whereas Kyd was seeking to turn history to tragedy, Marlowe in this play sought to turn tragedy back towards history.'[17]

History, tragedy, historio-tragedy or homoeroticism, the Polonius-like generic confusion which *Edward II* excites depends not only upon the prejudices of the critical community at any given moment, but also on the indeterminacy of classification itself. In the introduction to his edition of *Edward II*, W. D. Briggs defines the genre of chronicle history thus:

> a dramatic composition purporting to draw its material from the chronicles (or from an equivalent source), treating those materials in a way to bring about their accidental (particularly their chronological) relations, recognizing as a rule no other principle of connection than those of personality, and having the general character of a survey of a more or less arbitrarily limited period.[18]

Briggs continues to argue that 'the chronicle history passes into the historical drama when the emphasis is shifted from accidental to organic relations, from *post hoc* to *propter hoc*'.[19] Although both types of drama described by Briggs are based on source material, he distinguishes chronicle drama from historical drama according to whether events are connected casually or causally. However, in his attempt to determine the mediated from the unmediated use of secondary sources, Briggs seems to mistake the genre of chronicle drama for the chronicles themselves; for like Briggs's definition of a chronicle play, the annals rely on historical sources to describe chronologically the reigns of kings. The more sophisticated act of interpretation and reconstruction, which Briggs reserves for the history play, is actually a prerequisite of the practice of adaptation which all drama based on historical texts must negotiate. Exegesis remains the thin line between chronicle and play. The critical reading and writing of the inscribed past is consequently the characteristic which defines the chronicle history play and which confirms *Edward II*'s membership of that genre.

From Source to Stage

Briggs's definitions of chronicle and historical drama radically underestimate not only the unavoidable process of adaptation which dramatization demands, but also the highly ambiguous and sometimes contradictory nature of the historical sources themselves. The chronicles failed to achieve the description of a univocal past. Instead, they disclosed the impossibility of writing an impartial and stable narrative, even when that story was meant to be based upon fact. The inconsistencies contained in the works of authors such as Hall, Fabian and More did not pass unnoticed by Tudor writers. In the 1563 edition of *Mirror for Magistrates* William Baldwin complains of 'the varyaunce of the cronycles',[20] which is an impediment to historical accuracy and that most elusive of postmodern phantoms, truth. He explains:

> This disagreynge of wryters is a great hinderaunce of the truthe, & no small
> cumbrauns to such as be diligent readers, besides the harme that may happen
> in succession of herytages. It were therfore a wurthye and a good dede for
> the nobilitie, to causc al the recordes to be sought, & a true and perfecte
> cronicle therout to be wrytten.[21]

It would seem that Baldwin's recommendation was never taken to heart by historians; 'a true and perfect' record of the past remained an unachievable goal. Even the most ecumenical of writers, such as Holinshed and Stow, produced accounts which varied not only from their sources but also from edition to edition. In *Divine Providence in the England of Shakespeare's Histories*, H. A. Kelly remarks that the 1587 edition of the *Chronicles*, upon which Shakespeare based his plays, was extensively rewritten by Abraham Fleming, who radically altered Holinshed's views as embodied in the original 1577/78 copy.[22]

The textual instability of the chronicles, which the variations in the two editions of Holinshed illustrate, is boldly underlined by the three versions of Stow's *A Summarie of Englyshe Chronicles* printed before *Edward II* was probably composed. Condensing previous accounts of the past, Stow's *Summarie* forms an attempt to encapsulate and popularly communicate all other historical works. However, Stow's effort to abridge and to edit documents with diverse historical viewpoints, produces not one abbreviation of the past but several, each telling a slightly different tale of bygone days. Stow's enterprise is inherently self-defeating, placing yet more layers of ambiguity between the originary moment and the description of that moment.

Demonstrating this tendency towards obfuscation, the three editions of Stow's *Summarie* available to Marlowe contain versions of Edward II's fall which agree neither upon the name of the king's murderer, nor the nature of the king's death. The 1565 edition simply states that 'About the rri day of September Edward the second was murdered in ye castell of Barkley by Sir Roger Mortymer, & was buried at Glocester.'[23] However, by 1575 this rendering of the past is expanded beyond all recognition to occupy almost two pages of print. Stow's normally hasty narrative style pauses to delineate the particulars of history which Marlowe almost certainly consulted prior to his own composition. Unlike the other editions, the 1575 text describes Edward's death in detail, including his treatment at the hands of Gurney and Matrevis, the contents of the Latin letter and the method of the murder itself. Preceding Holinshed's own account by at least two years, Stow's description warrants lengthy quotation:

> the Quene being perswaded by ye Bishoppe of Hereforde and other, that ye Erle of Lecester to muche fauored the olde king her husband, they appointed Thomas Gourney and Sir Maitravers to have him in theyre custodye, who conuaied him from Kenelworthe Casttell, to the Castle of Corfe, from thence to the Castle of Bristow, and then to Barkley. By ye way on their iourney, Thomas Gourney put a Crowne made of haye on the olde kinges head, and the more to deforme hym that he might not bee knowne, they made hym to alight, and set him on a molehill by a dyche where they cut his heare and shaved his beard with the colde water of the same diche, save yt he bytterly weeping shede pleintye of warme teares from his eyes. After they had shutte him up in the Castell of Barkley, the Quene and Bishop wrote chiding letters, blaming hys kepers, for that they kepte him not streyghte ynough, the same Bishoppe in his letters sophistically written has as foloweth.
>   *Edwardum occidere nolite timere bonum est.*
>   which may be Englished thus.
>   *To seeke to shede, King Edwardes blood, Refuse to feare, I compt it good.*
> Which Ridle they enterpreting to the worste scence, conueyed him into a most filthy dongion of the Castell, where they thought he shoulde have died of the stenche, but hee escaping this, as he had ofte by purging either up or doune escaped such poisons as they had geven hym, they came sodainly in the night (he lying in his bed) the xxij of September, and with heavye feather beddes first choked hym then put into his fundament a holow instrument, throughe whiche they brent his bowels, so that no outwarde wounde could be seene, his cry did move many of the castell and Towne of Barkeney to compassien, as them selves reported, the Quene and Byshoppe

that their tiranny mighte bee hyd, outlawed and Banyshed Thomas Gourney and John Maltraver, Thomas flyinge into Marseis, three yeres after being knowe, was taken & brought towarded Englande, was beheaded on the sea, least hee shoulde accuse the chiefe doers. John Maltravers (repentinge himselfe) laye long hidden in Germany.[24]

Refusing to shy away from the most anatomical details of the crime, Stow produces an informative and thorough record of regicide which places the onus of guilt squarely on the shoulders of the queen. Perhaps proving too uncompromising in its apportioning of blame, this account was excised from the 1590 edition of Stow. In the wake of Elizabeth's act of legal regicide, the execution of Mary Stuart in 1587, the past possibly became too sensitive to rehearse. Whatever the political implications of this recourse to rewriting, the *Summarie* printed in 1590 dealt cursorily with Edward's death, dispersing criminal culpability by naming three accomplices:

The 22 day of September at night K. Ed, the second was cruelly murthered, in the castel of Barkley, by the practise of the Q, his wife, the Lord Mortimer, and the Bishop of Hereforde, he was buried at Glocester.[25]

It is evident from the disparity between Stow's editions that Elizabethan chronicling was neither a univocal nor a consonant science.

The historical sources for *Edward II* consequently provide a precedent for the adaptation and manipulation of the past through rewriting. Revealing history as a textual performance which is constantly modified and mutated every time it is played, the chronicles disclose the textuality and therefore instability of what was popularly thought to be invariable fact. A licence for staging the past, Stow's and Holinshed's textual promiscuity encouraged dramatists to select and prioritize events from their sources and even to invent others anew. For instance, two of the most prominent features of Holinshed's description of Edward's reign are omitted from the theatrical retelling of the story. Edward's constant domestic feuds with the Knights Templar and the repeated border invasions by Robert Bruce which occupy much of the *Chronicles*' narrative are excluded from the play. Although Mortimer senior never returns from the Scottish wars to which the king dispatches him (I.iv.358–62), the play makes no further reference to a political situation which dominated Edward's reign. Disregarding not only the prevailing historical details of the reign, the theatrical rendering of the past is also unmindful of potentially dramatic moments described by its sources. Holinshed's depiction of the pretender John Poydras's claim to the throne is surprisingly overlooked by the narrative of *Edward II*.[26] Instead, the play creates a tightly-woven narrative web which gives definition to images of geographical isolation, personal rivalry and secret machinations.

Removing entirely many of Holinshed's characters, the dramatic version of Edward's reign refocuses upon others. As many critics have pointed out,[27] the historical figures of Edward's reign are often recast socially or professionally in the drama. Most strikingly, the play presents the Spencers as ambitious members of the court entourage, when according to Holinshed they were actually mighty counsellors.[28] The *Chronicles* record that Edward was persuaded by the Spencers' influence to appoint Sir Robert Baldock Lord Chancellor of England.[29] Baldock and the Spencers therefore constituted the political driving force in the country. Omitted, altered and adapted, the information contained in Marlowe's sources is employed theatrically with scant respect for chronological accuracy or memorial exactitude. As if in recognition of history's status as text, the playwright foregrounds narrative opportunity rather than fidelity to source material.

Letters, Letters, Everywhere

The narrative opportunity which history offers drama is, of course, the same for any literary retelling of the past; the process of selection and prioritization which occupies Marlowe's rendering of history is consequently no different from any other dramatization of source material. However, what *Edward II* does do differently is to extrapolate from this basic process of adaptation a narrative expression of the instability of textuality and hence of historical sources. By punctuating the action with an excess of official documents, political messages and letters, *Edward II* stages the textually-derived nature of its genre. What is more, the play's self-conscious dramatization of the ambiguity of those sources on which knowledge of the past is based, gives rise to textual debates about the nature of identity and the perpetuity of intent. These debates find their focus in a highly politically-charged question: does the will of the monarch outlive his death in writing? The resolution of this question, which was of such importance to the Tudor monarchs, is expressed through *Edward II*'s textual cabaret of competing letters which the opening moments of the play initiate.

Edward II begins significantly with Gaveston's entrance, reading a letter brought from the king. As history is conventionally considered to be the recorded words of kings or of their counsellors, this scene may be interpreted as a literalization of the process of rereading the past with which the play is concerned.[30] It is important to note here that *Edward II* stages the play of history with three interrelated features; it is composed of the absent king's words, conveyed to a present person, in written form. History is therefore, in the most fundamental way, premised upon inscription. For as a discipline which tells the story of the past to an anticipated future, history necessarily requires writing to communicate its narrative. It is writing's ability to preserve the words of long dead generations which makes it the principal tool of the historian.[31] In *History/Writing* Albert Cook illuminates the inevitable connection between the possibility of describing the past and inscription. He claims that history 'may be said to call for writing insofar as it stands at a fixed remove from the past for the shaping and heightening of its patterns'.[32] The reading of the king's letter at the start of *Edward II* consequently realizes the textuality of history in its most inchoate form. Moreover, it highlights the complex negotiations texts introduce between their absent authors and present readers.

Reading the king's words aloud, Gaveston recites:

> 'My father is deceased; come Gaveston,
> And share the kingdom with thy dearest friend.'
> (I.i.1–2)

This textual performance complicates notions of absence and presence crucial to an understanding of inscription's nature. Conventionally, writing is a reminder of the writer's absence; its marks belie the fact that the author has been at work and is now no longer there. This inscriptional characteristic is most obvious in the epistolary form which is overtly designed to communicate a message when the sender cannot be present. The circumstance on which all letters are based is, however, also a necessary condition of any act of inscription, which inevitably requires the loss of its writer. The letter which Gaveston reads apparently serves to underline the textual theory of authorial absence; it is not only marked by its author's absence but also by a moment of absolute loss: the death of the writer's father. The king's letter is consequently doubly facilitated by absence; it is made possible by the metaphorical death of its author, as well as the actual death of that author's father.

The letter's reinforcement of the concept of authorial absence is, however, more contradictory than it at first appears. Complicating the polarities of absence and presence, the letter describes the king's death when the king still lives. The sender of the letter is, in a political sense, at once dead and alive, extant and extinct. The death of Edward's father has made him king, and consequently the king has never really died; monarchical rule has continued seamlessly. The king is dead: long live the king. Further confusing matters, the king is not only simultaneously absent and present because he is both alive and dead, he is also the bearer of a constant identity, an unchanging name. Edward II succeeds his dead father Edward I, just as his son ultimately succeeds him at the end of the play as Edward III. The sender of the letter is therefore at the same time absent and present both in terms of his kingly title and his name, Edward. The letter's destabilization of the apparently mutually-exclusive terms of absence and presence also finds expression in Gaveston's claim that:

> The sight of London to my exiled eyes
> Is as Elysium to a new-come soul
> (I.i.10–11)

Characterizing himself as deceased, Gaveston describes his lover's realm as the mythic Greek abode of the dead. Even Edward's kingdom is inscribed with loss and absence. This confusion of ontological certainties raises important issues about textual and authorial authority; it asks whether or not, like his identity, the king's word lives on as a potent force even after his death.

Attempts to discern the potency of the word largely depend on the vagaries of textual interpretation. This circumstance is amply demonstrated by Gaveston's reaction to the king's letter. Investing the king's words with an absolute authority which the play's narrative fails to bear out, Gaveston exclaims that Edward's letter makes him 'surfeit with delight' (I.i.3). The king's words are described by his lover as immediately and excessively affecting. Gaveston therefore bestows upon Edward's language an emotional forcefulness which he paradoxically denies other texts addressed to him. Only a few lines later, Gaveston dismisses the Third Man's curse to 'perish by a soldier's hand' as ineffectual (I.i.36). Brushing aside the pauper's execration, Gaveston boasts:

> [*Aside*] Ay, ay these words of his move me as much
> As if a goose should play the porpintine
> And dart her plumes, thinking to pierce my breast.
> (I.i.38–40)

Comparing the Third Man's words to feathers, Gaveston disdains their potency. Unlike the king's text, then, which he claims can effect a feeling of physical satisfaction, Gaveston believes the curse to be inert. Ironically, however, it is the beggar, not the king, who is in some sense able to keep his word in the play; never sharing the kingdom, Gaveston does die at the hands of a rebel warrior. From the opening moments of *Edward II*, the written word becomes the site of dramatic conflict. Indeed, as notions of textual identity and linguistic autocracy become increasingly complicated, the play lays bare the processes by which the word can be created and, more importantly, kept.

Preaching on Poles: The Reanimation of the Dead

The identification of a text's authority is fraught with difficulties because writing is always physically authorless and therefore without a voice which can be held accountable. Consequently, it can be argued that those texts which are considered commanding are actually no more than works upon which the community of readers have decided to bestow authority, like the Bible or the American constitution; in reality, of course, all texts are endowed with the same lack of agency. However, upsetting ontological norms, *Edward II* problematizes the notion of authorial absence by creating a power struggle in which the words of a dead, non-present author are set in opposition with those of a living one. On his coronation, Edward II seeks to overturn his father's authorship of the law by calling his lover, Gaveston, back from exile. The king's claim to textual supremacy meets with defiance; his barons decide to ignore his word and uphold the will of the literally and metaphorically absent author, Edward I. Mortimer tells Edward II:

> Mine uncle here, this Earl, and I myself,
> Were sworn to your father at his death
> That he should ne'er return into the realm:
> And I know my lord, ere I will break my oath,
> This sword of mine that should offend your foes,
> Shall sleep within the scabbard at thy need,
> And underneath thy banners march who will,
> For Mortimer will hang his armour up.
> (I.i.81–8)

Explaining that the barons will remain faithful to the word of the previous king, Mortimer dismisses Edward II's attempt to write his own kingship, to make his own history. It is this conflict between the dead and living word of the king which precipitates the action of the play and which ultimately produces Edward II's downfall. Although Edward I is physically absent from the world of the play, his word is ubiquitous; he is not only alive in the barons' loyalty but also in the identity of his patronymically named son. Edward II's sovereignty is therefore circumscribed by his dead father's will.

Dramatizing the way in which the past holds the present to ransom, *Edward II* disrupts notions of life and death with images of ontological confusion. It is as if the interruption of Edward I's exequies by Gaveston's imprisonment of the Bishop of Coventry (I.i.196) creates a realm in which the dead can become a formidable force in the present. Contributing to this state of limbo, Gaveston repeatedly images himself as a dead soul, not only upon his entry to London which he likens to Elysium (I.i.10–11), but also in his comparison between the torments of hell and his banishment from the king (I.i.145–6). Becoming an increasingly tangible presence in the play, the dead are eventually depicted as actually reanimated. Like history, the dead in *Edward II* make extinguished voices articulate once more. In the first scene Kent introduces the image of the speaking yet severed head. He tells the king to punish the rebel barons and 'let these their heads/Preach upon poles for trespass of their tongues' (I.i.116–17). Echoing this sentiment a couple of acts later, Spencer also advises the king to 'Strike off their heads and let them preach on poles' (III.ii.20). In 'Sovereignty, Disorder and Fetishism in Marlowe's *Edward II*', David Thurn attributes the play's emphasis upon headlessness to the emblematization of power. He maintains that the decapitated head is 'the sign of power over one's enemies' in *Edward II*.[33] The heads which preach on poles are, however, more than a symbol of absolute might; they are an expression of the refusal of the past to be silenced. The act of decapitation significantly fails to muzzle the outspoken. Instead death, paradoxically, renders the dead more capable of speech. Indeed, in death the traitors do not simply talk, they preach. In other words, the decapitated are imaged in the play as the deliverers of sermons or moral lessons; they are the teachers of the present. Like history which makes the past pertinent to the present, the dead in *Edward II* educate those who have executed them.

The clamorous nation of the dead, which threatens to overwhelm Edward's kingdom, finds expression not only in the vociferous severed heads, but also in the many absent father-figures who people the play; Edward's father is dead, as is Baldock and Spencer's master, while Mortimer's uncle is captured by the Scots, never to be returned. Despite their physical absence from the play, these 'fathers' precipitate much of the action; just as the barons fight to keep Edward I's word, they also declare war on the king because he refuses to ransom Mortimer senior. In response to Mortimer's demand that he pay his uncle's ransom, Edward exclaims: 'Shall I still be haunted thus?' (II.ii.154). The king seems to recognize here that his authority is directly subject to the absent and dead, or at least, to the upholders of their rights.

Perhaps in an effort to overcome the past's stranglehold on the present, Edward sets about reinventing himself as a dead father. The king twice alludes to his relationship with Gaveston in mythic paternal terms. At the start of the play Edward tells his returning lover that:

> Not Hylas was more mourned of Hercules
> Than thou hast been of me since thy exile.
> (I.i.143–4)

Hercules murdered Hylas's father before assuming his role. Edward consequently refashions himself as simultaneously the killer of Gaveston's father and his surrogate parent. Edward's attempt to father his own past is therefore riven with contradictions. Later in the play, Edward pictures Gaveston as both his lover and his daughter:

> Thy absence made me droop and pine away,
> For as the lovers of fair Danaë,
> When she was locked up in a brasen tower,
> Desired her more and waxed outrageous,
> So did it sure with me
> (II.ii.52–6)

Fearful Acrisius imprisoned his daughter, Danaë, to confound the prophecy which foretold that a son born to her would kill him. Ostensibly comparing himself with one of the lovers of the unjustly incarcerated Danaë, Edward cannot conceal his resemblance to Acrisius, her father. For just as Acrisius imprisoned his beloved daughter, so too did Edward command his beloved Gaveston's banishment. Confusing his own identity by seeking the status of a dead father, Edward importantly fails to understand that it is not really the past that he must master, but rather the uses of it by the present. In reality, the dead cannot preach upon poles unless the living choose to ventriloquize them. Like Acrisius, Edward is not undone by the prophetic texts of the past, but rather by his willingness to become their slave. History can only become destiny when it retells what has happened with hindsight.

The Fantasy of Perpetuity

Ultimately revealing the impossibility of the actual revivification of the dead,[34] *Edward II* discloses the ways in which the present seeks to naturalize its re-invention of the past; it is not that the past can live on, but rather that the present can give birth to it anew. History's apparent ability to give voice to the dead is, therefore, just as illusory as Edward I's ability to be resurrected after his own death. The king and his history are complicit in legal and textual myths which recreate the past with a sort of perpetuity which no man and no text can ever really possess, as men must die and texts cannot retain a fixed and stable meaning over time.[35] In political terms, however, Edward I can live on; he is a monarch and consequently part of a corporate entity which defies mortality: the body politic.

According to the law, the monarch could not die; his natural body might be destroyed by time, but his body politic would on his physical death be instantaneously invested in his successor.[36] Embodying the persevering spirit of the people, the land and the crown, the king's body politic was legally not allowed to die; it simply assumed another face, that of its heir. Although physically extinct in the play, Edward I is a corporate presence whose word lives on. Despite Edward I's death, his desires persist in the concept of the body politic which the nobles claim to represent when they defy the new king, Edward II. In *Sodomy and Interpretation*, Gregory Bredbeck claims that 'Mortimer's affront to the king is actually an allegiance to the politic king'.[37] As Edward II's rescinding of Gaveston's exile is in direct contravention of the desires of his body politic, the barons are justified in opposing him. Edward II's sovereignty is, therefore, paradoxically limited by a legal mechanism designed to provide his office with unimpeachable authority. The conflict between monarch and body politic which *Edward II* rehearses was of particular importance to Elizabethans. Questioning the responsibility of the queen to her body politic, parliament asked whether or not Elizabeth's choice of successor was to be constrained by the inscribed wishes of her dead father.

In an unprecedented move, Henry VIII sought to inhibit his line of succession by inscribing it in writing. Initially by statute and eventually by testament, Henry wrote and rewrote the identity of his heir. Unlike previous monarchs who customarily named their successors, Henry legitimized his offspring's right to the throne by inscribing it in law. Three Acts of Succession were passed during Henry's reign, each one revising his choice of heir as successive marriages altered the characters of history. The king's children were consequently named only to be unnamed later as the statutes determined the legality of their claims to the crown. The first Act of Succession of 1534 attempted to silence disapproval at Henry's divorce by commanding allegiance to Anne Boleyn and her daughter, Elizabeth. However, upon marrying Jane Seymour the king overturned this act and passed a second statute affecting the inheritance. The Act of Succession of 1536 made Mary and Elizabeth bastards, while any offspring of the new queen were to be legitimate heirs to the throne. In 1537 Jane was delivered of a sickly child, Edward. Fearing his only male heir might die before reaching adulthood, Henry initiated the final Act of Succession in 1544. This statute restored Mary and Elizabeth to the line of inheritance and created a regency council to advise Edward during his minority. The composition of the council was to be determined by Henry's last will and testament.

The heterodoxy of this textual approach to inheritance meant that the king's testament had to be endorsed in advance by the legislature; Henry was only given *carte blanche* to redraw the line of inheritance if his preferences were written down and signed. This process of textual verification, however, created more problems than it resolved. Henry's last will and testament radically failed to fix his dynastic desires. On 26 December 1546, Hertford, Lisle, Paget and Denny were summoned to the king's sickbed to revise his will. Fighting for his life, Henry named his successors: Edward, Mary and Elizabeth were to inherit the crown in that order, and a regency council of sixteen members was nominated. No provision was made at this stage for a Protector. However, on 28 January, as Henry's sickness rendered him unconscious, the will remained unsigned. Hertford, Paget, Herbert and Denny decided to stamp the will to make it legally binding; they also added several clauses which gave the regency council absolute authority and which provided for the king's debts to be met in full after his death. Both these clauses were obviously of benefit to Henry's nobles, who were effectively bequeathed the right to govern as they pleased and to pay themselves for doing so. Moreover, it is possible that Henry's will was actually altered after his death to create the office of Lord Protector for Hertford.[38] John Guy seems to favour this reading of events and mentions in his study, *Tudor England*, that Hertford's son 'admitted that his father was "his own carver"'.[39] Whether or not Henry's will was actively tampered with is, in textual terms, beside the point. It is not the fact that the king's will was unsigned which made it unable to fix the succession, but rather, that it was inscribed.

The extravagant measures Henry took to clarify the succession were ironically thwarted by their textuality. Written down, Henry's deathbed desires for the succession raise the same problems of interpretation and authentication which every text must negotiate. The importance of the will's textuality is reinforced by the uses to which it was later put. During the Elizabethan succession crisis of the 1580s, Henry's will was marshalled by parliamentarians and supporters of the queen alike. Henry's testament was employed by each of the competing factions as proof of their particular right to decide who should inherit the crown. Commenting upon the parliamentary cause in *Shakespeare and the Politics of Protestant England*, Donna Hamilton explains that because Henry's will had been made law it was claimed that the succession should be determined by 'the jurisdiction of parliament'.[40] Henry's attempt to resolve ambiguity consequently became its very cause; the king's words were hijacked for political purposes he could not possibly have foreseen. The uses to which Henry's will was put illustrate the myth of textual and monarchical perpetuity: the king's will does not live on after his death, it is simply reinterpreted and thereby rewritten depending on the political needs of the moment. In this way, history is created and recreated as simultaneously an example for and a justification of the present. Staging this process, *Edward II* shows that even historical texts cannot fix the identity nor the desires of their authors. Edward I's word can only outlive him because the barons reinvent it to serve their peculiar ends.

Naming Names

The realization that the perpetuity of the king's will is a politically expedient myth is rehearsed in *Edward II* through the numerous moments of naming and signing which question the possibility of identity to live on. The barons subscribe their names to Gaveston's banishment, Arundel pledges his name in return for a prisoner, Edward tears Mortimer's name to pieces, and the king witnesses the transfer of his name to another man. The play's concentration on the name develops notions of identity to which the concepts of textual and political perpetuity are intimately linked. Introduced in the first scene when Gaveston reads from the king's letter, the problem of embodying a stable and repeatable identity in writing is examined by *Edward II*. In contradiction with the play's disruption of the polarities of absence and presence in the images of the speaking dead, the examination of the name reinforces the impossibility of the word to retain the character or intention of its author. However, it is the conflict between the actual and the mythic power of the name which at once epitomizes the play's political and textual concerns about identity. The action is largely created by the characters' desire to assume a name whose very acquisition proves its lack of authority; if the king's name can be usurped then it cannot bestow absolute power. Edward's enforced inscription of his name at the start of the play stages this dilemma.

Threatening the king with deposition if he will not sign the document banishing Gaveston, Mortimer exclaims:

> Curse him if he refuse, and then may we
> Depose him and elect another king.
> (I.iv.54–5)

Paradoxically demanding to exercise the potency of the king's name, while at the same time reminding Edward that his title can be rescinded, Mortimer discloses the instability of identity. The transferability of both Edward's Christian name and his kingly title, to which the play ultimately bears testimony, illustrates the proteanism of the name. The nature of the proper noun, which cannot convey individuality nor retain character over time, finds expression in *Edward II*'s examination of naming. Proper nouns are consequently shown to be just another type of word which like all forms of language are subject to interpretation. Revealing the contradictions of the signed name, which is meant to indicate personal intent but which actually belies the impossibility of inscribing individuality, the scene undermines not only Edward's name but also those of his titled noblemen. Apparently uncomprehending of the implications this has for the stability his own name, Edward ironically responds to Mortimer's threats by offering titles to the barons. In his effort to placate the unhappy nobles, Edward suggests that he gives them new names:

> My lord, you shall be Chancellor of the realm,
> Thou Lancaster, High Admiral of our fleet,
> Young Mortimer and his uncle shall be earls,
> And you lord Warwick, President of the North
> (I.iv.65–8)

The Bishop of Canterbury rejects Edward's offer, saying: 'Nothing shall alter us' (I.iv.74). These words importantly incorporate the barons' abiding intent with their refusal to change their identity. The play thereby foregrounds notions of perpetuity, identity and intentionality in one phrase. Edward, of course, eventually accedes to the barons' demands and, in contradiction with his desire to have Gaveston, signs the decree banishing him. *Edward II* consequently questions the usefulness of the signature as a mark of binding intent.

Contemplating what it means to be named and to sign that name, the play recites not only the issues surrounding Henry's will, but also the circumstances contingent upon the Elizabethan Bond of Association. In 1584, while Mary Queen of Scots was still a presence to inspire assassination attempts upon the childless Elizabeth, the nobility introduced a so-called Bond of Association. In 'The Monarchical Republic of Queen Elizabeth I', Patrick Collinson describes the bond:

> This document engaged those who were sworn to its terms and who had applied to it their signatures and seals to pursue 'to the uttermost extermination' anybody attempting by any act, counsel or consent to bring harm to the queen's royal person, their comforters, aiders and abettors: and to resist the succession of any individual on whose behalf such acts might be attempted or committed.[41]

Designed to give the nobles authority over the succession, the bond provided for its signatories to punish would-be assassins and to elect a new monarch. The bond thereby created a form of vigilante justice. Ostensibly a gesture of obeisance to the monarch, the bond was actually an opportunity for Elizabethan noblemen to decide who should be handed the reins of government next. Inscribing one's name, therefore, need not mean what it superficially appears; a signature does not express an individual's intent.

Although a signature is conventionally considered to be a mark of identification and authentication, the inscribed name is actually a text which is by definition indeterminate. A signature cannot convey personal desires, as writing is incapable of perpetuating the identity of its author. Consequently, Edward's signature on the document decreeing Gaveston's banishment does not communicate a freely-given guarantee of assent; the king does not actually want his lover to be exiled. Similarly, the signatures appended to the Bond of Association did not necessarily express the unselfish loyalty of their writers. The potency of Edward's title relies, in reality, upon the interpretation of its readership; if the community of readers agrees to invest the king's name with a special authority then his signature is meaningful. The king's sovereignty depends, therefore, on the permission of his citizens; his name is always in need of consent. Illustrating the subjection of the name to its subjects, *Edward II* stages the barons' loss of faith in the king's title.

In anticipation of the eventual dissolution of Edward's name, the play demonstrates the gradual failure of the king's name to command his nobles. Sent to beg the barons to release Gaveston temporarily, Arundel is initially denied by Mortimer who does not believe the king's word. Arundel is thereby forced to give his own pledge for Gaveston's safe return. The king, however, does not get to see Gaveston before his execution, as the nobles renege upon their promise and seize their prisoner once more. Arundel explains to Edward that despite pledging 'the honour of my name' (III.ii.98), the nobles would not consent to Gaveston's release. Thus anticipating the cogency of his monarch's and his own name, Arundel is disappointed. The effectiveness of the characters' names as terms of honour or as promises is repeatedly shown by the narrative to be both inconsistent and capricious.

The instability of the name, which is significant at one moment only to be rendered meaningless the next, is examined more fully by the play's consideration of patronage. The allocation of titles in the play accentuates the processes by which names are usually given and hence writes large the act of christening. Returning from exile at the beginning of the play, Gaveston is renamed by his lover. Creating Gaveston as Lord High Chamberlain, Chief Secretary to the State, Earl of Cornwall, King and Lord of Man (I.i.153–5), Edward employs the name as a parent might; he renames Gaveston as a sign of his love for him, but more importantly, as a mark of his ownership of him. Relying upon the biblical belief that the act of naming can control the thing named, Edward seeks to refashion his lover as simultaneously a socially acceptable partner and the property of a king. Just as Adam named the birds and the beasts of Eden as an expression of his sovereignty over them, Edward renames Gaveston in an effort to control his citizens' perception of him and thereby ensure his presence in the kingdom.

The mythic power of the name to reshape reality is, however, ultimately shown to be illusory in *Edward II*. Despite having lavished honourable titles upon his lover, Edward importantly fails to transform him into a worthy consort for a king; the barons are not prevented from banishing and executing Gaveston. Naming is consequently unable to define, change or fix identity in the play. Instead, the process of naming and the name itself are revealed to be indeterminate and transferable. When Edward offers the barons new titles to dissuade them from banishing Gaveston (I.iv.65–73), he unwittingly discloses the fact that names can be applied and reapplied without bearing the mark of their occupier; titles and names are radically without individuality. Failing to convey either ownership or identity, the name can be invented and re-invented by anyone. As proof of this circumstance, Isabella renames her son, Edward, the Lord Warden of the Realm (IV.v.35). The right to name is therefore not exclusive to the king, while the name itself is not the peculiar property of the named. Existing for anyone to conjure with, confer, or convert, names are without either a sovereign or an owner; they are simply words.

The transpositive quality of the name is most obviously expressed in *Edward II* by the displacement of the king's title. Initially, Edward transfers his own name to Gaveston's use, but eventually his title is transferred by others in the moment of his deposition. In the first scene, Edward puts his name at Gaveston's disposal. Apparently unmindful of the implications of his offer, the king tells his lover to 'Save or condemn, and in our name command' (I.i.168). In this moment, Edward ironically introduces a process which will ultimately rob him of his kingdom, his office and his life: the act of transplanting a name from one man to another. For by underlining the availability of his title for others' use, the king instigates his own downfall. Consequently, when Mortimer wants to legitimize his authority, he attempts to appropriate Edward's name. Explaining to Isabella the necessity of crowning her son, Mortimer says: 'our behoof will bear the greater sway/Whenas a king's name shall be under-writ' (V.ii.13–14). Doubly underwriting his actions with the names of Edward II and Edward III, Mortimer exposes the rupture between king and title, person and signature, author and text which makes usurpation possible; they are not one and the same, but rather many and various. The separation of the name from the named is, moreover, foreshadowed by Edward's dismemberment of Mortimer's signature. Renouncing Mortimer's authority to remove him from Leicester's charge, Edward rips apart the decree bearing his name. However, tearing Mortimer's signature to shreds, Edward realizes that he has executed a 'poor revenge' (V.i.141). Although he desires Mortimer's limbs to 'be torn as is this paper' (V.i.142), Edward cannot actually inflict violence on his rival's body by destroying his signature; the name and the named are unconnected and hence cannot affect one another.

Like Edward I, the name marks its own physical absence from the play; able to live on after the person named has either gone away, or has actually died, the name importantly lacks presence. It is consequently a sort of *memento mori* or reminder of a limited textual perpetuity which mortal beings can never possess. Expressing this circumstance, the proper noun 'Mortimer' undergoes a series of transformations or puns in the play which each indicate the physical absence of the named from the name, or, metaphorically speaking, the name's deadliness. Most obviously, the word 'Mortimer' actually means 'dead sea' in French (II.iii.21–4). Linguistically premised on the notion of loss or death, Mortimer's name contorts into other words which suggest not only the deadliness of the name but also its very textuality; the name is a text which is open to interpretation. Elaborating the aside 'That villain Mortimer! I'll be his death' (I.i.80), Gaveston develops the pun '*Mort Dieu!*' (I.i.89) or 'by the death of God'. Mortimer's name is consequently contorted by Gaveston to produce deadly new meanings. Similarly, Lancaster's shield bears the Latin motto '*Undique mors est*' (II.ii.28) or 'death is on all sides'. The tag alludes to Lancaster's accomplice, Mortimer, who is preparing to murder the newly-returned Gaveston. The proper noun 'Mortimer' is thereby transformed into different anagrams which mark and re-mark the physical absence signposted by the name. Only able to communicate its non-presence, then, the name is importantly unable to convey identity or intent over time. It is, however, this inability which renders the name infinitely transferable and consequently able to make and unmake kings. In the final scenes of *Edward II*, the play's discussion of textual identity culminates as one king is killed and another one crowned. The textual themes which have preoccupied the rest of the play are ultimately incorporated in a single document, the Latin letter. Unsigned, unpunctuated and unclear, the text which draws the action to its close involves those issues of textual perpetuity and interpretation crucial to *Edward II*'s staging of the past.

Authoring Kingship

Wishing Edward dead while at the same time refusing to take responsibility for his murder, Mortimer devises a letter which he believes to be not only untraceable but also so equivocal it cannot be produced as evidence against him. Inscribing his desire for Edward's murder in an unsigned and unpunctuated Latin phrase which means fear to kill the king, or fear not to kill the king (V.iv.6–16), depending on the emphasis of the reader, Mortimer apparently understands the instability of textual identity and intentionality which the narrative has taken such pains to express. The cleverness of the Latin letter must, however, be questioned when it is remembered that the play ends not with Mortimer's uncontested governorship of England but with his execution for Edward II's murder. Mortimer's severed head is placed on his victim's hearse to appease the erstwhile king's murdered ghost (V.vi.95–102). Far from lacking its author's identity and intent, the Latin letter bears striking testimony to Mortimer's crime; the character and desires of the writer seem, exceptionally, to have lived on in his writing.

If the play's ending is to be read as a reassertion of writing's ability to convey an unchanging message over time, then Edward's murder may also be interpreted as a moment of stable and lasting inscription: an event of fixed historical significance. Commenting on the method by which Lightborn kills Edward, Gregory Bredbeck notes that 'The murder of Edward by raping him with a red-hot poker – quite literally branding him with sodomy – can be seen as an attempt to "write" onto him the homoeroticism constantly ascribed to him.'[42] Interpreting Edward's violent murder as an act of inscription which turns the king's body into an unproblematic text, Bredbeck importantly fails to recognize two aspects of the crime. Firstly, the nature of Edward's murder is not a dramatic invention; the play's chronicle sources record in detail the method employed to kill the king. Secondly, the manner of Edward's murder was designed not to leave a lasting message on his body, but rather to ensure that his corpse was unmarked and consequently unable to attest to its unlawful killing. The murder which Mortimer's letter incites does not, therefore, reinforce a notion of textual perpetuity. Instead, it further complicates the play's prior discussions of identity and intentionality.

Claiming sovereignty at the end of the play, Edward III accuses Mortimer of murdering his father. Significantly, his accusation relies on two authorizing myths which the play has already examined and found to be illusory: the perpetuity both of the king's will after his death and the writer's individuality after the moment of writing. Initially, Edward III tells Mortimer that he knows him to be responsible for Edward II's murder because he is now part of the body politic and therefore able to speak with his father's voice. The new king protests:

> Traitor, in me my loving father speaks
> And plainly saith 'twas thou that murderedst him.
> (V.vi.41–2)

Appealing to the authority bestowed upon him by the corporate entity of kingship, Edward claims to vocalize the will of the dead. Unlike Edward II, whose dead father overwhelmed his own reign, Edward III manages to make the voices of the past coincide with his own. This ostensibly happy coincidence does not, however, necessarily prove that the young king has deferred to the abiding will of his ancestors. This moment more likely confirms Edward III's pragmatic ability to ventriloquize his own desires through the mouth of the body politic. Apparently scornful of the new king's attempt to condemn him with little more than a mythic notion of royal perpetuity, Mortimer inquires: 'But hath your grace no other proof than this?' (V.vi.43). Undeterred by this retort, Edward III immediately produces the Latin letter as proof of the crime. Making his second appeal to an authorizing myth, Edward III claims that the unsigned and utterly ambiguous note clearly identifies Mortimer as the murderer of his father. The king maintains that 'if this be the hand of Mortimer' (V.vi.44) then he is responsible for regicide. Before acknowledging the handwriting as his own,[43] Mortimer importantly exclaims 'False Gurney hath betrayed me and himself' (V.vi.45). In this outburst, Mortimer seems to recognize that his guilt does not actually depend upon the authenticity of the letter, but rather upon the forced confession of an accomplice. Writing has not suddenly become able to convey identity and intentionality over time at the end of the play. It is not that Edward III can prove textually that Mortimer ordered his father's murder, but that as king he can impose his reading of the letter and of the voice of the body politic to suit his own political ends. Like the barons at the beginning of the play, Edward III uses myths of perpetuity to justify his actions in the present.

A matter of reading, Edward III's victory over Mortimer discloses the fact that textual instability initiates rather than invalidates interpretation. Through its examination of the processes by which the past is reread and thereby re-invented, *Edward II* stages the writing of history, the articulation of no longer present events. Consequently, when Edward III places Mortimer's decapitated head on his father's hearse, he literalizes the play's metaphorical representation of history, the speaking yet severed head. However, at the end of *Edward II* this motif does not confuse the ontological certainties of absence and presence by depicting the dead as reanimated to speak in the present. Instead, the play's closing tableau belies the textual and political myths of perpetuity which have preoccupied the narrative to show that the dead are only able to speak when the present speaks for them; Mortimer's head is only meaningful when Edward III makes it so. Reaching its conclusion, *Edward II* witnesses the emergence of a consummate historian and politician; Edward III is born into the world of the play as a man capable of exploiting the past in order to invent the present and circumscribe the future.

Notes

1. The edition of *Edward II* used in this chapter is edited by W. M. Merchant, for the New Mermaid series. London: A. & C. Black, 1967.
2. Charlton, H. B. and Waller, R. D., eds (1930), p. 1.
3. Brennan, M. (1988), p. 94.
4. Chambers, E. K. (1923), vol. 2, p. 129.
5. Murray, J. T. (1910), vol. 1, p. 71.
6. Chambers, E. K. (1923), vol. 3, p. 425.
7. Brennan, M. (1988), p. 94.

8.   Chambers, E. K. (1923), vol 2, p. 128.
9.   Charlton, H. B. and Waller, R. D., eds (1930), p. 1.
10. Charlton, H. B. and Waller, R. D., eds (1930), p. 1.
11. Charlton, H. B. and Waller, R. D., eds (1930), p. 3.
12. Ribner, I. (1957), p. 128.
13. Ribner, I. (1957), p. 127.
14. Ribner, I. (1957), p. 110.
15. Sanders, W. (1968), p. 125.
16. Tyler, S. (1985), p. 66.
17. Hattaway, M. (1982), p. 144.
18. Briggs, W. D. (1914), pp. xxi–xxii.
19. Briggs, W. D. (1914), pp. xxi–xxii.
20. Campbell, L. B. (1938), p. 267.
21. Campbell, L. B. (1938), p. 267.
22. Kelly, H. A. (1970), p. 138.
23. Stow, J. (1565), pp. 111–12.
24. Stow, J. (1575), pp. 258–9.
25. Stow, J. (1590), p. 275.
26. Holinshed, R. (1577), vol. 2, p. 856.
27. Briggs, W. D. (1914), p. ciii.
28. Holinshed, R. (1577), vol. 2, p. 852.
29. Holinshed, R. (1577), vol. 2, p. 869.
30. Of course, this definition of history fails to take into account oral history and social and economic history, which are both less obviously derived from the words of kings. Nevertheless, the point remains relevant in the case of Elizabethan history.
31. For a discussion of the limited perpetuity of writing see chapter one on the plays of *Doctor Faustus*.
32. Cook, A. (1988), p. 16.
33. Thurn, D. H. (1990), p. 122.
34. See chapter one on the plays of *Doctor Faustus* for a discussion of other instances in which the resurrection of the dead, which writing seems to promise, is shown to be illusory.
35. The impossibility of writing retaining a fixed and permanent meaning over time is evidenced in the plays of *Doctor Faustus* by the blood contract which Faustus reiterates in the final act. Were his initial contract binding, it would not be possible, nor desirable, to repeat it at the end of the plays. See chapter one on the plays of *Doctor Faustus* for a more thorough examination of this.
36. For a fuller examination of the concept of the body politic see Marie Axton's study *The Queen's Two Bodies* (1977), pp. 27–8, in which she explains that kings do not die like other men: 'To prove how radically royal *succession* differed from ordinary *inheritance* Plowden proposed legal cases and historical episodes showing the finality of a subject's death as opposed to the momentary disjunction of the king's body natural from the body politic which was then instantaneously vested in his successor. Demise, in legal terminology, was not equivalent to death. A single legal term described both the extinction of Henry VIII and the deposition of Richard II.'
37. Bredbeck, G. (1991), p. 61.

38. For a more complete consideration of the last days of Henry's reign see John Guy's discussion in *Tudor England* (1988), pp. 198–9.
39. Guy, J. (1988), p. 199.
40. Hamilton, D. (1992), p. 44.
41. Collinson, P. (1987), pp. 413–14.
42. Bredbeck, G. (1991), p. 76.
43. It is important to remember that Mortimer initially claims that the letter has been written 'by a friend' (V.iv.6). Does he therefore acknowledge the handwriting as his own because he knows that he cannot defend himself against Edward III's manipulation of his body politic and of history? The king's word overrides notions of authenticity.

Repetition

Chapter 3

Tamburlaine: A Timely Sequel

Unlike *Edward II* and the plays of *Doctor Faustus*, which explicitly examine the processes of writing and reading, the two parts of *Tamburlaine* do not stage inscription and reception. The dramatization of textual creation which preoccupies the plays already discussed is consequently only to be noted in the two parts of *Tamburlaine* by its absence; battles are won and lost, kings are made and unmade, messages are sent and received, but not in writing. It would be wrong, however, to conclude from the circumstances that the two parts of *Tamburlaine* do not consider notions of textuality. While refusing to place writing centre stage, the parts of *Tamburlaine* nevertheless draw attention to an issue of great textual significance: the complexities of repetition. Of course, this concern is most overtly examined by the connections developed between the first *Tamburlaine* play and its sequel; by the reverberances between the original and its reiterated copy. The negotiations incumbent upon the second part's repetition of the first *Tamburlaine* play are, moreover, expressed by the dramas on the microcosmic level of language. Examining the effect of repetition on words, the plays stage the realization that language has temporal as well as spatial co-ordinates which defy simple notions of linearity. On both a structural and a linguistic level, the two parts of *Tamburlaine* consider how the processes of repetition affect art.

The *Tamburlaine* plays' concern with repetition and originality is introduced by the prologues of both parts, printed in tandem below:

From jigging veins of rhyming mother wits,
And such conceits as clownage keeps in pay,
We'll lead you to the stately tent of war,
Where you shall hear the Scythian Tamburlaine
Threatening the world with high astounding terms
And scourging kingdoms with his conquering sword.
View but his picture in this tragic glass,
And then applaud his fortunes as you please.
(I: prologue 1–8)

The general welcomes Tamburlaine received,
When he arrived last upon our stage,
Hath made our poet pen his second part,
Where death cuts off the progress of his pomp,
And murderous Fates throws all his triumphs down.
But what became of fair Zenocrate,
And with how many cities' sacrifice
He celebrated her sad funeral,
Himself in presence shall unfold at large.
(II: prologue 1–9)[1]

By reciting these prologues side by side, it is possible to examine not only how each play locates its originality in relation to its dramatic antecedents, but also how the notion of mimesis, or the artistic representation of reality by imitation, is shown to be problematic.

With their borders almost touching, the prologues bristle with correspondences, the most obvious of which include the repeated 'Where' at the start of line four in both plays and the image of Tamburlaine's 'high astounding terms' which is reversed in the sequel to the triumphs the Fates throw 'down'. Similarly, both prologues begin by carving a place for their plays in relation either to previous dramatic styles, the 'jigging veins of rhyming mother wits', or to a previous drama, when Tamburlaine 'arrived last upon our stage'. The first part is designed to grab audience attention by being unlike those plays which have come before it, while the second part claims its dramatic appeal by resembling the play which precedes it; the originality, or at least novelty, of part one becomes the successful dramatic formula, or convention, of part two. The prologues apparently indicate their play's unproblematic progression from convention to innovation, from original to copy, from play to sequel.

This is, however, a rather superficial reading of the prologues. Examined more closely, they reveal a number of contradictions which question the very possibility of a stable and linear relationship between an original and its copy. Imaging the process by which life is turned into art, the prologue of part one complicates the conventional notion of imitation. Inviting the audience to 'View but his [Tamburlaine] picture in this tragic glass', the verse describes a creative process in which Tamburlaine is already a work of art, a fiction, before he is made into the play's protagonist by the poet's tragic glass. By representing Tamburlaine not as a real man whom fiction dramatizes through imitation, but rather as a picture for the poet to reflect in his creative mirror, the prologue disrupts traditional linear ideas about how art depicts life. It introduces the possibility that the thing which art is supposed to imitate or repeat may not in fact be real or original; it may be a fiction already. According to the prologue, then, part one is an imitation of art rather than of life. What is to be played in front of the audience is the copy of a copy, the echo of an echo, the reflection of a reflection; the moment of creative origination is thereby lost.

Consolidating this confusion of the relationship between original and copy, the prologue of part two implies that it has been written by someone other than the dramatist of the plays. Claiming that the praise which the first part enjoyed 'Hath made our poet pen his second part' (II: prologue 3), the prologue dislocates the connection between its writer and the plays' author. By describing the poet in the third person, the prologue implies that its author is not the dramatist himself. This disruption of assumptions about the authorship of the prologues renders the location of an unproblematic moment of origination by a single author almost impossible. Developing this challenge to traditional notions of creativity, the prologue further destabilizes the mimetic model by transforming Tamburlaine from the reflected picture described in part one to a real man who will 'in presence' unfold the narrative of part two. This reversal importantly fails to reassert conventional ideas of imitation. The prologue still refuses to posit an artistic imitation of a real man, but instead offers its audience the man 'Himself' (II: prologue 9). The polarities of life and art, of original and copy, of play and sequel are radically disrupted by the prologues of the *Tamburlaine* dramas.

The ultimate cause of these disruptions is the impulse which, paradoxically, also makes possible the genre of the sequel, initiating the second part of *Tamburlaine* – repetition. Conventionally, it is thought that art imitates life to create an original, or one-off, work. However, in the case of these plays, Marlowe writes *Tamburlaine the Great* only to write it again a year or so later. Repetition consequently facilitates the plays at their most fundamental level. It is, moreover, this circumstance which makes the plays so pertinent to textual theories of originality. For by staging the consequences of repetition on character, narrative and language, the plays of *Tamburlaine* interrogate the assumption that a work of art can ever be truly and singularly original or, in other words, unrepeatable. The self-professed originality which the prologue of part one claims for its play is questioned not only by its own unfolding drama, but also by the drama it inspires to be repeated. It is therefore the formal and substantial repetitions which develop both between and within the plays which will be the subject of this examination. Before presuming to analyse the plays together, it should be noted that Marlovian criticism of the dramas is largely concerned with determining whether or not the parts of *Tamburlaine* should be considered the sum of its whole.

Two Parts or One?

Despite the precedent of the earliest extant edition of the plays, in 1590, which prints both parts together, many Marlovian scholars maintain that the dramas should be analysed independently. Typifying this critical standpoint, Malcolm Kelsall argues:

The 'second part' of *Tamburlaine* is declared in the Prologue to be a sequel written because of the success of what we now call 'part one'. Since a continuation was not an integral part of Marlowe's original conception any interpretation which endeavours to account for the earlier work retrospectively in the light of the latter has got the cart before the horse.[2]

Kelsall notes here that to interpret part one in relation to its unanticipated sequel is to fly in the face of chronological common sense; if the plays were not initially planned together, then they should not be considered together. Similarly, other Marlovian critics contend that parts one and two are 'distinctly separate plays',[3] because the sequel is 'an afterthought rather than a completion of a projected ten-act drama'.[4] Those critics who favour the critical segregation of the plays must consequently prove that part two is 'irrelevant to any consideration' of part one.[5] Describing this circumstance, Paul Kocher maintains that the first part is a 'self-subsisting play' whose meaning 'must be sought within its own borders, not imported from the second part'.[6] Thus the parts of *Tamburlaine* present a design dilemma; scholarship must decide whereabouts to place the structural full stop: at the end of part one or part two?

Those critics who maintain that the two plays should be considered together usually do so by arguing that part two fulfils the generic expectations introduced by the first play; the sequel completes the tragic structure which the prologue of part one initiates. In *Marlowe's 'Tamburlaine'*, Roy Battenhouse devotes an entire study to proving that the two plays form a generic whole. He claims:

> The unity of the two parts of *Tamburlaine* has not always been recognized … But if the prologue is read through attentively to the end, it will be noted that the … lines suggest that the poet's motives in writing part II were not wholly commercial. There is the implication at least, that Tamburlaine's history needs to be brought to its appropriate end, and that Fortune's wheel must now complete its circuit.[7]

Battenhouse justifies his dualistic approach to the plays structurally. He maintains that because the ending of part one does not meet the conventional requirements of tragedy which part two ostensibly fulfils, the plays must form a preconceived whole. Similarly, Peter LePage proposes that because the *Tamburlaine*s 'leave an impression of integrity',[8] they should be considered a single drama in ten acts.

In spite of their contradictory conclusions, the two schools of *Tamburlaine* criticism disclose a common preoccupation with order, be it temporal or generic. Consequently, those critics who view the plays separately must sacrifice generic fullness for the sake of chronological regularity, while those critics who view the plays in unison must abandon sequential common sense in favour of structural closure. The exception to this circumstance is Joel B. Altman, who argues not only that the two plays should be considered separately, but also that part one consummates its tragic genre. He claims that part one 'represents not the tragic fall but the tragic *rise* of a great man'.[9] The mental gymnastics which scholarship performs to prove either the generic or temporal wholeness of the plays testifies to the self-imposed conceptual parameters which constrain criticism's perception of the dramas. Moreover, it seems that it is these parameters into which the plays will never comfortably fit. Perhaps, then, it is not the *Tamburlaine* plays themselves, but rather criticism's totalizing preconceptions which render the plays problematic? Indeed, much of the dramatic novelty and tension of the plays depends on their ability to encourage expectations of artistic propriety which they never really satisfy; the plays mark their generic and temporal boundaries while refusing to observe them.

The structural fluidity of the plays finds expression not only in their publication history, but also in the records of their performance. Therefore, despite their initial publication together in the black letter octavo of 1590,[10] the plays were produced by their fourth edition in successive, yet separate, volumes; part one was published in 1605, while part two was issued in 1606.[11] It seems that as demand increased the presentation of the plays became proportionately more lavish, and consequently unconnected. Divorced not only spatially but also temporally, the *Tamburlaine* quartos reiterate the theatre's treatment of the two parts for over a decade. First mentioned in Henslowe's *Diary* in 1594, the plays were apparently produced without a uniform dramatic approach. Part one was performed fourteen times between 18 August 1594 and 12 November 1595, while part two was staged on just seven occasions between 19 December 1594 and 13 November 1595.[12] Despite their clearly playing as a series on 12 and 13 November, the parts were evidently not always acted in tandem. As there are not enough performances of *Tamburlaine I* to support *Tamburlaine II*, the plays were perhaps produced independently or, as is more probable, part one was played alone and part two only in unison with the first drama. Redrawing, time and again, the borders which criticism would prefer to write in stone, the publication and performance histories of the plays rehearse their thematic challenge to structural certainty.

Bearing a forceful testimony to the questionable value of generic coherence and chronological exactitude, the dispute which characterizes *Tamburlaine* scholarship calls for a fresh approach to the dramas. The parts of *Tamburlaine* must now be reassessed across the very borders which have been erected around them; borders which have, moreover, limited and skewed the plays' critical receptions. Ultimately, then, determining whether or not the plays were designed as a whole seems rather beside the point. Criticism cannot read the first play without knowing how the second play develops and revises its outcome. It is this circumstance which makes it impossible to consider the plays independently. What is more, as the purpose of this analysis is to examine how the plays dramatize the effects of repetition on genre, narrative and language, the plays must be considered in a way which highlights their reiterative structures. In other words, the present study requires that the two parts of *Tamburlaine* be considered in unison.

Riding in Triumph or How to Keep your Word in Part One

According to traditional artistic notions, repetition is the blight of creativity. In *Repetition and Semiotics*, Stamos Metzidakis explains that repetition has a bad reputation because it is conventionally considered to be stasis, boredom and even, in Freudian terms, death. He writes that 'for the sake of originality or difference, it [repetition] must be avoided at all costs. Repetition in literature is thus considered by many to be the sign of a dull mind, and of an even duller pen.'[13] The condemnation of repetition is, however, somewhat ironic when it is noted that all art is, in some sense, reliant upon the recitation of previous forms, structures and ideas. It is the repetition, even by omission, of these forms, structures and ideas which enables criticism to appreciate and categorize a work of art. Originality is consequently a highly deceptive notion.[14] It requires that a work is spontaneously generated without the influence of anything or anyone else. A work cannot be created without a network of prior artistic conventions, just as a child cannot be born without a mother and a father. It is therefore as impossible to create an original work, or a work uninformed by repetition, as it is to create a work which exists outside time.

It is the unwelcome, and yet inescapable, nature of repetition which makes the reiterated plays of *Tamburlaine* so crucial to theories of textuality. Lawrence Benaquist's study of the plays takes for granted their repetitive structure. He notes:

> That the *Tamburlaine* plays display repetition is a common observation, and one which is traditionally considered to be the plays' major weakness. However, it seemed possible that this repetition might be the source of the

plays' appeal, that their very power lay in subtle variations played upon major themes.[15]

Performing a critical volte-face, Benaquist's work dismisses the conventional association of the plays' scenic duplications with ineffectual artistry. Instead, he recognizes that the very source or fountainhead of the *Tamburlaine* plays' dramatic potency is located in their repetitions. What is more, approximating artistic worth with repetitiveness, Benaquist's hypothesis enables the unification of the plays' external dramaturgy with their internal thematic concerns. Repeatedly dramatizing disputes in which Tamburlaine defeats a succession of increasingly troublesome enemies, the plays' reproductivity is not only an opportunity for the formulaic re-presentation of crowd-pleasing action, but also, and more importantly, the actual means of conquest on the stage.

Having helped Cosroe to usurp his brother's throne at the start of part one, Tamburlaine delivers the conquered Mycetes' crown to his ally, announcing: 'Hold thee Cosroe, wear two imperial crowns' (I: II.v.1). Repeating the coronation of Cosroe which initiates the action of part one (I: I.i.179), Tamburlaine creates an excessive display which doubly glorifies another man; he makes Cosroe the proud owner of not one, but two diadems. However, introducing a second repetitive movement, Tamburlaine seeks to reclaim the crown he has just given away. Repeating Menaphon's departing line, Tamburlaine exclaims:

> And ride in triumph through Persepolis?
> Is it not brave to be a king, Techelles?
> Usumcasane and Theridamas,
> Is it not passing brave to be a king
> And ride in triumph through Persepolis?
> (I: II.v.50–54)

First quoting Menaphon's line, and then reciting it at the conclusion of his own speech, Tamburlaine establishes a refrain with which both plays come to resound. Menaphon's words are appropriated and transformed by Tamburlaine as he establishes a policy of martial achievement through linguistic repetition. Duplicated and thereby emphasized, Menaphon's line is transferred into Tamburlaine's possession while it is at the same time converted from an ostensibly inconsequential aside into a kind of incantation or magical recitation.

By repeating the line, Tamburlaine endows it with a peculiar puissance; he successfully renders it seemingly ever more effective, more equivalent, more referential. Both the on- and off-stage audiences are consequently persuaded that if Tamburlaine pronounces a desire enough times, it will eventually be satisfied. In other words, if Tamburlaine repeatedly proclaims himself a king, he will become one. It is therefore only to be expected that when a few scenes later Tamburlaine defeats Cosroe, it is without a display of physical violence; for it is not military force which has achieved Tamburlaine's victory, but rather rhetorical might. Repeating the scene of coronation for a third time, Tamburlaine crowns himself with the same diadem he once gave away. In this way, Tamburlaine's verse acquires the appellation of 'working words' (I: II.iii.25).

Tamburlaine's working words have become the subject of much critical attention. As early as the 1960s, scholars have noted the plays' manipulation of conventional processes of signification. In an article from 1965, Susan Richards claims that by repeating certain images, words 'become equated, almost identified with their referent' in the *Tamburlaine* plays.[16] Richards describes a process here in which words become the things they are meant to denote. Hence, instead of standing in for things, words are transformed into the things themselves through Tamburlaine's rhetoric. Consequently, Tamburlaine assumes military mastery by sweeping communication free from ambiguity, by achieving the unhindered correspondence of the signifier with its signified. This process, however, defies the most basic rules of linguistic theory; it requires that words become what they are not: concrete, fixed, and unchangeably repeatable. Tamburlaine's working words are therefore a contradiction in terms, an oxymoron. Words cannot work or be active because they are words, because they are simply aural or visual signs which take the place of real, active things. Nevertheless, what part one stages is the ever-increasing ability of Tamburlaine to keep his word, to make his language immediately effective. Unlike Gaveston in *Edward II*, whose curses fail to produce their desired outcome, Tamburlaine makes a succession of promises which he manages to fulfil. For instance, as promised, Tamburlaine defeats all his rivals, carries out the threats indicated by his colour-coded tents, and produces crowns and kingdoms for his accomplices. In the most literal sense, Tamburlaine is able to keep his word.

Challenging Tamburlaine's Working Words

Despite the undeniable military success it produces in part one, Tamburlaine's rhetorical strategy is brought into question by the play's unfolding narrative. The potential for words to be made determinate is challenged in scenes which reveal the perverse, contingent and, ultimately, unsustainable nature of Tamburlaine's linguistic enterprise. For instance, having conquered Bajazeth and his wife Zabina, Tamburlaine turns their curses against them in a way which belies the unnaturalness of his working words. As Tamburlaine's use of language requires the removal of the thin veil which separates metaphor from that which it supplants, words become so immediate and concrete that they eventually assume the physicality of flesh. Tamburlaine removes the protective shield of substitution from imagery and thereby leaves nothing mediative to part the idea from the action it describes. The most shocking consequence of this process may be seen during the scarlet banquet, when Tamburlaine invites his captive to eat his own flesh.

Asked whether or not he has 'any stomach' (I: IV. iv.10) or appetite for the meal his captor is about to eat, the starving Bajazeth responds with a play upon a secondary meaning of the word stomach. Widely held in the Renaissance to be the organ which produced choler, the stomach mentioned by Tamburlaine not only denotes hunger, but also anger. Bajazeth emphasizes the magnitude of his fury against Tamburlaine by exploiting the less obvious meaning of the word introduced by his captor. He retorts that he has 'such a stomach, cruel Tamburlaine, as I could/Willingly feed upon thy blood-red heart' (I: IV.iv.11–12). Surpassing his captive's eloquence, however, Tamburlaine appropriates and repeats Bajazeth's comparison between outrage and eating by making anger and appetite synonymous. He therefore concludes that Bajazeth should eat his own flesh: 'pluck out that,[Bajazeth's heart]/And 'twill serve thee and thy wife' (I: IV.iv.13–14). Refusing Tamburlaine's suggested repast, Bajazeth is threatened with enforced cannibalism. Tamburlaine instructs him to eat 'or I will make thee slice the brawns of thy arms into carbonadoes, and eat them' (I: IV.iv.43–4). Peeling away the subtleties of signification in favour of linguistic equivalence, Tamburlaine renders the word and the thing identical. Bajazeth is required to realize fully his own metaphor; if he images his appetite for vengeance as so great that he could make a meal of human flesh, then that is what he must actually do. A startling expression of the unnaturalness of Tamburlaine's attempt to make language literal, the scarlet banquet concludes with yet another perverse display. The cannibal feast initiating the banquet is reversed in its final moments as Tamburlaine presents his followers a dessert of crowns. Placing another inedible platter before his diners, Tamburlaine metonymically realizes his earlier characterization of kingly ambition as an appetite demanding satiation: 'The thirst of reign and sweetness of a crown' (I: II.vii.12). Tamburlaine only succeeds in making language tangible and consequential by making it what it is not, by rendering language unlinguistic.

The unnaturalness of the working words employed in part one must ultimately beg the question: if language is not literal, physical and direct then how does Tamburlaine make it so? The answer to this question seems to lie in the colour-coded tents the play describes and presents. The tents are initially introduced verbally in part one as the Soldan's messenger explains the significance of their different colours. He informs his master that when Tamburlaine lays siege to a city, he indicates his intentions towards it by the colour of his tents. On the first day of a siege, Tamburlaine's tents are white 'To signify the mildness of his mind,/That satiate with spoil refuseth blood' (I: IV.i.52–3). On the second day of a siege, the tents are changed to red to show that Tamburlaine's anger must 'be quenched with blood,/Not sparing any that can manage arms' (I: IV.i.56–7). Finally, on the third day of a siege, the tents are changed to black to indicate that Tamburlaine means to 'razeth all his foes with fire and sword' (I: IV.i.63). The significance of the tents is therefore seemingly direct and unequivocal; if Tamburlaine pitches a black tent then all the citizens will die. Of course, the narrative of the play apparently bears testimony to the realization of the black tents' meaning; the citizens of Damascus are shown no mercy when they surrender on the third day of Tamburlaine's siege (I: V.ii). However, it is important to note here that it is not the tents which precipitate the slaughter of the virgins, but rather the citizens' acquiescence to Tamburlaine's tyranny of meaning. It is because the citizens of Damascus believe that Tamburlaine can keep his word, that they surrender and appeal to his mercy. Tamburlaine's language system is consequently reliant upon consent, rather than an ability to coerce. Tamburlaine achieves his desired outcome at Damascus, not because he has created a realm of absolute meaning, but because he has made the citizens believe he has. What is more, according to contemporary critics the tents are not unambiguous, they are actually highly indeterminate. For instance, in 'Marlowe's Technique of Communicating with his Audience', S. Wyler maintains that the black tents are meant to be reminiscent of the black cloth used in the theatre to signify tragedy.[17] Alternatively, J. P. Cutts argues in 'The Ultimate Source of Tamburlaine's White, Red, Black and Death?' that the tents represent the three horsemen of the apocalypse.[18] The tents are therefore an ironic expression of the impossibility of creating a system of meaning which is eternally repeatable without alteration. The colour-coded tents reveal that Tamburlaine's success does not depend on a new form of language, but rather upon an elaborate confidence trick.

The unsustainability of the protagonist's linguistic confidence trick is eventually realized at the end of part one when Zabina repeats and alters Tamburlaine's working words. Discovering her husband Bajazeth with his brains dashed out against the side of his cage, Zabina falls into a fit of grief which develops and deteriorates from verse into prose:

> What do mine eyes behold, my husband dead?
> His skull all riven in twain, his brains dashed out?
> The brains of Bajazeth, my lord and sovereign?
> Bajazeth, O Turk, O emperor, give him his liquor? Not I, bring milk and fire, and my blood I bring him again, tear me in pieces, give me the sword with a ball of wildfire upon it. Down with him, down with him! Go to my child, away, away, away! Ah, save that infant, save him, save him! I, even I speak to her, the sun was down. Streamers white, red, black, here, here, here! Fling the meat in his face. Tamburlaine, Tamburlaine, let the soldiers be buried. Hell, death, Tamburlaine, hell, make ready my coach, my chair, my jewels, I come, I come, I come!
> (I: V.ii.241–54)

Revealing the infinitely protean nature of words, which are always altered whenever they are recited, Zabina effectively refutes Tamburlaine's linguistic strategy. The erstwhile empress repeats the events and words which have preoccupied the play's recent past in a way which discloses the impossibility of making repetition return the same. Replaying the scarlet banquet, for instance, Zabina shows how words are of necessity changed by recontextualization. She repeats her husband's and her captor's words to create a patchwork of quotations which refuse to disclose their original intentions, and instead serve to condemn the behaviour of the protagonist they once glorified. Consequently, the false premise of Tamburlaine's rhetoric is exposed: the impossibility of uncomplicated repetition.

Repetition and Difference

An expression of repetition's refusal to return the same, to reiterate an exact duplicate of an original, Zabina's speech highlights one of the defining features of language. Words are only useful, or usable, because they can be transplanted into different contexts, because they can be repeated. Available for anyone's use, words are, by their very nature, promiscuous. It is this force of promiscuity, however, which renders words unable to retain a fixed meaning. For if they were constant, unchangeable and clearly defined, words could not be used by different speakers in the service of different causes and in different contexts. Unable to say the same thing twice, because they can never occupy exactly the same context twice, words are infinitely repeatable, while at the same time being unable to duplicate or re-present an original. It is, therefore, possible to imagine all words framed by virtual quotation marks as an indication of their eternally transferable character. One of the consequences of language's fickle nature is the inability of repetition to aid identification; repetition cannot bring about recognition because a word cannot be reiterated without becoming different, without becoming a copy and therefore not identical to the original. As Steven Connor notes in *Repetition, Theory and Text*:

> there can never be any such thing as pure or exact repetition. In order to be recognizable as such, a repetition must, in however small a degree, be different from its original. This 'difference' is invisible except in the fact of its pure differentiality. Functioning in this way, repetition becomes a kind of weak point in the principle of identity.[19]

Like an amnesia victim, repetition cannot remember itself; it cannot repeat an original without making a copy and, consequently, creating something unlike itself.

It is this circumstance which renders problematic the notion of originality. As if acknowledging this, part one concludes by reciting the mirror metaphor of the prologue which describes the processes of artistic creativity. Seeking to make significant the scene of slaughter before his on- and off-stage audiences, Tamburlaine claims that the dead bodies are 'All sights of power to grace' his victory (I: V.ii.410). He continues:

> And such are objects fit for Tamburlaine,
> Wherein as in a mirror may be seen
> His honour, that consists in shedding blood,
> When men presume to manage arms with him.
> (I: V.ii.411–14)

The glass, which in the prologue actually embodied the genre of the play, becomes only similar to it in Tamburlaine's speech. The bodies on stage are like a mirror because they can create a picture of Tamburlaine's honour. By transforming a metaphor into a simile, the play makes more apparent the difference between word and thing; at the end of the play, the image is like, but not the same as, the thing it describes. What is more, the difference between the original and its copy is not only disclosed verbally, it is also revealed contextually, by the very indeterminacy of Tamburlaine's speech. The scene of slaughter is not an obvious mirror of Tamburlaine's honour. The speech, which comes after Bajazeth's on-stage suicide, Zabina's expression of grief, and Zenocrate's exclamation of horror at yet 'another bloody spectacle' (I: V.ii.275), is profoundly ambiguous. The full stop in a series of criticisms of the play's protagonist, Tamburlaine's speech is radically open to interpretation; the mirror which it cites is consequently an ambivalent one. Despite Tamburlaine's efforts to make the play's closing tableau singularly significant, it cannot innocently endorse his reputation.

An original cannot be simply repeated to form an exact copy, just as a word cannot be simply repeated to transform it into the thing it describes; original and word can only be recited to produce something different. It is this conclusion which *Tamburlaine* part one realizes at its end. Traditional readings of the play's depiction of conquest through rhetorical repetition, therefore, only tell half the story. Thwarting the notion that the components of linguistic and creative systems are related in an unproblematic, linear fashion, part one initiates the breakdown of structures of order which its sequel develops and exaggerates. Part one therefore concludes with an expression of its refusal to depict uncomplicated repetition. Instead of repeating the conventional structure of tragedy and ending with the death of its protagonist, the play closes with Tamburlaine's coronation of the silent Zenocrate, accompanied by a speech which looks forward to their marriage and to the burial of the dead left on the stage. Part one is, consequently, unable to repeat the tragic genre it cites at its beginning. Rescinding traditional assumptions about repetition by performing them, *Tamburlaine* part one paves the way for its sequel to challenge yet further notions of generic exactitude and chronological accuracy; writing his play once more, Marlowe could not help but make it different.

Riding in Triumph or How to Change your Word in Part Two

Transforming the scenic and linguistic repetitions of the original play into the generic structure of its second part, Marlowe invented the secular sequel. Conventionally, of course, the genre of the sequel leaves much to be desired. According to traditional notions of creativity, great art is unrepeatable, and hence original. Consequently, to create a work by self-consciously imitating an already established piece of art contravenes the most basic rules of literary success. Nevertheless, this is exactly what Marlowe does in *Tamburlaine the Great Part Two*. Even bearing the same title as its predecessor, the sequel openly recites its origins from the first line of its prologue which refers to 'The general welcomes' received by the first play (II: prologue 1). However, taking its lead from the conclusion of part one, the sequel illustrates the impossibility of pure, utterly identical, repetition; part two cannot stop itself from being different. It is this difference, contingent upon repetition, which the sequel analyses. From the use of its sources to its relocation of lines from the original play, part two stages not only the inevitability of difference, but also the necessity of repetition. Questioning the possibility of a truly original work, a work without any precursors or successors, the sequel bears witness to the unavoidable nature of repetition.

At the most obvious level, part two examines repetition by reciting lines from the first play. The most famous instance of this must surely be the sequel's transformations of Tamburlaine's 'And ride in triumph through Persepolis' line which undergoes at least five recitations in the second play. The line is initially repeated at the beginning of the sequel by Bajazeth's incarcerated son, Callapine. The metaphorical significance of the multiple sons who appear in part two will be discussed in greater detail later in the chapter. Nevertheless, it is worth noting here that the negotiations incumbent upon the creation of a sequel from an original drama are staged by the second part's representation of generational friction. Consequently, the differences played out between Tamburlaine and his heirs realize the sequel's own challenge to its father play. Appropriating the line which his captor once acquired from Menaphon, Bajazeth's son attempts to persuade his gaoler to release him. Callapine conjures the promise of a victory procession for Almeda if he will help him to escape from Tamburlaine. He describes how Almeda's courage will be honoured 'as thou rid'st in triumph through the streets' (II: I.iii.41). Transplanting the line from part one, Callapine also transforms it. Most explicitly, Callapine alters the line's grammar, by changing the verb morphology from a simple infinitive to a direct and personal description in the second person. Less obviously, Callapine also alters the original implication of the line; what in part one was a call to manage arms for Tamburlaine becomes, in part two, a seductive request to defy him. Thus, the repeated line is linguistically and contextually different. The ease with which Tamburlaine's most reverberative rhetoric is turned against him in the sequel illustrates the infinitely transferable nature of language, the promiscuity of words.

Despite Callapine's successful deployment of the repeated line, which achieves his release from captivity, Tamburlaine's phrase is reiterated at least four more times in the play by his erstwhile captor. Reclaiming the line at the end of the sequel, Tamburlaine employs it to describe the even greater victories to which he looks forward. In his chariot drawn by kings, Tamburlaine pictures the palace he will build at Samarcanda, where he will 'ride in golden armour like the sun' (II: IV.iii.115). He even repeats the line again in the same speech, as he concludes 'So will I ride through Samarcanda streets' (II: IV.iii.130). Having taken Babylon one scene later, Tamburlaine transforms the line twice more as he notes 'Where Belus, Ninus, and great Alexander/Have rode in triumph, triumphs Tamburlaine' (II: V.i.69–70), and again, 'in the streets, where brave Assyrian dames/Have rid in pomp like rich Saturnia' (II: V.i.76–7). Compulsively repeating Menaphon's line from part one, the sequel discloses the impossibility of repetition without difference, and consequently the impossibility of sustaining Tamburlaine's repetitive rhetorical strategy; Tamburlaine cannot keep repeating Menaphon's line and expect it to make the same thing happen twice.

Challenging the notion of exact, identical repetition on a scenic as well as a linguistic level, the sequel repeats episodes from part one with different characters and with radically different outcomes. Apart from the sequel's numerous scenes of conquest which repeat the structural climaxes of the first play, part two also repeats Tamburlaine's wooing of Zenocrate in the form of Theridamas's love for Olympia. Like Zenocrate, whom Tamburlaine takes captive in part one only to fall in love with, Olympia is captured by Theridamas who is immediately enamoured of her beauty. Unlike Zenocrate, however, Olympia is not seduced by her captor's words and rejects Theridamas's advances. The happy consummation which the audience has been led to expect from the scenario of female captivity in part one is, consequently, denied. Theridamas does not succeed in winning Olympia's love. The inability of the sequel to repeat exactly events from the first play is accentuated by the tragic ending which the sub-plot does realize. Instead of being rewarded with Olympia's love, Theridamas becomes the victim of a terrible trick; Olympia persuades him to stab her under the pretence that her throat is anointed with a balm that defies injury. Theridamas's unintentional murder of Olympia is heavy with irony; he has killed the woman he loves and disappointed the structural expectation of the female captivity plot. In the most dramatic of ways, Theridamas fails to duplicate the success of his master.

Similarly, Olympia's murder of her son in an attempt to evade capture by Theridamas, sets in motion another repetitive structure which the sequel ultimately frustrates. Looking forwards to the end of the sequel, rather than back to the first play, Olympia's act of infanticide anticipates Tamburlaine's own killing of his eldest son, Calyphas. However, what is an act of mercy and honour when it is first performed in the play becomes, upon its repetition by Tamburlaine, a brutal and unnatural murder. The sequel disrupts the expectation that the repetition of the same act or the same line in another context and with different characters can ever produce something the same. Repetition simply refuses to adhere to a linear notion of con-sequentiality; a repeated act does not necessarily produce an anticipated outcome.

Failing to Persuade or Words Which Are Not Working in the Sequel

Repetition's outcome, the fact that signifier and signified, original and copy, act and outcome, are not connected in an unproblematic and linear fashion, has far-reaching repercussions for more general linguistic theory in the sequel. Therefore, even though Zenocrate's death and the broken truce of Sigismund and Orcanes are not implicated in repetitive structures initiated by the earlier play, they nevertheless show that words are indeterminate and irresolute: that words are not con-sequential. Unlike part one, in which the actual means of conquest on the stage is rhetorical, part two exposes the ineffectual nature of words. Introduced by a plot which describes how easily promises may be broken, the sequel dwells on the impossibility of making words concrete and active.

Requesting the confirmation of their truce, Orcanes asks the King of Hungary to 'swear in sight of heaven and by thy Christ' (II: I.ii.55). Sigismund replies:

> By him that made the world and saved my soul,
> The Son of God and issue of a maid,
> Sweet Jesus Christ, I solemnly protest,
> And vow to keep this peace inviolable.
> (II: I.ii.56–9)

The efficacy of Sigismund's word is, however, short-lived. When, a few scenes later, Tamburlaine's forces divert the attention of Orcanes's army, Sigismund is easily persuaded to break his oath and attack his erstwhile ally. Frederick, one of the king's counsellors, claims that it is a 'superstition' (II: II.i.49) to believe that a Christian should keep faith with a non-Christian.

Another adviser, Baldwin, argues more importantly that 'with such infidels' (II: II.i.33) Christians are not bound by normal rules of social and martial engagement; for the religion by which non-Christians swear is 'not by necessary policy' to be considered a valid bond for a Christian (II: II.i.38). Because the Turk swears by a faith alien to his Christian hearer, the potency of his promise is brought into question. Redefining the very notion of giving one's word, Baldwin's argument locates vows on a sliding scale of observance, depending on whether or not the hearer is part of the same religious community as the speaker.

Conventionally, the introductory episode of Sigismund and Orcanes's broken truce is read, like *The Jew of Malta*, as a satirical commentary on Christian hypocrisy. It may also be interpreted, however, as an important instance of the inability of language to achieve its expressed aims, to be of consequence. Despite the ostensible gravity of Sigismund's oath of allegiance, his words do not make real his intention. The king's words are not of necessity the communicators of his truthful intent, nor the realizers of his desires. Instead, like all language acts, Sigismund's promise is unstable, indeterminate and irresolute. It is this linguistic circumstance which Orcanes highlights when he appropriates Sigismund's god as guarantor of his own oath. Upon hearing of Sigismund's broken vow, Orcanes swears by the Christian king's saviour to conquer the Christian king. He calls upon Christ for retribution against the duplicitous Christians: 'If there be Christ, we shall have victory' (II: II.ii.64).

Paradoxically, by using the name of his enemy's protector to attack his enemy, Orcanes demonstrates the absence of a direct connection between word and thing, expression and intention, disciple and deity. The term 'Christ' is thereby shown not to be the sole property of the Christians. Instead, the word 'Christ' is realized as just another proper noun, able to operate in the service of any speaker. A similar realization of the lack of potency of the name occurs in *Edward II*, when the king distributes names and titles to his nobles with such alacrity that the authority usually thought peculiar to his own kingly title is brought into question.[20] By swearing the name of Christ, Orcanes shows the unstable and transferable nature of words, which can be marshalled in the service of any cause. Lacking a definite meaning or intent, words are radically impotent. They cannot independently initiate a domino effect of action, because they cannot convey a stable and resolute meaning which might then become of consequence. Thus, when Orcanes's army does defeat Sigismund in the ensuing battle, it is not because Christ has switched his allegiances to the non-Christians, but rather because the sequel persistently refuses to complete sequences of signification, to return the anticipated outcome.

Serving to underline this example of the ineffectual nature of words, the narrative succeeds Orcanes's victory with a scene in which even Tamburlaine is dramatically unable to make his words of consequence. The great orator of the first play is rendered linguistically impotent in the sequel by the death of his wife, Zenocrate. Unable to assuage mortality, Tamburlaine rails absurdly against the gods while Zenocrate dies before his very eyes. Pointing out the futility of his master's lengthy and ornate speeches, Theridamas advises Tamburlaine to 'be patient, she is dead,/And all this raging cannot make her live' (II: II.iv.119–20). The death of Zenocrate staged against the backdrop of Tamburlaine's ineffectual words poses a direct challenge to the rhetorical assumptions established by the first play. Indeed, refuting the idea of a communicative domino effect, the sequel highlights the impossibility of creating an active chain of signification which might make things happen. What is more, because the word and the thing it describes are not connected in a stable, predictable and linear way, words can only reveal their inconsequentiality, their refusal to return an expected outcome.

The sequel's self-conscious rupturing of the anticipated relationship between event and consequence is most obviously staged in the final act at the siege of Babylon. Reiterating the circumstances of the siege of Damascus from part one, the sequel's representation of the defeat of Babylon nevertheless refuses to comply with the details of the earlier episode. In the first siege depicted in part one, Damascus yields to Tamburlaine on the third day, when his tents are black to indicate his determination to 'razeth all his foes with fire and sword' (I: IV.i.63). In the sequel play, however, the city of Babylon refuses to yield and has to be taken by force, while Tamburlaine's tents are still 'vermillion' (II: V.i.86) and 'bloody' (II: V.i.103): in other words, red. According to the first play, Tamburlaine's tents are only red on the second day of a siege, when he means his anger to 'be quenched with blood,/Not sparing any that can manage arms' (I: IV.i.56–7). Therefore, despite the First Citizen's claim that it is Tamburlaine's 'last day's dreadful siege/Wherein he spareth neither man nor child' (II: V.i.29–30), the colour of the tents seems to indicate that it is actually the second, and not the third, day of the conflict. Accentuating the sequential confusion, Tamburlaine ignores the meaning of his red tents, which only signify death to those capable of bearing arms, and instead instructs Techelles to 'drown them all, man, woman, and child/Leave not a Babylonian in the town' (II: V.i.168–9). In this way, not only do the colour-coded tents no longer convey Tamburlaine's intentions, they also belie the inevitability of disruption in supposedly consequential systems of meaning in the play. The sequel, therefore, reveals that signs and words cannot unproblematically lead an interpreter through a chain of fixed significances to a moment of absolute meaning; there will always be interruptions, inconsistencies and disruptions.

Tracing Disruption in the Sources of the Sequel

According to poststructuralist linguistic theory, units of language are not related to one another in a sequential fashion; words do not stand in for things, creating a network of linear substitutions which bestow meaning. Instead, theorists maintain that 'meaning is nowhere punctually present in language'.[21] This means that signs can never coincide with the things they describe and, consequently, meaning is always detoured and delayed through language. In other words, a sign cannot contain meaning, it can only gesture towards it; absolute meaning is always located in an unattainable place beyond signification. The word *différance* has been coined by Jacques Derrida to describe the way that a sign simultaneously differs from itself and defers its meaning.[22] In keeping with this revised theory of linguistics, the sign is replaced by the trace; a unit of language which, unlike the sign, does not pretend to retain presence and instead disrupts the linear progression from thing to word. The trace is neither absent, nor present; it simply recites itself in different temporal and spatial contexts in which it is always altered. Enabled by the force of repetition, the trace is constantly playing somewhere else. The sequel's examination of repetitions which produce different outcomes and which disrupt sequentiality therefore stages the processes of *différance*.

The sequel's disruption of consequentiality is evident not only from the repeated lines and scenes which refuse to realize an anticipated conclusion, but also from the play's deployment of sources which fail to observe chronological order. The second play relies on historical episodes, while showing scant respect for historical accuracy. For example, the sequel opens with an incident based on events which occurred after the death of the drama's historical protagonist. The introductory anecdote describing how a Christian reneges on a truce with a Turk is probably derived from Bonfinius's account of the battle of Varna in 1444. Sigismund and Orcanes are therefore the fictitious representations of King Vladislaus of Poland and Hungary and Amurath II, respectively.[23] The date of the battle, however, post-dates the life of the play's protagonist; the historical Tamburlaine died in 1405, almost almost forty years before the broken truce of Varna. This temporal blunder has excited considerable critical attention. In Roy Battenhouse's examination of the source for this sub-plot, the critic desperately wonders, 'But why did the playwright thus transpose history?'[24] Offering an answer to his own question, Battenhouse maintains that Marlowe adopted a narrative precedent from Foxe's 1583 edition of his *Book of Martyrs*, in which Sigismund's treachery is cited out of its proper order.[25] According to Foxe's retelling of history, the Council of Constance of 1415, where Sigismund broke his oath, occurred before his encounter with Bajazet. Overriding chronology, however, this account ignores the date of the Council of Constance which happened at least fifteen years after the death of Bajazet. Battenhouse argues that Foxe is treating Sigismund's earlier defeat at the hands of the Turk as 'a providential consequence of his misbehaviour at Constance' some years later.[26] Misreading the temporal co-ordinates of cause and effect, Foxe's narrative offers a distorted and partisan account which resembles the sequential thoughtlessness to be found in the *Tamburlaine* sequel. However, what in *The Book of Martyrs* is a way to see Sigismund's defeat as punitive is in the *Tamburlaine* sequel a means to illustrate how repetition disrupts notions of linear order and consequentiality.

Another example of the sequel's disruption of chronological order comes after the death of Zenocrate, when Tamburlaine takes his three sons to one side to offer them military advice. Tamburlaine explains 'the way to fortify' (II: III.ii.62) in a speech which is taken almost word for word from a manual on warfare which did not appear in print until after the play's production. When Tamburlaine's speech (II: III.ii.62–82) is viewed in unison with the relevant section from Paul Ive's *Practise of Fortification*, the indebtedness becomes evident.[27] Published in 1589, Ive's *Practise of Fortification* post-dates most critical estimates of when the *Tamburlaine* sequel was composed and first performed. The reference to Ive's treatise in the sequel is, consequently, temporally impossible. In an effort to account for the historical incongruity of Tamburlaine's speech, critics have posited two hypotheses. Characteristic of the first, Fredson Bowers argues in his introduction to the *Complete Works* that Marlowe had access to the treatise while it was still in manuscript.[28] This theory finds support from Charles Nicholl, who notes in *The Reckoning* that *The Practise* is dedicated to Sir Francis Walsingham, the Elizabethan spymaster, with whom *Tamburlaine*'s playwright was also connected.[29] It is therefore possible that the playwright was given Ive's work to read by his patron prior to its publication. Representing the second theory, Frederick Boas maintains that Marlowe probably revised the two plays before their publication, inserting not only the speech based on Ive's work, but also passages from Spenser which he contests 'are little more than embroidery'.[30]

A variation on the chicken and egg dilemma, the critical wrangling over which came first, play or source is, although intriguing, nevertheless insoluble. The Ive reference may be more usefully considered as an expression of the reproductivity of the sequel which dwells on the temporal disruptions incumbent upon repetition. Moreover, the Ive quotation is only one in a network of references to works which are themselves based on yet other texts. For example, the Sigismund and Orcanes story is recounted by Bonfinius and Foxe, as well as Thomas Fortescue in *The Foreste* (1576), which is a translation of Pedro Mexia's *Silva de varia lección* (1544) and which is largely retold by George Whetstone in the *English Myrror* (1586).[31] By highlighting, through its chronological discrepancies, the proliferation of source texts and consequently originary moments, both before and after the production of part two, the sequel challenges the very possibility that a work can be created without the influence of other texts. The sequel therefore undermines the notion that a work of art can ever be truly original or without influence or, in human terms, without a father.

Re-Productivity in the Sequel or A Bastard Copy

The *Tamburlaine* plays are located at the centre of a network of texts, some of which are sources and some dramatic successors. The plays' repetitive dramaturgy has therefore become a source of inspiration for other dramas which seek to imitate the success of Marlowe's works by repeating their structure, characterization and versification. On the most obvious level, lines and scenes from the two plays are repeated and transformed in other dramatic works of the period. Most famously, in William Shakespeare's *Henry IV* part two, Pistol makes his entrance to a line which parodies Tamburlaine's triumphant cry of 'Holla, ye pampered jades of Asia' (II: IV.iii.1).[32] Similarly, in *Dido, Queene of Carthage*, Marlowe recites the scene of Olympia's frustrated suicide bid on a bonfire of her own making (II: III.iv.31–3); instead of falling on Aeneas's sword as Virgil states, Marlowe's heroine kills herself by throwing her body into a fire which has already consumed all remnants of her lover.[33] On a larger scale, the *Tamburlaine* plays also initiated complete new works. According to Peter Berek in '*Tamburlaine*'s Weak Sons', 'Of the 38 extant plays for the public theater performed in England between 1587 and 1593, 10 show clear debts to *Tamburlaine*'.[34] The dramatic repertoire of the Elizabethan theatre bore witness to the impulse of re-production on which the *Tamburlaine* plays dwell.

The fact that the *Tamburlaine* plays spawned a whole host of dramatic offspring is significantly anticipated by the sequel's concentration upon children. The five sons who people the sequel dramatically realize not only the influence of the dramas on works by other dramatists, but also the familial relationship between the first and second parts of *Tamburlaine*. The generational conflict which characterizes part two, from the moment Callapine determines to revenge his dead father and raise an army against Tamburlaine (II: I.iii), consequently comments upon the necessary negotiations a copy must make with its original play, or a sequel with its first part. Indeed most, if not all, of the scenes involving children in part two focus on the theme of generational sequentiality, or the maintenance of a proper hierarchical order between father and son. Tamburlaine's education of his children to become worthy of their birthright is, according to this reading, the very literalization of the first play's efforts to make its sequel deserving of the original's title. However, Tamburlaine is not satisfied with simply creating an heir to perpetuate his military success. Instead, he wants a successor who will be as much like himself as possible; Tamburlaine wants a son who will duplicate him. Expressing this sentiment at the start of the play, Tamburlaine is worried to find that his children's 'looks are amorous,/Not martial as the sons of Tamburlaine' (II: I.iv.21–2). Here, Tamburlaine posits the idea that his sons have a fixed and eternal identity to which his actual children must aspire; Tamburlaine's sons must live up to an ideal notion of Tamburlaine's sons. Thus, Tamburlaine destabilizes the identities of his children rendering them simultaneously like and unlike themselves. The subsequent failure of Tamburlaine's sons to duplicate their father stages the sequel's inability to replicate its own dramatic progenitor; the sequel is as different from its parent play, as Calyphas is different from Tamburlaine.

In an effort to make his sons more like himself, Tamburlaine encourages his children to compete for rhetorical supremacy.[35] Responding to his father's delight at Zenocrate's story of his bravery, Celebinus boasts that he will imitate Tamburlaine's martial exploits and 'Have under me as many kings as you' (II: I.iv.55). Tamburlaine replies:

> These words assure me boy, thou art my son.
> When I am old and cannot manage arms,
> Be thou the scourge and terror of the world.
> (II: I.iv.58–60)

Celebinus's legitimacy is only confirmed for Tamburlaine by his words; Celebinus must be Tamburlaine's own child because he can speak like him.

This ability to imitate his father's most dominant feature earns Celebinus the right not simply to name himself after Tamburlaine, but rather to assume Tamburlaine's identity utterly. Celebinus is told that he will not just take over from 'the scourge and terror of the world', he will actually be 'the scourge and terror of the world'. Of course, in a play whose genre relies on the impossibility of identical repetition, Tamburlaine's attempt to have Celebinus repeat his character is inevitably doomed; at the end of the play Amyras assumes Tamburlaine's throne, not Celebinus.

Having unwittingly demonstrated that which the sequel is at pains to stage, the unlikeliness of ever achieving exact repetition, Tamburlaine goes on to confuse sequential order. Tamburlaine tells his children that his choice of successor will depend not upon the order of their birth, but rather upon his assessment of their worth:

> If thou exceed thy elder brothers' worth,
> And shine in complete virtue more than they,
> Thou shalt be king before them, and thy seed
> Shall issue crowned from their mother's womb.
> (II: I.iv.50–53)

Tamburlaine explains to his youngest son, Celebinus, that if he proves a deserving successor, he will be made king before his brothers. Showing as little respect for chronology as the sequel in which he speaks, Tamburlaine overturns the conventional sequence of succession; ignoring the rules of primogeniture, Tamburlaine offers to make his youngest child his heir. However, challenging the sequential order which also empowers his own position at the top of the family tree, Tamburlaine disrupts not only the idea of succession, but also the notion of parental supremacy. Indeed, by offering to overturn the generational hierarchy, Tamburlaine unwittingly undermines his own role as head of the family. In metadramatic terms, this is tantamount to promoting a copy over its original, or a sequel over its first part.

Tamburlaine's disruption of the supposedly natural order is made yet more evident when he kills his eldest son.[36] The first instance of infanticide in the play occurs when Olympia acquiesces to her son's demand to 'dispatch me, or I'll kill myself' (II: III.iv.26). An explicitly merciful and honourable act, the murder of Olympia's son anticipates Tamburlaine's infanticide by being similar in structure, but radically different in execution. When Tamburlaine kills Calyphas some acts later, the manner of the murder and the immediate reaction to it leave little doubt that it is an act the play seeks to condemn. Like Callapine, the vengeful son of Bajazeth, Calyphas rebels against Tamburlaine.

The similarity in the sound of their names may be a phonic reminder of their thematic association in the play. Unlike Callapine, however, Calyphas's rebellion takes a form which profoundly subverts Tamburlaine's achievements in both play and sequel; Calyphas refuses to take up arms. Indeed, from his first appearance in the play, Calyphas obstructs and mocks his father's attempts to make him like the mighty Tamburlaine.

Initially protected by his mother, Calyphas tells Tamburlaine that his brothers can 'conquer all the world/And you have won enough for me to keep' (II: I.iv.67–8). Later in the play, after Zenocrate's funeral, Tamburlaine cuts his own arm to show his children that 'A wound is nothing be it ne'er so deep' (II: III.ii.115). Invited to admire his father's display of bravery, Calyphas responds: 'I know not what I should think of it. Methinks 'tis a pitiful sight' (II: III.ii.130–31). Significantly ridiculing Tamburlaine's exhibition of wounding in one of the few prose lines in the play, Calyphas challenges both his father's military temperament and his rhetorical verse.[37] Consequently, when at the battle against Orcanes Calyphas refuses to fight and instead sits playing cards and talking about women, Tamburlaine becomes so incensed he kills his eldest son. Making explicit that it is Calyphas's unwillingness to be like him which causes his anger, Tamburlaine exclaims: 'villain, not my son,/But traitor to my name and majesty?' (II: IV.i.87–8). In spite of pleas for mercy from the assembled kings and sons, Tamburlaine stabs Calyphas, while swearing to take vengeance on Mahomet for sending him such a cowardly offspring (II: IV.i.101–35). Calyphas does not speak throughout the scene; his silence, therefore, opposes Tamburlaine's excessive eloquence and underlines the barbarism of his father's behaviour. Tamburlaine stabs the heir to his empire in a moment which disrupts the notion of appropriate sequentiality. The ultimate break with the fideism of orderly succession in the sequel, Calyphas's death marks the final movement of the play in which events become yet more disconnected and eventually utterly without consequentiality.

The Map and the Book

Having taken Babylon by storm, Tamburlaine instructs Usumcasane to collect all the 'superstitious books' (II: V.i.173) in the city and prepare to burn them. Possibly still angry with Mahomet for providing him with such an inadequate heir, Tamburlaine rails against his erstwhile deity. As Tamburlaine burns the Koran, he challenges Mahomet:

> if thou have any power
> Come down thyself and work a miracle
> Thou art not worthy to be worshipped,
> That suffers flames of fire to burn the writ
> Wherein the sum of thy religion rests.
> (II: V.i.185–9)

Some twenty lines later, Tamburlaine exclaims: 'But stay, I feel myself distempered suddenly' (II: V.i.216). The sequence of these events has encouraged some critics to argue that they are causally linked, that Tamburlaine's unexpected sickness and eventual death are as a direct result of his Islamic blasphemy.[38] However, in a play which revises the assumption that an original and a copy, a word and a deed, a father and a son, can ever be unproblematically connected in a linear way, one should be wary of leaping to obvious conclusions. As Judith Weil complains, Tamburlaine's illness cries 'out for the kind of explanation Sigismund and Orcanes would gladly provide, but it never comes'.[39] The reluctance of the sequel's characters and structure to pass an explicit judgement on Tamburlaine's sickness creates a moment of what Ian Gaskell calls 'cognitive dissonance',[40] or a deliberate disturbance of understanding. The sequel tantalizingly stages a series of events which defy simple notions of con-sequentiality. Instead, the play introduces a moment of absolute ambiguity, an instance which radically refuses resolution by conventional processes of signification.

When Tamburlaine seeks to restore some sort of order to the narrative of his exploits by tracing them on a map at the end of the sequel, he is dramatically unable to rescind the play's persistent disruption of consequentiality; he cannot reinstate a sense of causally-connected action. Beginning at his 'march toward Persia' (II: V.iii.126), the dying Tamburlaine attempts to impose a simple linear story upon his life. These efforts, however, prove ultimately futile. Tamburlaine cannot make his words unproblematically consequential; he cannot draw his narrative to an unambiguous close. Instead, Tamburlaine ends his second play on a note of terrible sequential uncertainty. Despite reintroducing conventional notions of primogeniture by making his eldest surviving son, Amyras, his heir, Tamburlaine fails to create a convincing successor. Indeed, Tamburlaine describes his newly crowned son in terms which anticipate Amyras's eventual loss of his father's empire. Once again returning to the theme of generational conflict, Tamburlaine images himself as Clymene, the sun-god, whose heir, Phaeton, stole his chariot and drove it out of control. Tamburlaine explains to Amyras that the chariot drawn by kings which he has inherited is as valuable 'As that which Clymene's brain-sick son did guide' (II: V.iii.231). Consequently, when Tamburlaine dies only moments later, the ending of the drama is profoundly irresolute. Like the first play, the sequel refuses to repeat the conventional processes of dramatic closure and instead raises the possibility that Amyras's reign will imitate Phaeton's rather than his father's; in other words, Tamburlaine's heir will jeopardize his inheritance. Left with the image of a potentially unsuccessful successor, the sequel restates not only the unlikeliness of Amyras being able to repeat Tamburlaine's conquests identically, but also the impossibility of predicting what the consequence of Tamburlaine's final description of his heir will be. The complexities of the impulse to repeat which informs both parts of *Tamburlaine* are thereby staged at the sequel's conclusion.

Notes

1.   Harper, J. W. (1984). I have used this edition in this chapter.
2.   Kelsall, M. (1981), p. 112.
3.   Summers, C. J. (1974), p. 74.
4.   Harper, J. W. (1984), p. ix.
5.   Martin, R. A. (1978), p. 249.
6.   Kocher, P. (1946), p. 69.
7.   Battenhouse, R. W. (1941), pp. 252–3.
8.   LePage, P. V. (1965), p. 605.
9.   Altman, J. B. (1978), p. 323.
10. Cunningham, J. S. (1981), p. 20.
11. Jump, J. D. (1967), p. xxv.
12. Geckle, G. (1988), p. 15.
13. Metzidakis, S. (1986), p. 1.
14. See chapter four, on *Dido, Queene of Carthage*, for a fuller explanation.
15. Benaquist, L. M. (1975), p. i.
16. Richards, S. (1965), p. 379.
17. Wyler, S. (1967), pp. 306–16.
18. Cutts, J. P. (1985), p. 147.
19. Connor, S. (1988), p. 7.
20. See chapter two, on *Edward II*.
21. Norris, C. (1987), p. 15.
22. See Derrida's 'Différance' in *Speech and Phenomena: And Other Essays*, trans. David B. Allison (1973). Evanston: Northwestern University Press.
23. Battenhouse, R. W. (1973), p. 30.
24. Battenhouse, R. W. (1973), p. 30.
25. Battenhouse, R. W. (1973), p. 32.
26. Battenhouse, R. W. (1973), p. 33.

27. See Ive, P. (1589), chapter two, pp. 2–3: 'Who so shall fortifie in playne ground, may make the Fort he pretendeth of what forme or figure he will, and therefore he may with lesse compasse of wall enclose a more superficies of ground, then where that scope may not be had. Also it may be the perfecter, because the angles that do happen in it, may be made flatter or sharper. Moreouer the ground in plaines is good to make ramperts of, and easie for cariage, but where water water wanteth, the building is costly and chargeable, for that a Fort situated in a dry playne, must have deepe ditches, high walles, great bulwarks, large ramparts, and cavalieros: besides, it must be great to lodge fiue or sixe thousand men, and have great place in it for them to fight, ranked in battaile. It must also haue countermines, priuie ditches, secret issuings out to defende the ditch, casmats in the ditch, couered wayes round about it, and an argine or banke to empeache the approach, will require great garrison, much artillerie, powder, victuals, and other things necessarie for the keeping and mainteining of it.'
28. Bowers, F. (1973), vol. 1, p. 74.
29. Nicholl, C. (1992), p. 120.
30. Boas, F. S. (1940), p. 73.
31. Bevington, D. (1962), p. 203.
32. Geckle, G. (1988), p. 17.
33. For a fuller discussion of the significance of this moment in relation to the play's use of its source see chapter four, on *Dido, Queene of Carthage*.
34. Berek, P (1982), p. 58. According to Berek the ten plays are Green's *Alphonsus King of Aragon* (1587), Peele's *Battle of Alcazar* (1589), the anonymous *Locrine* (1591), the anonymous *The Taming of a Shrew* (1589), Greene's *Orlando Furioso* (1591), *The Wars of Cyrus* (1588), Lodge's and Greene's *A Looking-Glass for London and England* (1590), Lodge's *Wounds of Civil War* (1588), *Selimus* (1592) and Shakespeare's *Henry VI* plays.
35. See Lisa Hopkins '"Lear, Lear, Lear!"': Marlowe, Shakespeare, and the Third', in *The Upstart Crow* vol. xvi (1996), pp. 108–23, in which she compares the relationship between Tamburlaine and his children to Lear's relationship with his three daughters and his rhetorical love test.
36. Despite there being no explicit references to the order of the sons, it is clear that Calyphas is the oldest and Celebinus the youngest, from the ordering of their names in the original stage directions, and Tamburlaine's reference to Celebinus's 'elder brothers' (II: I.iv.500), which is in the plural.
37. Note that Calyphas again speaks at length in prose in his final scene (II: IV.i.). Compare Zabina's deconstruction into prose at the end of the first play, which also challenges Tamburlaine.
38. See, for example, J. B. Steane, who claims that while the historical Tamburlaine died peacefully with his children, Marlowe's hero 'dies in fevered madness, justly punished for his sins'. Steane, J. B. (1964), p. 72.
39. Weil, J. (1977), p. 122.
40. Gaskell, I. (1985), p. 185.

Chapter 4

Fathering Virgil: *Dido, Queene of Carthage* and Originality

The play of *Dido, Queene of Carthage* is informed by the same impulse which gives shape to the *Tamburlaine* dramas – repetition. Like the *Tamburlaine* sequel, *Dido, Queene of Carthage* is based on an existing work. Consequently, both *Tamburlaine* part two and *Dido, Queene of Carthage* repeat a group of characters and a set of dramatic circumstances with which their audiences are already familiar. In the case of the *Tamburlaine* plays, it is the very fact of this familiarity which licenses the second play, which makes the sequel a viable dramatic genre. Unlike the second *Tamburlaine* drama, however, which reiterates the same characters and form as its source text in order to extend and develop the plot of the original play, *Dido, Queene of Carthage* repeats the story on which it is based with almost exact precision; it even quotes directly from its source. The remarkable exactness with which *Dido, Queene of Carthage* renders its source story, coupled with the nature of its artistic progenitor, involves the play in contentious debates about imitation which are largely irrelevant to the *Tamburlaine* plays. For while the *Tamburlaine* sequel repeats features of a dramatic work by its own author, *Dido, Queene of Carthage* repeats the story of a non-dramatic source written by a revered classical author. What in the *Tamburlaine* plays is ostensibly a simple matter of cashing in on one's own success becomes in *Dido, Queene of Carthage* an issue of absolute indebtedness to a much-celebrated non-dramatic poem by a non-Christian poet. *Dido, Queene of Carthage*'s engagement with the theme of repetition is therefore more complex than the *Tamburlaine* sequel's; *Dido, Queene of Carthage* is involved in an artistic process which is directly at odds with the imperative of originality, while at the same time being part of a contemporary humanist debate about the validity of imitating and thereby elevating the works of pagan or non-Christian writers.

The most overt expression of the play's problematic relationship to its classical source occurs at the end of the action, when Aeneas bids farewell to Dido for the last time. In a moment of exaggerated generic self-consciousness the drama stages its origins by quoting directly from its source, Virgil's *Aeneid*.

As its characters move seamlessly from Renaissance English to classical Latin, the drama reveals its indebtedness:

> DIDO. By this right hand, and by our spousall rites,
> Desires *Aeneas* to remaine with her:
> *Si bene quid de te merui, fuit aut tibi quidquam*
> *Dulce meum, miserere domus labentis: & istam*
> *Oro, si quis adhuc precibus locus, exue mentem.*
> AENEAS. *Desine meque tuis incendere teque querelis,*
> *Italiam non sponte sequor.*
> (V.i.134–40)[1]

It is at this point that the drama's repetition of Virgil's poem is at both its most explicit and its most exact. The source text irrupts into the play, making it impossible to ignore the drama's indebtedness. Like *Edward II*, which also culminates in a Latin phrase taken from another text, *Dido, Queene of Carthage* reaches its climax in the language and genre from which it is derived. Thus the drama recites its origins as classical poetry.

Those critics who do not read this episode as an example of Marlowe's weariness with translation tend to interpret the scene as the dramatist's eventual recognition of his inability to surpass, or even to match, the artistry of his source text.[2] According to this reading, by quoting from the *Aeneid*, *Dido, Queene of Carthage* openly surrenders to the superiority of its original. This interpretation, however, does not tell the whole story. It is equally possible that the play recites its origins as a direct challenge to them, as an acknowledgement of the battle for textual primacy which has been waging throughout the rest of the drama. For the act of imitation does not necessarily indicate a deferential attitude towards the text imitated. The terms of imitative engagement are too complex and too paradoxical to conclude that imitation consistently implies artistic deference. The contradictory nature of imitation, especially when based on non-Christian sources, was noted as early as the thirteenth century when Pierre de Blois imagined the imitators of classical authors like 'dwarfs mounted on the shoulders of giants; with their assistance we can see further than they can; clinging to their works, we restore a new life to their more elegant thoughts, which time or the neglect of men had already left as dead.'[3] De Blois explains to an unnamed critic that the imitation of texts by non-Christian authors is justified because it revivifies valuable concepts which would otherwise be lost. Moreover, characterizing imitation as a process which resurrects the past, de Blois endows the imitative enterprise with a Christian agenda; for de Blois the imitation of classical texts is a Christ-like activity which gives life to dead ideas. Similarly, de Blois's depiction of himself as a dwarf mounted on the shoulders of a giant discloses that the act of imitation is more self-aggrandizing than it is deferential. Although de Blois pictures himself as physically inferior to his classical predecessor, as a dwarf, it is paradoxically by virtue of his diminutive stature that he is able to see further than the mentor on whose shoulders he perches. Commenting upon the irony of this circumstance, Louis Dupré notes that 'Posterity reaps what its ancestors sowed. *Quanto juniores, tanto perspicaciores*. The younger, the wiser!'[4] For the medieval author, imitation was an activity which revealed contemporary, not ancient, genius.

Despite the eloquence of de Blois's defence, the necessity of his letter cannot help but reveal the widespread mistrust of imitation. Indeed, setting aside the tortuous problem of the use by Christian authors of pagan works as exemplar, Renaissance writers were still faced with both classical and biblical edicts against imitation. The banishment of poets from Plato's idealized state in the *Republic* caused considerable concern for Renaissance exponents of imitation. In his famous *Apology for Poetry*, Sir Philip Sidney attempts to argue that Plato does not condemn poetry as such, but rather, its abusers.[5] However, Plato's exclusion of poetry depends on a wholesale condemnation of imitative art; the philosopher maintains that because artists copy man-made works which are themselves mere imitations of ideal forms, art operates at a third remove from the truth.[6] Masking what it should illuminate, art is, according to Plato, guilty of distracting mankind from the pursuit of the ideal.

Similarly concerned with the wrongness of emulating ideal forms, the Old Testament also prohibits imitation. At the foot of Mount Sinai the chosen race flouted the taboo against imitation and constructed a golden calf to worship. Ignoring God's second commandment, 'You shall not make for yourself a graven image, or any likeness of anything that is in heaven above, or that is in the earth beneath, or that is in the water under the earth; you shall not bow down to them or serve them; for I the Lord your God am a jealous God' (Exodus 20: 4–5), the Israelites committed perhaps the greatest and most often repeated sin of all – imitation. Even Lucifer's fall from grace is ascribed to his desire to copy God: 'I will make myself like the Most High' (Isaiah 14: 12). The classical and biblical rules prohibiting copying ultimately depend not upon the evils of imitation, but rather upon the sanctity of originality. An original must be beyond reproduction or it is not original. Like Moses's God, the original cannot countenance imitation as every copy detracts from its uniqueness, from its singularity, and hence from its value. Consequently,

Marlowe's rewriting of part of the *Aeneid* as *Dido, Queene of Carthage* can be read as a direct challenge to Virgil's originality; copying that which should be beyond reproduction, Marlowe threatens the primacy of Virgil's text. It is *Dido, Queene of Carthage*'s dramatization of this artistic debate about imitation and originality which the present chapter will elaborate. However, before examining the drama's self-conscious indebtedness, it will be useful to consider the twentieth-century reception of *Dido, Queene of Carthage*, which reveals the critical dis-comfort induced by works dependent upon imitation.

Translation, Imitation or Dramatization? The Uncategorizable Nature of *Dido, Queene of Carthage*

The critical, editorial and theatrical history of *Dido, Queene of Carthage* has been characterized by neglect. Between the moment of its composition and 1825 it was printed only once, in 1594, and since the nineteenth century it has been included in editions of Marlowe's complete works but seldom printed separately as a play in its own right. Consequently, *Dido, Queene of Carthage* is rarely awarded a literary status beyond that of Marlovian juvenilia; the play is considered to be essential to the construction of the dramatist's canon, while not a work of independent value. The almost unanimous scholarly disregard for *Dido, Queene of Carthage* is ostensibly due to critical anxieties concerning its generic and chronological categorization. D. C. Allen notes that *Dido, Queene of Carthage* 'has been curiously unprized by critics partly because they do not know where in the Marlovian chronicle it belongs and partly because it seems not to move in the great swinging orbits of the universal tragedies'.[7] Apparently neither one thing nor another, *Dido, Queene of Carthage*'s critical reception is everywhere inscribed with an uneasiness about the drama's literary standing. For Matthew Proser this problem can only be resolved by viewing the play as an anomaly within the canon: an expression of a minor aspect of the writer's talent which produced a stylistic refinement and equipoise absent from his other works. Proser maintains that:

> *Dido, Queene of Carthage*'s style shows signs of control and wit, a rationalistically oriented urbanity, and a neo-classical respect for balance and limits, and these in a variety of scenes and passages. Yet such are actually the reflections of a subordinate dimension of Marlowe's personality.[8]

Proser is therefore only able to classify *Dido, Queene of Carthage* by its very resistance to classification, as an atypical work. The premise on which Proser erects his argument is, however, highly dubious. By marginalizing the technical control and eloquence apparent in *Dido, Queene of Carthage*, Proser simply constructs an alternative view of Marlowe's canon which reveals more about his own aesthetic assumptions than the dramatist's actual style. Proser thereby draws a portrait of Marlowe as a Promethean artist which is in keeping with Harry Levin's influential analysis of the dramatist in *The Overreacher*. Ignoring the qualities of elegance and self-discipline to be found not only in *Dido, Queene of Carthage* but also in *Hero and Leander* and *Edward II*, Proser refuses to accommodate aspects of the dramatist's work which do not conform to his preconceptions of Marlowe's personality. In a similar attempt to peripheralize the play, some critics dismiss *Dido, Queene of Carthage* as a juvenile work. Examining the drama as a premature and ultimately abortive effort, J. B. Steane argues that the dramatic promise of *Dido, Queene of Carthage* had to wait until Shakespeare's treatment of ancient history to be brought to fruition. Steane claims that *Dido, Queene of Carthage*'s 'glorying in romantic love' produces an 'immature' version of *Antony and Cleopatra*.[9] In an effort to render the play classifiable, Steane must transfer it to a more comfortable niche in the canon of a dramatist more commonly associated with the expression of passion.

Generically unsatisfying, stylistically anomalous and chronologically immature, *Dido, Queene of Carthage* stands accused of artistic irregularity. Under cross-examination, however, the charges against *Dido, Queene of Carthage* rapidly dissolve. Far from being uncategorizable, *Dido, Queene of Carthage* is extant in an early edition (1594) which clearly states a genre and a dramaturgy on its title page:

> The Tragedie of Dido/*Queene of Carthage*:/Played by the Children of her/*Maiesties Chappell.*/Written by Christopher Marlowe, and/*Thomas Nash. Gent.*[10]

Refusing to conform to twentieth-century artistic tastes, *Dido, Queene of Carthage* defines itself as a tragedy based on a classical legend, designed to be played at court by a boys' company. Presuming a specific theatrical and literary context, it cannot be the paucity of information about the play which confuses criticism, but instead its very particularity. It is *Dido, Queene of Carthage*'s intractable categorization within a genre and a dramaturgy to which modern criticism is unsympathetic that ultimately depreciates the artistic value of the play. However, it is possible that the features which modern scholarship finds so difficult to accommodate are actually the primary interest of the drama; it is *Dido, Queene of Carthage*'s dramaturgy which enables the play to dwell upon its generic indebtedness. It will therefore be useful to note the effect of the play's genre and dramaturgy on its prior reception and present interpretation.

A Genre of Indebtedness

In denial of the drama's explicit indebtedness many critics maintain that *Dido, Queene of Carthage* is nothing more than a translation of a work by another author. The most recent edition of the play, produced in 1987 by Roma Gill as part of her *Complete Works of Christopher Marlowe*, includes *Dido, Queene of Carthage* in the volume entitled *Translations*, where it appears alongside Marlowe's renderings of 'All Ovid's Elegies', 'Lucan's First Booke' and 'Hero and Leander'.[11] Gill explains in her introduction to the volume that the works contained within it 'find their common denominator in the fact that all are translations from a classical language into English'.[12] Gill goes on to categorize *Dido, Queene of Carthage* according to Dryden's terms as a 'paraphrase, or translation with latitude'.[13] She concludes that apart from the addition of the Anna and Iarbus sub-plot 'with its ludicrous climax', the dramatist 'is true to his original: Virgil is always "kept in view"'.[14] Characterizing Marlowe's composition as an unproblematic 'Englishing' of a classical narrative, Roma Gill's classification of *Dido, Queene of Carthage* differs surprisingly little from C. F. Tucker Brooke's own appraisal some half a century earlier. Tucker Brooke maintains that *Dido, Queene of Carthage* is a 'work of borrowed plot and rather composite style' in which 'we see the impact of Vergil's splendid gravity upon the most exuberantly romantic of the Elizabethan dramatists'.[15] Gill and Tucker Brooke both dismiss the drama as no more interesting than an historical artefact; the play is an example of the use of a classical source by a young poet who was later to dispense with such formalism.

Dido, Queene of Carthage's 'untypical Marlovian dependence on a widely known literary source' has therefore been a stumbling-block for scholarship's appreciation of the drama.[16] In response to the play's generic and dramaturgical challenge, critics have either emasculated *Dido, Queene of Carthage*'s dramatic vigour by pronouncing the work a translation, like Roma Gill, or dismembered the drama's narrative to produce a poetic fragment reminiscent of Virgil, like Tucker Brooke. *Dido, Queene of Carthage* has been repeatedly refashioned by scholarship in an effort to account for, and ultimately to ignore, its indebtedness. However, even more problematic than the drama's reliance on a classical author is the title page's attribution of *Dido, Queene of Carthage* to not one, but two, playwrights. By naming Thomas Nashe as co-author, the earliest edition multiplies points of origination in a process which only serves to accentuate critical anxieties about indebtedness.

The authorial dilemma presented by *Dido, Queene of Carthage* has often been cursorily dismissed by critics. According to Roma Gill in her introduction to the drama, Nashe's part-authorship 'has never been seriously entertained'.[17] Moreover, despite the 'surprisingly high' number of verbal connections with Nashe's work which occur in the first scene of *Dido, Queene of Carthage*, Gill maintains that 'the phrasing is undoubtedly Marlowe's'.[18] The editor concludes, therefore, that 'if there is any significance in these parallels, it is for the student of Nashe'.[19] Reinforcing the argument of earlier Marlovian scholars such as Fredson Bowers,[20] as well as C. F. Tucker Brooke,[21] Roma Gill denies Nashe's contribution to *Dido, Queene of Carthage*. Gill is even less flexible than F. S. Boas, who speculates in his *Biographical and Critical Study* that Nashe may have prepared the text for publication after Marlowe's death, his name being thereby appended to a work not his own.[22] Notwithstanding the weight of critical opinion opposing Nashe's co-authorship of *Dido, Queene of Carthage*, it should be noted that there is no firm evidence to disprove the title page's claim that he contributed to the play. Moreover, as the only extant drama definitely attributed to Thomas Nashe is *Summer's Last Will and Testament* (1593) which was composed, like *Dido, Queene of Carthage*, for performance by a boys' company, it is possible that Nashe's involvement with Marlowe's play either initiated or extended an interest in the dramaturgy of children's theatre. Insoluble as the authorship question remains, it nevertheless offers the opportunity to note not only modern scholarship's failure to accommodate multiply-influenced works, but also the impossibility of recuperating the figure of the author in any determinate way. The attribution problem is most reasonably addressed by H. J. Oliver in his 1968 edition of the play. Having examined Nashe's grammar, spelling and literary style, Oliver concludes: 'in the notes on *Dido, Queene of Carthage* and sometimes in the remainder of the Introduction, I have referred to "Marlowe", as have earlier editors, where "Marlowe" is only a kind of shorthand for "the author or authors of the play, whoever he or they may have been at this point"'.[23] Following Oliver's lead, I will also refer to the author/authors of *Dido, Queene of Carthage* under the simplifying name of Marlowe. Thus *Dido, Queene of Carthage*'s reception is everywhere inscribed by scholarship's unwillingness to acknowledge works indebted to more than one author, more than one influence. What is more, this problem is only exacerbated in the case of *Dido, Queene of Carthage* by a dramaturgy which self-consciously draws attention to the play's parentage.

A Theatre of Self-Consciousness

Challenging conventional twentieth-century notions of dramatic originality with its humanist genre and collaborative authorship, *Dido, Queene of Carthage* is similarly perplexing in its dramaturgy. The title page inscription states that *Dido, Queene of Carthage* was performed by the Children of the Chapel which indicates that the drama was probably composed for the court revels. According to Michael Shapiro, the Chapel Boys enjoyed such commercial success in the last quarter of the sixteenth century that their master Richard Ferrant, a temporary replacement for William Hunnis, was able to open a theatre for them at Blackfriars in 1576.[24] This theatre became the subject of a lengthy legal dispute as the owner, Sir William More, fought to reclaim his property. In 1584 More's efforts proved successful and Blackfriars passed from the hands of the Chapel Boys. It was not until 1597, more than ten years later, that the boys were able to return to Blackfriars in a new theatre.[25] Indeed, in *Playgoing in Shakespeare's London*, Andrew Gurr notes that 'From 1590–1600 no boy companies and no indoor playhouses, except possibly the occasional hall or a city inn, were available in London'.[26] The closing of Blackfriars and subsequently all indoor playhouses means that *Dido, Queene of Carthage*, which is usually dated between 1585–88,[27] was possibly never performed before a public audience in Marlowe's lifetime.

However, H. J. Oliver records in his edition two references made by Henslowe to a Dido and Aeneas play, performed after Marlowe's death by an adult company. He writes:

> There are no surviving records of any one performance of *Dido, Queene of Carthage* by the Children of the Royal Chapel, but it may be the play to which Henslowe refers in two entries in his *Diary* for 1598. On 3rd January 1597/8 he laid out 29s 'for copr lace for the littell boye and for a valle for the boy Ageanste the playe of dido and eneus' and five days later he lent the company 30s 'when they fyrst played dido at nyght'. Also an inventory of the property of the Lord Admiral's Men, printed by Malone and since lost, included on 'the 10 of March 1598', 'j tome of Dido', 'Cupides bowe, and quiver' and Dides robe'. This performance, or these performances of a Dido and Aeneas play could have been, but were not necessarily, performances of

the work written by Marlowe and Nashe; and if so they would have been revivals by an adult company of a play not written originally for them.[28]

Although Marlowe's *Dido, Queene of Carthage* does not require a tomb for its protagonist, Oliver ascribes Henslowe's references to the children's company play of his edition. Of course, the likelihood of an adult revival of the text is important; it is nevertheless of even more interest to consider how Oliver's research transposes *Dido, Queene of Carthage* from a highly stylized and self-conscious dramaturgy to a more naturalistic and acceptably modern one: from the boy players at court to the adult company at the public playhouse.

Part of a tradition we can only glimpse in the annual school production, the Elizabethan children's companies practised a style of drama which was visually lavish and verbally formal. Often performed as a series of static tableaux in which set speeches were delivered, the boys' dramas did not aspire to mimetic realism. Indeed, as G. K. Hunter conjectures in his study of *John Lyly: The Humanist as Courtier*, the 'boys' companies must have provided an extreme case of the formality of Elizabethan acting. There could be no question of it being supposed that they were living rather than acting the roles they portrayed'.[29] What is more, specializing in the depiction of classical legends such as *Sappho and Phao*, and ancient histories such as *Campaspe*, boys' companies made no attempt to disguise the youth of their players. Casting the boys in roles they could not possibly portray convincingly, their masters instead used the children's physical incongruity to emphasize the artificiality of their dramatic venture. In this way, the gap between life and art was consciously accentuated by the boys' companies.

Constantly deflecting attention away from the particulars of *Dido, Queene of Carthage*'s generic and dramatic contexts, modern criticism belies an ostrich-like mentality, a wilful refusal to acknowledge the more knotty problems of Renaissance representation. Problems, moreover, which *Dido, Queene of Carthage* self-consciously stages in order to interrogate and ultimately perhaps to challenge. Consequently, it is possible to argue that it is the same generic and dramatic features which have inspired criticism to dismiss the play that are in fact the very source of its theatrical and intellectual value. *Dido, Queene of Carthage* is able to examine its genre through its dramaturgy; the play stages its indebtedness by being performed in a highly formalistic and metadramatic theatrical style. According to this reading, *Dido, Queene of Carthage* is not an unimportant 'Englishing' of a classical poem, but rather a significant dramatic contribution to the humanist debate about the revivification of the past. It is the play's dramatization of the activity of turning the past into the present, Virgil into Marlowe, and poetry into drama, which renders *Dido, Queene of Carthage* much more than a deferential translation. *Dido, Queene of Carthage*'s self-conscious presentation of the attempt to make Virgil's non-dramatic poem dramatic requires further examination.

Making Priam Live

At the beginning of Virgil's *Aeneid*, Aeneas happens upon a series of frescoes depicting the Trojan war, which decorate Juno's temple at Carthage.[30] Aeneas is, of course, moved by the sight of his recent past translated into art. By contrast, in Marlowe's retelling of the story, the Trojan general does not encounter two-dimensional wall paintings but rather a statue of Priam so lifelike that Aeneas mistakes it for the king himself: 'He is alive, *Troy* is not overcome' (II.i.30). This moment cleverly stages Marlowe's theatrical enterprise throughout the entire play; it reveals the way in which the playwright makes the *Aeneid* dramatic. Transforming Virgil's story from a descriptive tale to be read, into a theatrical show to be performed, *Dido, Queene of Carthage* reveals the negotiations necessary between page and stage. For, by quite literally making what in Virgil is two-dimensional and descriptive, here three-dimensional and almost alive,[31] *Dido, Queene of Carthage* gestures towards its origins while simultaneously refusing to realize them fully. Developing the theme of dramatizing the non-dramatic, Marlowe's play presents Aeneas's first meeting with Dido: an encounter in which the Trojan general tries to deny his own visibility, his own theatricality. Directed to watch the queen's approach, Aeneas maintains Dido will not be able to see him:

> ILLIONEUS. Looke where she comes: *Aeneas* view her well.
> AENEAS. Well may I view her, but she sees not me.
> *Enter* DIDO [*with* ANNA *and* IARBUS] *and her traine*.
> DIDO. What stranger art thou that doest eye me thus?
> (II.i.72–4)

In this exchange Aeneas seems to expect that he will be able to see others – himself unseen. It is almost as if Aeneas believes himself to be invisible. This lack of self-awareness is not, however, a sign of humility. Indeed, Aeneas's refusal to acknowledge his physicality is actually a refusal to participate in the theatrical world in which he finds himself; Aeneas is explicitly resisting the form in which his story is being retold. The drama must, therefore, keep reminding Aeneas that he is not the figure described in Virgil's epic poem, but rather a character portrayed by a living actor that the other characters and the audience are able to see. Aeneas's reluctance to be seen stages the competing narrative and dramatic impulses which inform *Dido, Queene of Carthage*.

According to Virgil's *Aeneid*, Aeneas enters Carthage swathed in a magic mist which does not lift until Dido requests his appearance.[32] Aeneas's problem with visibility in *Dido, Queene of Carthage* might therefore realize the requirements of the play's source text. A mist is, however, as theatrically realizable as a storm or an invisible spirit;[33] the playwright could have easily staged Virgil's fog by simply telling the audience that at this point in the play the Trojans cannot be seen by the Carthaginians. But this is not what happens in Marlowe's play. Instead of translating Virgil's story for the stage, Marlowe self-consciously dwells upon the nature of his theatrical enterprise; he draws attention to the drama's conversion of its source by depicting Aeneas's reluctance to become a physical presence in the play. Indeed, even before Aeneas meets Dido, his physicality is marked as a problem in the text. When the Trojan general encounters his followers in Carthage, they significantly fail to recognize him. Quite literally unable to see his general, Illioneus exclaims: 'I heare *Aeneas* voyce, but see him not' (II.i.45). By making Aeneas's visibility an issue, Marlowe develops and accentuates the differences between his source and his play. Consequently, Dido's desire to dress Aeneas in the clothes of her dead husband directly opposes the general's refusal to be visible. Stage-managing a piece of pure theatre, Dido insists that Aeneas is given a new costume to wear:

> Warlike *Aeneas*, and in these base robes?
> Goe fetch the garment which *Sicheus* ware: (II.i.79–80)

Dressing Aeneas in the borrowed robes of her dead husband, Dido creates an explicitly theatrical moment in which the visual is made meaningful. For by dressing Aeneas in Sicheus's clothes, Dido indicates not only the very visible nature of all theatre, but also her amatory intentions towards the general. Dido identifies Aeneas with her dead spouse, and thereby raises the possibility that in Marlowe's retelling of the story she has already fallen in love with the Trojan warrior before Cupid wounds her some scenes later. The visual and the verbal, the dramatic and the narrative, the copy and the original, are shown to be in competition in the play. However, snatching back textual control from the woman who has just made him a highly visible character, Aeneas resists Dido's theatricality with a speech which is apparently a Virgilian interruption;

the drama's momentum is temporarily suspended as the play's non-dramatic origins irrupt into the world of the theatre.

Aeneas's Troy Speech: A Poetic Fragment?

The so-called Troy speech is probably the most well-known and certainly the most often quoted piece of *Dido, Queene of Carthage*. Occupying over 167 lines of verse, the speech has, not surprisingly, been mistaken for a poetic fragment which can easily be detached from its dramatic context and unproblematically anthologized elsewhere. In keeping with this reading of the speech, Richard A. Martin maintains that 'the story of the fall of Troy creates a miniature epic within the dramatic world'.[34] The ostensibly incongruous nature of the speech, however, does not necessarily render it non-dramatic. Indeed, Aeneas's description of the fall of Troy is delivered within an ongoing theatrical production to an on-stage audience whose anticipated relationships impact upon its significance. In spite of the Troy speech's seeming anti-theatricality, the monologue actually cannot help but be theatrical because it is performed in the context of a play. Consequently, the speech dramatically fails to turn the play back towards its Virgilian origins; Aeneas's attempt to freeze the drama in a moment of already determined narrative does not succeed. Instead of confining his narrative to the one described by Virgil, the Aeneas of the play raises questions about both his role in the eventual Greek victory and his single-mindedness in escaping from Troy.

Introducing a series of interpretative questions, Aeneas's 'sad tale' (II.i.125) initially encourages the audience to wonder how the Trojan general is able to describe Priam's murder in such intimate detail. With a narrative completeness more typical of an omniscient narrator than a dramatic character, Aeneas recounts the fall of Troy. He describes how '*Achilles* sonne' (II.i.233), Pirrhus,[35] finds the King of Troy sheltering with his wife Hecuba at Jove's altar. There Priam pleads to the boy to be allowed to live but Pirrhus 'strooke off his hands' (II.i.242). Aeneas continues:

> At which the franticke Queene leapt on his face,
> And in his eyelids hanging by the nayles,
> A little while prolong'd her husbands life:
> At last the souldiers puld her by the heeles,
> And swong her howling in the emptie ayre,
> Which sent an eccho to the wounded King:

> Whereat he lifted up his bedred lims,
> And would have grappeld with *Achilles* sonne,
> Forgetting both his want of strength and hands,
> Which he disdaining whiskt his sword about,
> And with the wind thereof the King fell downe:
> Then from the navell to the throat at once,
> He ript old *Priam*
> (II.i.244–56)

Aeneas's account of Priam's murder is told with an intimacy only available to an eyewitness or an omniscient narrator. Consequently, in his article '"Unstable Proteus": *The Tragedy of Dido Queen of Carthage*', Brian Gibbons claims that the Troy speech does not reveal Aeneas's heroism, but rather his treachery; Aeneas can detail Priam's slaughter because it was he who led Pirrhus to the king and stood by while he was killed:

> The apparent hero, ancestor of the British race, loyal defender of Troy, founder of Rome, breaks down and betrays his cowardice! It is we may think, characteristic of Marlowe to treat Aeneas, a very 'type' of the Renaissance hero, with sardonic irreverence; but this is not mere caricature. Aeneas' account of the Fall of Troy combines Virgilian grandeur and range with Medieval details of horror and violence which derive from popular romances, especially the well-known *Troy Book* of Lydgate; and this must remind the audience that the Aeneas of Medieval legend was a notorious villain not an epic hero. Aeneas knows the frightful details of Priam's death because he and Antenor had led Pyrrhus to the king's place of refuge and stood by, consenting as he murdered.[36]

According to Gibbons, Aeneas's speech redirects his audience to texts other than Virgil's, to medieval works which describe the Trojan general's betrayal of the ancient kingdom. When Dido asks Aeneas whether Antenor sold Troy to the Greeks, 'Some say *Antenor* did betray the towne' (II.i.110), the queen is also turning a spotlight on the general's own dubious behaviour. Indeed, in John Lydgate's *Troy Book*, based upon Guido delle Colonne's Latin *Historia Destructionis Troiae*, Aeneas is described as a villain who has been wrongly glorified by ancient authors. Lydgate maintains:

> Virgile also, for love of Enee,
> In Eneydos rehersyth moche thyng,
> And was in party trewe in his writyng,

Exsept only that hym lyst som whyle
The tracys folwe of Omeris stile.[37]

Redressing the glorious narrative of the pagans, Lydgate depicts Aeneas and
Antenor seeking to save their own skins by betraying Troy.[38] Together they
engineer a false peace with the Greeks, allowing the wooden horse to enter the
city. Later, as the Greeks sack Troy, Antenor and Aeneas take Pyrrhus to
Priam's treasure where they find the king sheltering from the battle. Refusing
to intervene, Aeneas and Antenor watch while Pyrrhus slaughters Priam.[39]
Implied around the margins of the Troy speech, the alternative medieval
representation of Aeneas haunts *Dido, Queene of Carthage*. In a similar vein,
Mary E. Smith notes in *Love Kindling Fire* that the ambivalence produced by
Aeneas's account of the fall of Troy 'is not an accident, nor a sign of a
playwright who has insufficiently mastered the art of characterization'.[40]
Instead, Smith maintains that the Troy speech deliberately invites intertextual
comparisons which allow for the 'distortion, exaggeration, and mockery of the
legendary ancestor of the Britons'.[41] The speech and the play in which it is
spoken stage, not only the struggle between Virgil's epic version of events and
Marlowe's dramatic one, but also that between the classical and the popular
descriptions of Aeneas.

Opening Aeneas to yet more criticism, the Troy speech describes the
general's single-minded escape from the conquered city, which requires his
abandonment of three women. Aeneas explains that fleeing from Troy with his
wife Creusa, he was accosted by Greeks and 'there I lost my wife' (II.i.270).
Having abandoned his wife, the Trojan general goes on to rescue Cassandra
temporarily before being 'forst to let her lye' (II.i.279) so that he can reach his
ships. Finally, Aeneas maintains that he attempted to save Polixena from the
Greeks by swimming for shore but that he was too late to prevent Pirrhus from
sacrificing her (II.i.280–88). This narrative of female desertion even prompts
the women in Aeneas's on-stage audience to ask what happened to two further
female characters, Hecuba and Helen.[42] Refusing to answer Dido's and Anna's
questions, Aeneas redirects them to Achates who explains the women's fates
(II.i.294–9). Despite the general's apparent control of the Troy speech, the
dramatic context of the narrative cannot help but raise doubts about Aeneas's
involvement both in the murder of King Priam and the deaths of the three
Trojan women. Aeneas's abandonment of Creusa, Cassandra and Polixena is
dramatically significant because it exaggeratedly foreshadows his eventual
desertion of the woman who has been the primary audience of his words,
Queen Dido. A part of an ongoing theatrical plot, Aeneas's speech cannot help

but assume a series of dramatic meanings which simultaneously look back at the characterization of the Trojan general in previous texts and forwards to his theatrical realization in Marlowe's play as the archetypal deserter of women.

Looking even further forwards than the end of Marlowe's play, however, the Troy speech is recited in *Hamlet* when the eponymous hero requests that the Player performs 'Aeneas' tale to Dido' (II.ii.449). Almost certainly a parody of Marlowe's own speech,[43] the Player's rendition of the fall of Troy is importantly connected with *Dido, Queene of Carthage* not only in terms of its subject matter but also in terms of its thematic significance. The Player's soliloquy in *Hamlet* reflects upon anxieties about paternal influence which also inform Marlowe's own Troy speech. Consequently, the primary point of connection between Marlowe's text and Shakespeare's is the literal and metaphorical theme of fathers; Virgil, Priam, Old Hamlet and Claudius are the abstract and the actual fathers implicated in both the Troy speech and the Player's words. For while Hamlet employs the Troy speech to understand how father-figures may be dispatched, Aeneas employs it to reassert his parental text, to make the drama in which he finds himself revert from theatre into Virgilian poetry. The epic paternal struggle being waged between Virgil's and Marlowe's texts in the environs of *Dido, Queene of Carthage* is rehearsed by Hamlet to describe his murderous feelings towards his stepfather, Claudius. It should therefore come as no surprise that the paternally-preoccupied Hamlet desires to hear 'Aeneas' tale to Dido'. The story of Pyrrhus's triumphant slaughter of Priam offers the prince an exemplary model for his own beleaguered position. Like Pyrrhus, Hamlet has lost a father in murderous circumstances, and like Pyrrhus he must take revenge upon a man who is simultaneously a king and a father-figure. It is important to note here that Priam, the legendary producer of 100 sons, is actually referred to in the Player's speech as 'Th' unnerved father' (II.ii.470). However, the differences between Pyrrhus and Hamlet are more pronounced than the similarities; unlike Claudius, Pyrrhus's victim is an elderly and feeble man to whom he is not related, while unlike Hamlet, Pyrrhus is the very embodiment of ruthless and rash revenge. The Player's rendition of Aeneas's speech ventriloquizes the passionate emotions Hamlet is as yet unable to feel, and even more unable to express. When the players leave to prepare for *The Mousetrap*, Hamlet ponders what a coward he must be to remain unmoved by a real event when the actor is so readily moved by a fiction: 'What would he do/Had he the motive and the cue for passion/That I have?' (II.ii.554–6). Hamlet unwittingly discloses here that the Troy speech has been a substitute for his own action. Revenge has consequently been recited rather than enacted; narrative has taken the place of drama. In the same way that Aeneas attempts to suspend Marlowe's play by letting the drama lapse into its paternal narrative, Hamlet employs the actor to create the drama he is unwilling to act out himself. The Troy speech is repeated by Shakespeare at the moment when his play questions not only its hero's ability to be an active participant in the drama, but also his fraught relationship to his patrilineal descendants. It cannot be coincidental, therefore, that only moments before reciting Marlowe's Troy speech Hamlet dwells on an image of distorted inheritance which also involves the boys' companies, the theatrical troupes for whom *Dido, Queene of Carthage* was written.

Rosencrantz explains to Hamlet that the primacy of the players has been threatened by 'an eyrie of children, little eyases' (II.ii.337). The 'little eyases', or young hawks, are the boys' companies who have become so popular that they are putting the adult troupes out of business. Hamlet complains that 'their writers do them wrong to make them exclaim against their own succession?' (II.ii.351–2). In other words, the popularity of the children's companies, coupled with their satiric criticism of their dramatic progenitors, threatens to destroy the adult troupes, leaving the boys without a profession to inherit. Importantly, Hamlet characterizes the boys' companies as an interruption in the natural order of things; children are not meant to outstrip their parents, uncles are not meant to marry their sisters-in-law, and brothers are not meant to murder their father's sons. Epitomizing the chaotic inversions which have beset Denmark, the boys' companies are implicated in Hamlet's mind with Claudius's unnatural succession. Hamlet protests that the children's popularity is 'not very strange; for my uncle is King of Denmark, and those that would make mouths at him while my father lived give twenty, forty, fifty, a hundred ducats apiece for his picture in little' (II.ii.359–62). Hamlet condemns his uncle's succession by juxtaposing it with the child actors' success; both are evidence of sequential disruption. What is more, this analogy reveals yet another point of influence between *Hamlet* and *Dido, Queene of Carthage*, for like Shakespeare's play, Marlowe's interrogates notions of succession through the image of the child; while *Hamlet* considers the political ramifications of a son's desire to inherit his father's estate, *Dido, Queene of Carthage* considers the literary implications of the struggle between a new text and its artistic progenitor or father-figure. Thus *Hamlet* offers a more concentrated version of *Dido, Queene of Carthage*'s themes; it restages the earlier play's anxieties about literary succession through similar images of children supplanting adults. It is these images which require examination now.

Dandling Ganimed

From the very beginning of *Dido, Queene of Carthage*, the struggle between Marlowe's dramatic text and Virgil's poem is realized by the staging of generational inversion, of children overcoming parental figures. The opening image of Jupiter dandling Ganimed initiates this examination of the reversal of conventional sequential order.[44] Presenting the spectacle of an adult holding a child, the first scene of *Dido, Queene of Carthage* introduces an apparently innocent and utterly natural picture of parental affection. The apparent naturalness of the opening image is, however, disrupted as the dialogue of the characters reveals that they are not father and son, but rather lovers. Jupiter appeals to the boy on his lap:

> Come gentle *Ganimed* and play with me,
> I love thee well, say *Juno* what she will.
> (I.i.1–2)

With Jupiter's words the audience is informed that the child dandled on the god's lap is not only familially unrelated to him, but also considered a rival by his wife. Malcolm Kelsall's disgusted reaction to the sexualization of the initially paternal stage picture is typical of scholarly responses to the scene. Kelsall exclaims that 'the play begins with one of the most nauseous scenes in Marlovian drama. Perhaps only the buggering of Edward with a red-hot poker matches it. The subject is paedophilia.'[45] The vehemence of such reactions fails, however, to take into account two important points. Firstly, the scene crucially depends on two moments of manufactured mis-recognition: initially the misrecognition of the sexual nature of the characters' relationship and eventually the misrecognition of the actual nature of the actors depicting the characters. The emblem unravels itself by staging a sexual act involving a young child perpetrated by a god played by yet another young child. The drama thereby allays exclamations of disgust by reminding the audience that their outrage depends on a sexual knowingness absent from the actors who are ironically 'playing' at that which they cannot actually 'perform'. Permanently pre-coital, the dramatization of the scene by boy players effectively removes the sting from the tail of *Dido, Queene of Carthage*'s first scene. Secondly, within the context of the drama the relationship between Jupiter and Ganimed is not being deployed as an advertisement for paedophilia, but instead as a playful personification of the complex artistic negotiations inherent in the adaptation of a story by a previous writer, by a literary father-figure.

Throughout the play the initial image of an adult holding a child is repeated involving a variety of different characters in a variety of different scenarios, including Dido holding Ascanius, Dido holding Cupid, and the Nurse holding Cupid.[46] The audience is consequently invited to draw parallels between the Jupiter–Ganimed relationship and the interactions of the other adults and children. These scenarios develop and complicate conventional notions of appropriate adult–child relations. For instance, by the end of the first scene, the relationship between Jupiter and Ganimed is revealed as one of mutual satisfaction, not abuse. As the scene unfolds, Ganimed is not presented as Juptier's unwitting victim but rather as a cunning opportunist willing to exploit the god's sexual appetite. Exchanging his favours for gifts, Ganimed proposes:

> I would have a jewell for mine eare,
> And a fine brouch to put in my hat,
> And then Ile hugge with you an hundred times.
> (I.i.46–8)

Ganimed is here shown turning the tables on his abuser and manipulating Jupiter's affections for financial profit. What is more, this inversion of the conventional power relationship between an adult and a child anticipates Aeneas's own relationship with Dido, which is premised upon the general's need for maritime supplies. The drama therefore creates the initial emblem first as a locus of innocence, then of adult abuse and finally of exploitation by children. Assuming a position of dominance, Ganimed is paradoxically in charge of his abuser; the child ultimately masters the master. This inversion of conventional notions of generational order interestingly refers back to the very origins of the boy players who would have performed Marlowe's play. The children's companies probably developed from the annual ceremony of the Boy Bishop.

In *The Child Actors*, Harold Newcomb Hillebrand connects the tradition of the Boy Bishop with the birth of the children's companies. He explains that annually on Saint Nicholas's Day, 6 December, the Boy Bishop would have been elected from among the choristers and schoolboys of the parish. Some weeks later, on 27 December, or Holy Innocents's Eve, the chosen boy would become the bishop while his fellow choristers would take on the roles of the other church officials. For one whole day the children 'assumed complete control over the church'.[47] The Boy Bishop would conduct religious services, process through the streets and collect money; in some churches he would even celebrate Mass.[48] The ceremony proved so popular that statutes had to be passed to control the enthusiastic crowds who gathered to see the Boy Bishop.[49] The undoubted appeal of the festival probably depended on its ability to marry together the frivolities of the pagan Saturnalia with the religious respectability of a Christian festival. A sometimes unhappy marriage, however, as Henry VIII's proclamation of 1541 attests, the ritual was considered by Tudor authorities to 'resemble rather the vnlawfull superstition of gentilitie, than the pure and sincere religion of Christe'.[50] Uncannily expressing the humanist problem with imitation, the Boy Bishop straddled the fence between the sacred and the profane. This analogy notwithstanding, the ceremony is more important to a rereading of *Dido, Queene of Carthage* for what it has to say about inversion.

Established to commemorate Holy Innocents' Day, the rite of the Boy Bishop marked Herod's slaughter of newborn males and Christ's flight from Bethlehem. A martyrdom which prefigured Christ's own sacrifice, the death of the innocents was remembered as a precursor to the crucifixion. In place of the massacre of the boys, the medieval church temporarily elevated children to positions of power. By reversing accepted notions of hierarchical order, the Boy Bishop ceremony sought symbolically to make amends for past abuses. It should nevertheless be kept in mind that this amendment was emphatically symbolic and concertedly temporary. Thus, the dramatic context and text of *Dido, Queene of Carthage* redirect its audience to images of generational inversion, of the unexpected usurpation of parental figures by children. It is these images which cleverly realize Marlowe's own attempt in the drama to unseat his artistic progenitor, Virgil. Consequently, like the children who master their adults throughout *Dido, Queene of Carthage*, Marlowe masters his father text, the *Aeneid*, by consistently challenging the primacy of Virgil.

Replacing the Father with the Son or How to Make That Which Comes First Come Second

As noted at the beginning of this chapter, the critical discomfort produced by imitative works ultimately depends on a belief in the sanctity of originality, a belief in the absolute primacy of that which came first. This belief, however, may be somewhat misplaced. According to Françoise Meltzer in *Hot Property: The Stakes and Claims of Literary Originality* the belief in originality depends on 'the prose and economy of paranoia'.[51] This paranoia serves to disguise a 'basic anxiety that originality may be impossible and illusory'.[52] Meltzer goes on to claim that within the entire literary industry, creators and critics alike rely on the notion of originality to justify their work. Consequently, were the lie of originality to be revealed the literary edifice would crumble before its proponents' eyes. The illusory nature of originality can therefore only ever be glimpsed 'when anxiety about originality or about origin risks exposing the fraud it noisily conceals'.[53] According to Meltzer, creators and critics are complicit in a conspiracy which at once empowers and enthrals them. The academy must obfuscate its own work in order to hide from others, and also from itself, the truth that originality is a literary form of fool's gold, dazzling but ultimately deceptive. What is more, the concept employed to police this anxiety about originality is connected with Marlowe's dramatic presentation of his struggle to overcome his artistic father in *Dido, Queene of Carthage* – plagiarism. Derived from the Latin *plagiarius*, a plagiarist was quite literally a kidnapper of children or slaves.[54] The exchange of children as commodities, either to gain rigging for Aeneas's fleet or to make theatrical profits in the text and contexts of Marlowe's play, consequently allegorizes the very notion of literary larceny in familial terms.

Possibly influenced by plagiarism's derivation from notions of interrupted paternity, originality is often described in familial ways. As Joseph Kronick explains, 'The author who believes he is original also believes he can be his own parent'.[55] Kronick directly relates the concept of originality here to a disruption in the linearity of succession. Stepping outside conventional genealogies, according to Kronick, the originary author must have no predecessors, no fathers; he must effectively be at once his own father and son. A truly original author is, therefore, an impossibility. Kronick's statement seems to be appropriately indebted to Edward Young's *Conjectures on Original Composition* (1759) which is widely considered to be the first treatise on originality in English. In his *Conjectures*, Young describes the original in a way which foreshadows the Romantic correlation between artistic genius and impromptu creativity. Young notes: 'An *original* may be said to be of a *vegetable* nature; it rises spontaneously from the vital root of genius; it *grows*, it is not *made*: *Imitations* are often a sort of *manufacture* wrought up by those *mechanics*, *art*, and *labour*, out of pre-existent materials not their own.'[56] Dependent on notions of naturalness which would be given greater impetus by the industrial revolution, Young measures originality on a sliding scale, according to a work's lack of crafting. The original is consequently an artefact produced without recourse to artistry. It is important to notice here that although the concept of originality is commonly attributed to Romantic aesthetic philosophies, Young's artistic prejudices echo anxieties which can be traced to the Renaissance and before. Indeed, in John Heminges and Henry

Condell's famous letter 'To the Great Variety of Readers' of the First Folio (1623), William Shakespeare is awarded the status of a literary genius because 'His mind and hand went together, and what he thought he uttered with that easiness that we have scarce received from him a blot in his papers.'[57] Thus over a century before Young the requirement that an original be spontaneously produced was already in place.

Pausing for a moment, however, to contemplate the correspondences between Kronick and Young, it becomes apparent that the founding principle of originality is a naturalness which is profoundly unnatural. According to both Kronick and Young an original work must father itself; it must be immaculately conceived, in a way which openly flouts the Romantic idealization of nature as a force of order and coherence. Moreover, Young's notion of 'a vegetable nature' still presumes a period of growth which implies that an artefact can never be entirely self-sustaining. The paradoxical definition of originality as a lack of origins reveals the concept as an impossibility. In *Origin and Originality in Renaissance Literature*, David Quint underlines this point when he notes: 'The claim to historical priority is vitiated since no human work of art is absolutely prior, originating outside of history. Rather, the artist's individual greatness confers upon him an *originality* which makes him seem to transcend history.'[58] Ultimately, originality cannot help but reveal its illusory nature, it cannot help but disclose the impossibility of a work ever coming absolutely first, ever being produced without parents. In *The Light in Troy: Imitation and Discovery in Renaissance Poetry*, Thomas M. Greene claims that the anxiety generated by originality's impossibility is inscribed in Renaissance works. Instead of denying their debts to previous texts, Renaissance works are 'based upon a courage that confronts the model without neurotic paralysis and uses the anxiety to discover selfhood'.[59] It is this process which can be seen at work in Marlowe's *Dido, Queene of Carthage*. As the play presents a succession of children who despite being born after their parents eventually master them, the drama stages not only the lie of originality, but also the very relativity of art which is always produced in relation to something or to someone else.

Dandling Ganimed Again and Again

Remarking upon the play's initial image of Jupiter dandling Ganimed on his lap, Malcolm Kelsall maintains: 'The original emblematic scene imposes structural necessities upon the rest of the play. Marlowe returns to it with both verbal and visual allusions.'[60] Employing the tableau of infantile mastery to express the play's own flouting of its classical father, the image of an adult holding a child is repeated again and again in the play. With each new recitation the image becomes yet more familially and sexually complicated, and consequently more significant as a testimony to the inevitability of inversion and perhaps of perversion. The initial tableau of Jupiter fondling Ganimed is replaced on the stage first by Dido holding Ascanius and then by Dido holding Cupid. Importantly deviating from Virgil's account of the legend in the *Aeneid*, Dido holds Ascanius before Venus substitutes Cupid for him. During Aeneas's Troy speech Dido is shown embracing Ascanius whose first words to the queen are: 'Madam, you shall be my mother' (II.i.96). Therefore, prior to Venus's intervention in the plot, the mortals have voluntarily adopted familial and sexual roles towards each other; Dido has dressed Aeneas as her husband, while Ascanius has freely chosen to play the part of her son.

Later in the play, however, when Dido once more cradles Ascanius, the child in her arms is actually Cupid in disguise. Successively contaminating the parental tableau with each re-presentation, the image of Dido holding a child now encourages more sexual readings. What is more, accentuating the newly sexualized nature of Dido's affections for the boy on her lap, the scene depicts the queen being wounded by the god of love while she listens to her erstwhile lover's sexual frustrations. Iarbus complains: 'That love is childish which consists in words' (III.i.10). Iarbus's words are an ironic comment on the scene he is witnessing; he has unwittingly identified that love is indeed childish in this play as it is personified by Cupid, a boy. Moreover, allowing Cupid/Ascanius unhindered access to her body, the queen exchanges gifts for the boy's kisses in a scene reminiscent of the play's opening tableau:

> CUPID. Will *Dido* let me hang about her necke?
> DIDO. I wagge, and give thee leave to kiss her to.
> CUPID. What will you give me? now Ile have this Fanne.
> DIDO. Take it *Ascanius*, for thy fathers sake.
> (III.i.30–33)

Referring back to the first scene when Jupiter promises to give the child on his lap 'fannes wherewith to coole thy face' (I.i.35), the tableau of Dido and Cupid/Ascanius replays Ganimed's requests for presents in return for sexual favours. Unlike Jupiter, however, Dido showers the boy with affection because he is a surrogate for the man; Ascanius is being wooed in his father's stead. Hence the emblem of mother and child is fraught with sexual suggestions which are only rendered more perverse when it is noticed that the object of Dido's love is not Ascanius but Cupid, who shares the same mother as Aeneas and is therefore her prospective lover's own brother. Dido is shown simultaneously displacing her sexual desires for the Trojan general onto his son and his brother. The emblem of an adult holding a child is repeated once more in the play when the Nurse is left to tend the false Ascanius. In this scene the Nurse's thoughts turn, not surprisingly, to love as she fondles Cupid. Rebuking the old woman's fantasies, however, Cupid reminds the Nurse that she is past sexual delights. He cruelly jibes: 'A husband and no teeth!' (IV.v.24). Juxtaposing Dido's dandling of Cupid/Ascanius with the Nurse's, the play draws parallels between the queen's love for Aeneas and the old woman's rekindled sexuality. Ridiculing the Nurse's sexual longings, the text also invites a less sympathetic reading of Dido's desire for Aeneas; for if the Nurse is made to look foolish by the god of love then so too is the Queen of Carthage on whose lap he has been dandled.

The depiction of the child as master of the man in *Dido, Queene of Carthage* serves to disrupt audience preconceptions of sexual and familial normality which in turn invert conventional notions of artistic primacy, of the dominance of the model over the copy, the artistic father over the son. Further obfuscating the idea of traditional hierarchical order, the drama depicts Aeneas falling in love with a woman dressed as his mother. Clothed to go hunting, Dido is at pains to describe her appearance:

> My princely robes thou seest are layd aside,
> Whose glittering pompe *Dianas* shrowdes supplies,
> All fellowes now disposde alike to sporte,
> The woods are wide, and we have store of game:
> Faire Toian, hold my golden bowe awhile,
> Untill I gird my quiver to my side
> (III.iii.3–8)

Wearing a costume which resembles the one Venus dons to conceal herself from Aeneas in the play's first scene, Dido is theatrically identified with her potential lover's mother. Encountering her son in the 'shrowdes' (I.i.192) of 'one of chast *Dianas* fellow Nimphs' (I.i.194), Venus assumes a mantle which Dido takes up later in the play. Paradoxically wearing the robes of a virgin huntress, then, Dido preys not upon the beasts of the wood but upon the Trojan general in a cave. Marlowe consequently directs audience attention to the image of Aeneas acquiescing to the sexual advances of a woman dressed as his mother. The connection between Venus and Dido is even made explicit verbally, as Aeneas compares his meeting with the queen to classical legend:

> DIDO. Tell me deare love, how found you out this Cave?
> AENEAS. By chance sweete Queene, as *Mars* and *Venus* met.
> (III.iv.3–4)

Here Aeneas describes his own sexual liaison by alluding to his mother's marital infidelity with the god of war. The relationship between Dido and Aeneas is therefore brought into question by theatrical and literary precedence; the queen woos her lover's son who is actually his brother, while the Trojan general agrees to love a woman whom both he and the text have recognized as a type of his mother. Constantly returning to the issue of lineal appropriateness by staging the dilemma of sexual attraction between adult and child, parent and progeny, *Dido, Queene of Carthage* interrupts notions of artistic sequentiality fundamental to the concept of the original.

In *On Deconstruction: Theory and Criticism after Structuralism*, Jonathan Culler makes clear why originality is ultimately an utterly compromised principle. He notes that all works must be iterable or repeatable or they are left with no means of expression or classification. For instance, according to Culler:

> There is such a thing as an original Hemingway style only if it can be cited, imitated, and parodied. For there to be such a style there must be recognizable features that characterize it and produce its distinctive effects; for features to be recognizable one must be able to isolate them as elements that could be repeated, and thus the iterability manifested in the inauthentic, the derivative, the imitative, the parodic, is what makes possible the original and the authentic.[61]

Consequently, the only form of originality possible is paradoxically one which acknowledges the impossibility of uniqueness and admits the necessity of imitation and repetition: the necessity of having both literary fathers and sons. Of course, in conventional terms this definition of originality contradicts the most fundamental assumptions about what it means to be original. It nevertheless adequately describes the processes personified in Marlowe's *Dido, Queene of Carthage* in which the dominance of the inauthentic, the derivative, the imitative and the parodic is shown by the mastery of the adults by their derivative offspring or children. Acknowledging the inescapability of repetition and imitation, then, *Dido, Queene of Carthage* openly recites its origins by dramatizing the conflict between poem and play, by showing inverted familial hierarchies, and finally, by quoting directly from its Latin source. It is the reading of this climactic moment of recitation which ultimately determines how we interpret the dramatist's relationship to his artistic father; is the relationship one in which Marlowe expresses his anxious deference to Virgil or his triumphant dismissal of his classical father?

Quoting Virgil

Attempting to quit Carthage for the last time,[62] Aeneas is accosted by Dido who tries to persuade him to stay with her. Marked by Aeneas's silence in contradistinction to his usual epic stance, the final exchange between the lovers rehearses Aeneas's reluctance to participate in the drama any longer. Refusing to play a role in the dramatic dialogue, Aeneas only speaks in single lines while Dido pleads with him at great length to stay. Possibly losing a grip on the dramatic, Dido finally resorts to Virgil's text:

> DIDO. By this right hand, and by our spousall rites,
> Desires *Aeneas* to remaine with her:
> *Si bene quid de te merui, fuit aut tibi quidquam*
> *Dulce meum, miserere domus labentis: & istam*
> *Oro, si quis adhuc precibus locus, exue mentem.*
> AENEAS. *Desine meque tuis incendere teque querelis,*
> *Italiam non sponte sequor.*
> (V.i.134–40)[63]

The 1594 quarto of *Dido, Queene of Carthage* prints the Latin quotations in the same style as the proper names and stage directions; they are underlined by a single black line. By contrast, although Roma Gill's edition is an old-spelling one, she retains all the idiosyncrasies of the copy text while rendering the quotations into italics. In his introduction to the history of punctuation, *Pause and Effect*, M. B. Parkes notes that in the sixteenth century 'Because italic founts were used to indicate quotations from authorities they were also used to indicate gnomic utterances', consequently they assumed an 'emphatic force'.[64] Roma Gill's use of italicization therefore serves to emphasize the independence of the italicized words from the rest of the text. An accentuation of the differences between Marlowe's and Virgil's recitation of the Dido and Aeneas story, the Latin quotations, whether marked, italicized or underlined, wilfully refuse to be assimilated. In *Varieties of Poetic Utterance*, Nina Perlina argues that quotation 'necessarily challenges the validity and authority of the word'.[65] Indeed by enclosing words from another text within quotation marks the present text marks its own discomfort with their authority. A testimony to the uneasiness with which a text handles the words it quotes, the bracketing-off of phrases between apostrophes indicates that the expression cited is open to question, or uncertain. Consequently, quotation is, paradoxically, both deferential and demanding; deferring to another authority, to the extent that the words are extracted immaculately intact, quotation nevertheless demands the reappraisal of the phrases cited. Thus, by quoting Virgil, *Dido, Queene of Carthage* simultaneously holds up its hands and admits its debt, while at the same time inviting the interrogation of its source's authority and in turn the examination of its own textual sovereignty.

It should therefore come as no surprise that Marlovian scholars have met *Dido, Queene of Carthage*'s emphatic recourse to quotation with unease. In his study of the playwright, J. B. Steane maintains that Marlowe's readiness to quote from the *Aeneid* is a sign of hasty and inattentive composition. He claims that the dramatist is 'content merely to quote Virgil' because he 'is in too much of a hurry' and consequently 'doing a job, no more'.[66] However, it seems strange that Marlowe's lack of interest in his work should only materialize in the final moments of the play; having determinedly resisted the temptation to quote Virgil for the previous four acts it seems unlikely that the playwright would resort to it with the finishing post in sight. By contrast, considering Aeneas's one and a half lines of Latin, Roma Gill argues in her edition that 'the remarkable patterning of the first of these lines is possible only in an inflected language; and this is followed by the simplicity of one of the most famous half-lines in world literature. For such poetry there is no translation; and Marlowe is brave to resist any impulse to tamper with it.'[67] Conjecturing that the *Aeneid* is beyond translation, Gill proposes that Marlowe's unfitness to dramatize Virgil only dawns upon him at the end of his play when he is forced to return to his source text.

Characteristic of criticism's inability to deal with the challenge of this highly self-conscious textual moment, Steane and Gill both read *Dido, Queene of Carthage*'s recourse to the *Aeneid* as proof of Marlowe's artistic limitations and eventual dramatic failure. This need not, however, be the only interpretation. Alternatively, the scene can be read as the climax of a dramatic movement towards which the play has been working since Jupiter's first words to Ganimed. Disclosing originality's refusal to acknowledge its own origins, *Dido, Queene of Carthage* stages the impossibility of creation without a father.

By quoting from the *Aeneid*, Marlowe admits that his own work is derivative not because it is deferential, but rather because like all texts, including Virgil's, it cannot avoid imitation, indebtedness and repetition.

Whose End is it Anyway? Virgil's or Marlowe's?

In the *Aeneid*, Dido storms away from Aeneas, leaving their dialogue unfinished. By contrast, in Marlowe's play Aeneas leaves Dido without speaking:

> if thou wilt stay,
> Leape in mine armes, mine armes are open wide:
> If not, turne from me, and Ile turne from thee:
> > *Exit* AENEAS.
> For though thou hast the heart to say farewell,
> I have not the power to stay thee: is he gone?
> (V.i.179–83)

Aeneas's final action utterly erases his character from Marlowe's drama; he refuses to answer Dido and he refuses to be seen by her. Successfully leaving Marlowe's text, Aeneas fulfils his initial desire in the play to be unseen. A reversal of the lovers' first meeting when Aeneas wrongly believed Dido would be unable to see him, the final exchange between the characters stages Dido's inability not only to see the Trojan general but also to hear him. Coming full circle, the play reminds its audience that the conflict between Marlowe's and Virgil's telling of the classical story has been fought through a narrative and dramatic struggle focused on the issue of visibility. In the play's last scene, the drama departs from Virgil's anticipated ending in yet more significant and destructive ways which dwell upon the theatricality of Marlowe's adaptation of the *Aeneid*. Calling for a fire, Dido burns Aeneas's relics in an act which also annihilates those stage properties which have made the narrative both visual and dramatic. Directing the stage business, Dido laments:

> Here lye the Sword that in the darksome Cave
> He drew, and swore by to be true to me,
> Thou shalt burne first, thy crime is worse then his;
> Here lye the garment which I cloath'd him in,
> When first he came on shoare, perish thou to:
> These letters, lines and perjured papers all,

Shall burne to cinders in this pretious flame.
(V.i.295–301)

Remarking upon each item prior to its destruction, Dido burns the dramatic artefacts about which the play has turned: Aeneas's letters, clothes, and most importantly, his sword. The disposal of Aeneas's sword on Dido's funeral pyre is vital here as it punctuates Marlowe's ultimate resistance to Virgil's text. In the *Aeneid*, Dido kills herself by falling on Aeneas's sword. Instead, in Marlowe's play the theatrical world is put on display as a reminder that this is not Virgil's promised end, not his full stop.

The extant stage directions for the play's last scene are sparse and hence unhelpful. This means that the precise staging of the suicides remains open to interpretation. Evidence for the presentation of the final tragic movement can be gleaned, however, from the dramatic dialogue which demands a lighted funeral pyre on the stage, into which Dido must throw Aeneas's relics and finally herself. Dido's death by fire is confirmed in the text (V.i.314–15) when Anna calls out '*Dido, Queene of Carthage* in these flames/Hath burnt her selfe, aye me, unhappie me!'[68] Iarbus and Anna then follow the lead set by Dido: they commit suicide, probably also by jumping into the funeral pyre. Similarly ambiguous, the precise manner of these deaths is only available from the dialogue. Bemoaning Iarbus's death, Anna exclaims:

Iarbus slaine, *Iarbus* my deare love,
O sweet *Iarbus, Annas* sole delight,
What fatall destinie envies me thus,
To see my sweet *Iarbus* slay himselfe?
But *Anna* now shall honor thee in death,
And mixe her bloud with thine
(V.i.321–6)

Dido kills herself for Aeneas; Iarbus kills himself for Dido; Anna kills herself for Iarbus. Referring to a mixing of blood, this speech may imply that Dido's suitor murders himself with a knife. In this case Anna would have to take up the weapon in turn and also stab herself. Although this staging can be inferred from the word 'bloud', it is nevertheless more likely that Iarbus and Anna also fling themselves into the fire in emulation of Dido. The on-stage pyre required by the final scene could be realized with a fire contained in a brazier, or alternatively, by a smoking trapdoor through which the characters leap out of sight.[69] E. K. Chambers gives weight to the likelihood of a trapdoor in a private theatre for this purpose in *The Elizabethan Stage*. Drawing precedents from a number of court productions performed around the same time as *Dido, Queene of Carthage*, Chambers concludes: 'the addition of an elevated stage enabled traps to be used'.[70] Thus the actors and their properties could actually disappear from view through a trapdoor, rendering their extinction complete.

Having examined these staging difficulties, it becomes apparent that the important point is not to discover how the suicides would have been executed, but rather to notice the plethora of opportunities the text provides to underline the play's deviation from Virgil's narrative. Certainly devoured by fire, and probably utterly removed from the stage, Aeneas's relics and the bodies of Dido, Iarbus and Anna, bear a peculiar testimony to Marlowe's annihilation of those parts of the play for which the dramatist is solely responsible: the properties, the elaborated characters, the parallel love plots and the multiple suicides. Destroying the most blatant theatrical additions to Virgil's source, the playwright alludes to his own creativity in the very moment of its devastation. Thus the ending of *Dido, Queene of Carthage* dramatizes Marlowe's negotiations with his classical source. Articulating the trade-off the Renaissance had to make between the past and the possibility of its present, the play reveals that Virgil's words are as original as Marlowe's, as they are both implicated in the intricacies of influence. By conversing with the dead, then, humanists were finally forced to acknowledge that the voice in their ear was at once that of their ancestors, but also and more startlingly, their own.

Notes

1. Gill, R., ed. (1987). All references to *Dido, Queene of Carthage* are from this edition. The lines from Virgil are as follows, in English: 'If I ever deserved well of thee, or if aught of mine has ever been pleasant in thy sight, have pity on a falling house and, I pray you – if there is still a place for prayers – abandon this plan of yours' (Aeneid IV: 317–19). Aeneas's response comes forty or so lines later (IV: 360–61): 'Cease inflaming both yourself and me with these laments; it is not of my own free will that I search out Italy.' These and other references are from the *Aeneid*, edited and translated by H. Rushton-Fairclough (1974).
2. See chapter two for a fuller discussion of the critical reception of this episode.
3. See Greene, T. M. (1982), p 84: 'Nos, quasi nani super gigantum humeros sumus, quorum beneficio longius, quam ipsi, speculamur, dum antiquorum tractatibus inhaerentes elegantiores eorum sententias, quas vetustas aboleverat, hominumve neglectus, quasi iam mortuas in quandam novitatem essential suscitamus.'
4. Dupré, L. (1993), p. 152.
5. Sidney, P. (1966), p. 59.
6. Plato (1985), p. 288.
7. Allen, D. C. (1963), p. 64.

8. Proser, M. N. (1988), p. 94.
9. Steane, J. B. (1964), p. 29.
10. Marlowe, C. (1594), title page.
11. Gill, R., ed. (1987).
12. Gill, R., ed. (1987), p. xi.
13. Gill, R., ed. (1987), p. xiii.
14. Gill, R., ed. (1987), p. xi.
15. Tucker Brooke, C. F., ed. (1930), p. 123.
16. Martin, R. A. (1980), p. 45.
17. Gill, R., ed. (1987), p. 121.
18. Gill, R., ed. (1987), p. 121.
19. Gill, R., ed. (1987), p. 121.
20. Bowers, F., ed. (1973), vol. 1, p. 20.
21. Tucker Brooke, C. F., ed. (1930), p. 115.
22. Boas, F. S. (1940), p. 50.
23. Oliver, H. J., ed. (1968), p. xxv.
24. Shapiro, M. (1977), p. 14.
25. Shapiro, M. (1977), p. 18.
26. Gurr, A. (1987), p. 22.
27. Shapiro, M. (1977), p. 259.
28. Oliver, H. J., ed. (1968), p. xxxi.
29. Hunter, G. K. (1962), p. 94.
30. Virgil (1974), 1: 21.
31. Note that the statue would probably have been realized by an actual actor: compare the end of William Shakespeare's *The Winters Tale*.
32. Virgil (1974), 1: 27.
33. See William Shakespeare's *The Tempest*, for an example of Ariel as an 'airy spirit'.
34. Martin, R. A. (1980), p. 55.
35. I am using 'Pirrhus' in reference to Marlowe's play, but 'Pyrrhus' will be used in order to denote references to *Hamlet* and Virgil's character.
36. Gibbons, B. (1968), p. 41.
37. Lydgate, J. (1906), prologue, lines 304–8.
38. Virgil (1974), 4: 6530–32.
39. Virgil (1974), 4: 6389–91.
40. Smith, M. E. (1977), p. 6.
41. Smith, M. E. (1977), p. 6.
42. For Hecuba, see II.i.290, and for Helen II.i.292.
43. The lack of popularity described by Hamlet as 'caviar for the general' coupled with the brutal depiction of Priam's murder makes it likely that it is Marlowe's play and not Virgil's poem to which Hamlet is referring.
44. Compare *Tamburlaine*'s disruption of sequentiality.
45. Kelsall, M. (1981), p. 34.
46. The emblem of the adult holding the child will be discussed later in this chapter.
47. Hillebrand, H. N. (1926), p. 25.
48. Hillebrand, H. N. (1926), pp. 25–6.

49. In W. W. Wooden's article he notes: 'Attempts to curb the festivities are recorded as early as mid-thirteenth century where, at St. Paul's regulations were made to curtail the playing and processions.' See Wooden, W. W. (1981), p. 197.

50. Wooden, W. W. (1981), p. 198.

51. Meltzer, F. (1994), p. 6.

52. Meltzer, F. (1994), p. 6.

53. Meltzer, F. (1994), p. 6.

54. Mallon, T. (1989), p. 6: 'In classical times a "plagiary" had been one who kidnapped a child or slave'.

55. Kronick, J. (1981), p. 365.

56. Young, E. (1918), p. 7.

57. Wells, S. and Taylor, G., ed. (1988), p. xlv.

58. Quint, D. (1983), p. 4.

59. Green, T. M. (1982), p. 31.

60. Kelsall, M. (1981), p. 38.

61. Culler, J. (1983), p. 120.

62. It is noteworthy that Marlowe stages a first thwarted leave-taking in IV.iv which lacks Virgilian authority and seems to have been added to the narrative to emphasize the force of repetition and adaptation which the drama stages.

63. See the introduction to this chapter for translation from Latin.

64. Parkes, M. B. (1992), p. 55.

65. Perlina, N. (1985), p. 28.

66. Steane, J. B. (1964), p. 48.

67. Gill, R. (1987), p. xiv.

68. The fire could be considered a parodic adaptation of Aeneas's instruction to Dido not to become inflamed or *incendere* in the *Aeneid*. Marlowe is thereby staging his ultimate translation and adaptation of Virgil which makes his words ultimately visual and dramatic.

69. Shapiro, M. (1977), p. 170.

70. Chambers, E. K. (1923), vol. 3, p. 42.

Re-formation

Chapter 5

Forever Babel: The Canon, Translation and *The Massacre at Paris*

Unlike *Doctor Faustus* and *Edward II* which are overtly concerned with reading and writing, *The Massacre at Paris* does not stage the processes of reception and inscription. Unlike the two parts of *Tamburlaine* and *Dido, Queene of Carthage*, *The Massacre at Paris* is not concerned with issues of repetition, imitation and originality. Instead *The Massacre at Paris*, like *The Jew of Malta*, challenges those literary structures through which texts are conventionally read. In the case of *The Jew of Malta* the structure challenged is generic; the drama rehearses the impossibility of ever satisfying the generic requirements of Machevill's pronouncement in the prologue that the audience is about to see 'the tragedy of a Jew'.[1] In the case of *The Massacre at Paris* the structure challenged by the play is more complex and less obvious; *The Massacre at Paris* examines the transcendental, transhistorical and translational structure of the canon which serves to classify all literary artefacts. It is, moreover, this structure which has dictated the critical yardsticks by which *The Massacre at Paris* has been judged and by which it has ultimately been beaten. Indeed, according to Constance Kuriyama, the text of *The Massacre at Paris* represents 'the skeletal remains of what was probably never a very good play'.[2]

The supposed textual and artistic 'badness' of the play has only been exacerbated by a critical belief that the drama originally existed in a more complete and more artistically accomplished state.[3] This belief is reinforced by the existence of the so-called 'Collier leaf', an alternative manuscript version of the death of Mugeroun which was discovered by the editor John Payne Collier. In his edition of *The Jew of Malta* for Dodsley's *Old Plays* in 1825, John Payne Collier prints and describes the newly-found version of *The Massacre at Paris* as 'A curious MS. fragment of one quarto leaf of this tragedy'.[4] Collier goes on to suggest that the leaf 'perhaps formed part of a copy belonging to the theatre at the time it was first acted' and might even be 'in the original hand-writing of Marlow'.[5] Reprinting the leaf less than ten years later in his *History of English Dramatic Poetry* (1831), Collier produced a slightly different version of the text. According to J. M. Nosworthy the discrepancies between the first and second transcriptions of the manuscript may be attributed to a 'genuine perplexity over badly made letters'.[6] Subsequently passing through the hands of a number of institutions, the Collier leaf finally came to rest where it remains today, in the Folger Library, Washington. The significance of the leaf for the present discussion is twofold. Firstly, the leaf evidences the critical desire to rehabilitate an Ur-text of *The Massacre at Paris*, an ideal version of a play which the canon currently finds unsatisfactory. Secondly, the Collier leaf highlights the issue of authenticity which is central to the construction of the canon. Some thirty years after John Payne Collier's discovery of the manuscript version of *The Massacre at Paris*, he was scandalously exposed as a literary forger. When in 1852 Collier drew public attention to a Shakespeare Folio that contained extensive marginal notes confirming his own emendations of and assertions about the plays, his academic reputation was brought into question. Collier's Folio was subsequently proved a fake. However, as Thomas Dabbs notes, despite being 'completely exposed and disgraced' Collier 'never confessed to this or to many other forgeries that he committed during his career'.[7] The exposure of Collier's Shakespeare forgeries led in turn to the revelation that an entry in Henslowe's diary naming Marlowe as the author of *Tamburlaine*,[8] and a ballad entitled 'The Atheist's Tragedy' which referred to Marlowe as an actor, were also fabricated.[9] Brought down by the critical institution to whose taste he pandered, Collier was found guilty of remodelling the Marlowe scholarship desired.[10]

To date the leaf remains a Marlovian mystery; it has been neither substantiated nor categorically dismissed. Written, according to John Bakeless, on genuine Elizabethan paper containing a recognized watermark, the leaf may yet prove to be what Collier said it was: the one truth in a career of lies.[11] If the leaf is in fact a manuscript fragment from the period of the play's composition a number of questions nevertheless remain, the utmost being: did Marlowe write it? Arguing that the leaf records a 'tentative draft' of the drama,[12] Joseph Q. Adams fails to acknowledge that it could equally embody a post-performance revision or a discarded early version in a hand other than Marlowe's. Only able to maintain that the leaf was an autograph manuscript until a sample of Marlowe's writing was discovered, however, paleographers, including P. J. Croft, have since concluded that the author's signature and Collier's fragment bear no marked resemblance.[13] Finally, it is worth being reminded by Richard Altick that 'In the light of Collier's known habits, any item to which he refers is automatically suspect if its history cannot be traced before him.'[14] Whether or not the Collier leaf is a fake or a fact it is significant as a marker of the negotiations critics and editors are willing to make to create a canonically-acceptable version of *The Massacre at Paris*.

What is more, the leaf provides an excellent illustration of Pierre Macherey's argument in *A Theory of Literary Production* that the literary academy and the canon on which it relies ultimately depend for their survival upon the imposition of unachievable aesthetic goals which are proffered as judicious and impartial. Macherey maintains that 'all criticism can be summed up as a value judgment in the margin of the book: "could do better". Glimpsing but never attaining the "better", it looks beyond the real work to its dream image.'[15] Collier's leaf, whatever its veracity, is of course the critical institution's dream image of the actual text of *The Massacre at Paris*. According to Macherey, the academy must constantly negate in order to perpetuate itself. Apparently the sole arbiter of taste, criticism dangles its tape measure of excellence before a public spellbound by the possibility of perfection: perfection, that is, in criticism's terms. Eternally doomed to fall short of a mark always already drawn ahead of it, the work of art can only ever be a pale imitation of a mythic ideal. The treatment Marlowe's *Massacre at Paris* has received at the hands of the academy represents an extreme version of Macherey's theory. Consequently, the reception of Marlowe's play coupled with its internal concern with structures of authority renders it a useful text through which the critical institution itself can be examined. Before considering the drama's exposition of transformational and transhistorical notions central to the creation of the canon, the 'badness' of the text of *The Massacre at Paris* requires explanation.

So How 'Bad' is *The Massacre at Paris*?

Extant in an undated octavo, the earliest surviving edition of *The Massacre at Paris* names its author as '*Christopher Marlow*'.[16] Dramatizing the death of King Henry III which occurred on 2 August 1589 and referring to the bones of Pope Sixtus whose demise followed just over a year later,[17] the text was probably composed sometime between the summer of 1590 and the play's first recorded performance at the Rose on 26 January 1592.[18] As printing usually took place as a consequence of theatrical success, the octavo was probably set after 1592. Unhelpful to the resolution of the edition's precise date, the title page device which belongs to Edward Allde was employed by his printing house for more than two decades after 1592.[19] However, as the title page also records that the play was performed by the 'Lord High *Admirall* his servants' it is likely that the octavo was published before 1596 when the company was renamed the Earl of Nottingham's Men.[20] Although the play is not mentioned in the Stationers' Register,[21] causing some critics to suspect that the octavo represents a pirated copy, this does not of necessity make it any worse nor any better than the majority of rapidly-printed, cheaply-produced editions of the period.[22]

An outwardly unextraordinary Elizabethan text, the octavo nevertheless receives exceptional critical attention which has most frequently taken the form of unfettered disdain. Clearly attributed to Marlowe by its earliest edition, *The Massacre at Paris* demands consideration in relation to the author's other works. Unable simply to dismiss the play as the product of a theatrical novice, therefore, criticism has instead demoted it to the lowest rung of a ladder of ascending canonical achievement topped by *Doctor Faustus*. For example, as J. B. Steane maintains, *The Massacre at Paris* 'is probably the last of Marlowe's plays, and in its extant form certainly the least'.[23] In a similar vein, John Bakeless complains that 'No judgment, however charitable, can set down *The Massacre at Paris* as anything but one of Marlowe's failures'.[24] Failing to meet a critically preordained requirement of authorial quality, Marlowe's play has been wholeheartedly condemned.

Not content only to detract from the play's Marlovian status, however, criticism has simultaneously reserved for *The Massacre at Paris* the infamous title of the 'worst of the "bad" Elizabethan dramatic texts'.[25] As H. S. Bennett asserts in his edition, *The Massacre at Paris* 'is certainly one of the worst examples of garbled and mangled texts, and Dr. Pollard's general adjective of "bad" for such works seems all too weak to describe this confused and often-times barely intelligible play in its present form.'[26] According to Bennett, one of the few scholars diligent enough to edit the play, *The Massacre at Paris* actually redraws the boundaries of the bibliographical term 'bad'. Dropping off the conventional scale of textual worth, Marlowe's play sinks almost without trace into a realm of critical oblivion from which it has never been satisfactorily salvaged. Evoking extreme critical responses, commentary on the play remains one of the most memorable areas of Marlovian scholarship. A small body of criticism admittedly, but one of such hyperbole that it perversely encourages, even demands, the reconsideration of that which it so roundly dismisses. Floating to the surface of the critical ferment, questions emerge from the academic reception of *The Massacre at Paris*, the foremost of which must surely be: why is the text so 'bad'?

Arguments positing the textual 'badness' of *The Massacre at Paris* rest upon three criteria which will each be examined in turn: length, originality and good taste. A short text by Elizabethan standards, the octavo's 1263 extant lines have inspired criticism's pronouncement that the edition represents a severely curtailed version of an Ur-*Massacre*. Typical of this hypothesis is J. B. Steane's assertion that 'It is fairly certain … that our text is a shortened version, and that abridgment has cheapened the original'.[27] Marshalling the Collier leaf as proof of the existence of a missing, superior text of *The Massacre at Paris*, Steane continues: 'If the Collier leaf is in any way typical, it suggests that the places where attitudes might have been shaped and thought developed have been exactly the places cut'.[28] Although Steane sees a great play in the mutilated remains he considers the octavo to be, other critics are less visionary. In spite of the Collier leaf, scholars such as H. S. Bennett maintain that an originary, completed text of *The Massacre at Paris* would still be an artistic failure. Bennett argues that as 'Bad as the state of the text undoubtedly is, there is nothing about it that leads us to believe that, had we the perfect text, we should have a great play'.[29] Bennett therefore concludes that *The Massacre at Paris* 'is one of the weakest plays of its day'.[30] The 'weak' nature of the actual octavo as well as the arguably poor condition of an idealized Ur-*Massacre* depends largely upon the modern estimation of the play's subject matter.

A theatrical presentation of recent French history, Marlowe's drama utilizes the mass of publications which followed hot on the heels of Saint Bartholomew's day 1572. Adapting these sources freely, the play dramatizes events already detailed in print. Taking issue with this reliance on existing works, Wilbur Sanders complains that *The Massacre at Paris*

> is notable for crippling dependence on source material which was, in itself, vacuous: the public declarations, apologies and manifestoes published by the official parties; the flood of polemic ephemerae (pamphlets and newsbooks) dealing with European affairs between 1570 and 1589; and the various partisan histories of the Religious Wars in France.[31]

Disparaging the derivative nature of the play's composition, Sanders pictures an author lacking the Romantic Muse of spontaneous originality, an author willing to adapt in order to delight his audience. Sanders goes on to characterize Marlowe as 'a man who capitulates … to the lowest appetites'.[32] Accused of pandering to the 'lowest appetites', Marlowe's play contravenes the final and most subjective critical criterion – good taste. Not inappropriately perhaps for a piece entitled *The Massacre at Paris*, the drama depicts scenes of riotous slaughter which many critics find monstrous and sensational. In his 'Note' on the play, J. B. Steane concludes that at the end of the day *The*

Massacre at Paris 'is an unfeeling and rather tasteless play, cashing in on still recent suffering which it never really enters'.[33] Spanning the whole spectrum of 'badness', then, *The Massacre at Paris*, if critics are to be believed, is unfinished, unoriginal and uncouth.

Denied fame, the play has certainly been awarded infamy. An infamy, moreover, which Wilbur Sanders argues should be recognized by scholarship in order to expose fully the mediocrity of the dramatist's canon. As Sanders explains:

> I am continually astounded at the ease with which Marlowe's editors arrive at the conclusion that a certain passage is not Marlowe's but the work of an interpolator, yet do so without offering any account of the qualities they regard as specifically Marlovian ... this kind of editorial activity is not so much 'impressionism' as a systematic attempt to rehabilitate a poet whose reputation must suffer if all the texts published under his name are acknowledged to be his own.[34]

Encouraging the examination of those works which criticism would prefer to ignore, of which *The Massacre at Paris* is foremost, Sanders desires a totalizing reappraisal of Marlowe's canon in the hope that it will, paradoxically, de-canonize the author. Currently experiencing a resurgence of critical interest, however, Marlowe remains firmly within the canon among the limited number of authors whose works the establishment considers worthy of academic study and, consequently, the name of literature. Rather than execute Sanders's injunction to exclude the author from the 'Tradition', criticism has instead expelled the play. Rarely edited, seldom studied and almost never admired, *The Massacre at Paris* has been effectively omitted from Marlovian scholarship. Even Emily Bartels's recent (1993) book-length study of Marlowe and the marginalized Other, *Spectacles of Strangeness*, ironically refuses to consider a drama which in many respects epitomizes the peripheralization of the alienated subject.[35]

Justifying its rejection of the play in terms which ultimately rely on the theoretically redundant criterion of personal preference, scholarship seems to have blinded itself with a concept of 'badness' which fails to recognize more interesting and more productive ways to see the octavo. If it is remembered, moreover, that the highest takings of the theatrical season of 1592 were recorded at *The Massacre at Paris*'s première,[36] and that the play was revived three times during the next ten years,[37] the drama's contemporary popularity alone demands its reconsideration. Although many modern critics find the play incoherent and unintelligible, its original audience clearly did not. Possibly, as Judith Weil maintains, *The Massacre at Paris*'s rapid pace and 'switch back' style is a clever dramaturgical device in which 'the extreme variations in length of speech or scene seem functional. Leisurely murders or expositions of haphazard, confused motives scarcely seem called for'.[38] Elaborating upon this argument, Simon Shepherd rehabilitates the play's protean structure as a whole when he claims that 'we have been taught to see its [*The Massacre at Paris*'s] incompleteness in a negative way (the mangled text) not positively, with the suppression of the coherent sense of nation and of moral order as a counterstatement to providential histories'.[39] According to Shepherd, it is *The Massacre at Paris*'s 'incompleteness' which enables the play to criticize previous dramatic accounts of history, whose structures give the impression of the past working to create a new and improved Tudor present. A popular success, an innovative dramatic experiment, a teleological critique, such appellations hang uncomfortably on the frame of *The Massacre at Paris*, not because they are indefensible, but because they have been rendered unexpected by the scholarly response to the play.

Perhaps criticism will at last be forced to step back and scrutinize its treatment of Marlowe's drama when it is acknowledged that the octavo's supposedly garbled state bears a striking resemblance to that of the two texts of *Doctor Faustus*, the most highly praised and canonically-accepted of Marlowe's plays. Unwittingly drawing attention to the contradictions inherent in this circumstance, Emily Bartels notes that '*Faustus* has become the most canonical of Marlowe's plays and appears regularly and singularly in anthologies and course syllabi, despite the fact that, after *The Massacre at Paris*, its text is the least reliable in the Marlovian corpus'.[40] Indeed, the A-text of *Doctor Faustus*, which is only 250 lines longer than *The Massacre at Paris*, experienced a critical renaissance during the 1980s. Promoted in place of the longer B-text, the 1604 play was praised for its theatrically daring performance-oriented version. What is deemed 'bad' in *The Massacre at Paris* is, depending upon the fickle whims of criticism, esteemed significant and worthwhile in the *Doctor Faustus* A-text. In an effort to discover why the *Doctor Faustus* A-text is admitted to the canon, while *The Massacre at Paris* is excluded from it, the definition and history of the canon requires examination.

Who's In and Who's Out: A Loose Canon?

In *Cultural Capital*, John Guillory defines the literary canon as the concept
which 'names the traditional curriculum of literary texts by analogy to that
body of writing historically characterized by an inherent logic of *closure* – the
scriptural canon'.[41] Consequently, the notion of the canon involves three
elements: education, analogy and closure. The canon lists those literary texts
which are considered to be essential reading for anyone hoping to understand
the history of literature. The authority given to this list is created not only by
the passing of time, but also by comparison with the fixed canon of biblical
texts. The canonization of a text is therefore analogous to the canonization of a
saint; it requires that an institution reappraise and redefine a text or a person
and thereby elevate them beyond the vagaries of temporality into a realm in
which approbation remains fixed and constant. In order to maintain its
authority, the canon must appear to be closed. It must appear to transcend
personal preference and historical contingency or its contents will be radically
open to question by each new generation and each new reader. The
maintenance of this myth of closure is, however, extremely difficult; for it is,
paradoxically, only by constantly opening and closing its borders to new texts
that the canon can retain its relevance and consequently its viability as an
institution. The notion of transportation is essential to the definition of the
canon which must always take texts into itself.

In his lectures on *History and Value*, Frank Kermode describes the canon's
involvement with the processes of transportation and also transformation. He
argues that when books enter the canon they undergo changes:

> First, they are completely locked into their times, their texts as near frozen
> as devout scholarship can make them, their very language more and more
> remote. Secondly, they are, paradoxically, by this fact, set free of time.
> Thirdly, the separate constituents become not only books in their own right
> but part of a larger whole – a whole because it is so treated. Fourthly, that
> whole, with all its interrelated parts, can be thought to have an inexhaustible
> potential of meaning, so that what happens in the course of time – as the
> original context and language of the collection grows more and more distant
> – is that new meanings accrue (they may be deemed, by a fiction
> characteristic of this way of thinking, to be original meanings) and these
> meanings constantly change though their source remains unchangeable.[42]

According to Kermode, the canon requires the transportation of certain texts
into itself which are then transformed to create an impression of transcendental

value and meaning. The canon therefore attempts to convince onlookers that the impossible project of removing literature from time is possible. The ultimate confidence trickster, the canon tenders its wares as immutable and infinitely significant when they are actually the opposite; they are changeable and historically contingent. In reality, the canon operates more like an elaborate filing cabinet than a religious institution. It offers scholars and students alike access to literary works which its selection and transformation render easily retrievable and openly available to future generations.

In spite of the canon's limited usefulness, it has recently received considerable theoretical and political criticism. The New Historicist project to reclaim the works of marginalized authors, coupled with the theoretical objection to the classification of texts as either literary or non-literary, has rendered the concept of the canon largely redundant. Nevertheless, it is worth noting that while institutions of higher education are rewriting their courses to take on board changing attitudes towards the canon, schools are implementing the National Curriculum which legally requires pupils in state schools to study highly canonical authors, such as William Shakespeare and Jane Austen. Currently the canon may well be under review, but its replacement at universities by a new list of authors and texts from either the racial, sexual or historical margins constitutes more an extension than a break with the canonical structure of classification. Despite these points, the present chapter does not attempt to offer a canonically-redemptive re-examination of *The Massacre at Paris*; instead, it seeks to consider those notions of transportation, transformation and transcendence central to the drama, to the canon which refuses it entry, and to the period in which it was written.

According to Franklin E. Court the concept of the canon was already established by the time Marlowe wrote *The Massacre*. Court maintains that 'From the Renaissance, there has been a general critical consensus that some literary figures offer something of lasting intelligence to the culture'.[43] This assertion should come as no surprise when it is remembered that the Renaissance concern with the reclamation and translation of ancient authorities importantly involves the same notions of transportation, transformation and transcendence which also implicate the concept of the canon. Like the canon, the Renaissance is defined by a process of re-formation. Even the phrases coined by the period to describe its preoccupations involve a concept of conversion at their core. Although the term humanist was not introduced until the nineteenth century by German scholars,[44] the appellation *Humanista* or teacher of Latin was current during the Renaissance.[45] The expression

Humanista consequently reveals that the Renaissance considered the key to learning to be translation or linguistic conversion.

Thomas Hoby's dedicatory letter to his English version of Castiglione's *Book of the Courtier* (1588) testifies to the significance placed upon translation in the Renaissance. Hoby notes that 'the translation of Latin or Greeke authours, doth not onely not hinder learning but furthereth it, yea it is learning it selfe'.[46] Directly identifying translation as the primary means of learning, Hoby goes on to eulogize the translational project in yet more lavish terms. He claims that translation is

> a great stay to youth, and the noble end to which they ought to apply their wittes, that with diligence and studie have attained a perfect vnderstanding, to open a gap for others to follow their steps, and a vertuous exercise for the vnlatined to come by learning, and to fill their minds with the moral vertues, and their bodies with ciuill conditions, that they may both talke freely in all company, liue vprightly, though there were no lawes, and be in readinesse against all kinde of worldly chaunce that happen.[47]

Hoby maintains that translation does not simply enable less well-educated readers to access texts otherwise denied them, it also provides readers with the ability to express their views, to live moral lives, even when unregulated by the law, and finally to prepare to tackle any mishap which they may encounter. If Hoby's dedication is to be believed, translation will people England with eloquent, virtuous, self-regulating individuals. For humanists, translation was a philanthropic exercise. At the heart of the translational endeavour lies the selfless desire to communicate that which the translator can already understand to a readership which cannot. Making a similarly philanthropic statement in his 'Preface to the Reader' of his translation of the *Paraphrase of Erasmus upon the Newe Testamente* (1548), Nicholas Udall argues that there is 'a speciall regarde to bee had to the rude and unlettered people, who perchaunce through defaulte of atteignyng to the high style, should also thereby have been defrauded of ye profite & fruite of understanding the sense, which thyng that thei might dooe, was the onely purpose why it was first translated'.[48] Translation was, therefore, viewed by the Renaissance as a tool of social transformation and control; it was a means to communicate moral ideas to readers unable to read them in the original. What is more, according to James Winny, fired by 'an uneasy recognition of the cultural inferiority of England to the countries of Renaissance Europe' the reign of Elizabeth witnessed the feverish reclamation of ancient texts through translation.[49] Deemed a veritable treasure-trove, the works of the classical authors were plundered in search of paradigms which might transform society. As Martin Elsky explains: 'By imitating the language of exemplary eras, a nation preserves an eloquence that can transcend the vicissitudes of its political history.'[50] Thus, like the canon itself, translation provides shelter from the winds of change by creating the impression of transcendental permanence through the processes of textual transportation and linguistic transformation.

The illusion of transcendental permanence created by both the canon and translation may be noted in an entertaining anecdote from one of the possible sources for *The Massacre at Paris*. Simon Goulart's Protestant collection, *Mémoires de l'estat de France* (1576–77), includes a tale of switched paintings which can be employed as an allegory for the transportative and transformative nature of the canon and of translation. Goulart's story tells how the Pope was so pleased by news of Protestant suppression that he decided to send the head of the Guise family, the Cardinal of Lorraine, a painting of the Michelangelo *Pietá*. The painting was duly dispatched with a papal courier. However, when the courier fell sick, he was forced to persuade a merchant from Lucca who was already travelling to Paris to deliver the picture. Unluckily for the cardinal, the merchant bore an ancient grudge against him, and in seeking to settle an old score replaced the painting of the Virgin Mary weeping over her dead Son with a naked portrait of the Guise family women lustfully attending the cardinal. On receipt of the picture the cardinal organized a grand unveiling without having viewed the painting himself. When the picture was revealed at court the cardinal and his family were publicly humiliated.[51] This tale of a miscarried painting topically depicts the impossibility of either translating or canonizing something without at the same time altering it. Although translation should ideally provide the unmediated transfer of ideas from one language into another, in reality this is an illusion. Like the substituted painting, translation always recreates its subject as something different. With the ambivalent power of Midas, the translator always transforms whatever his pen touches; the act of translation creates a new and different text, however exact a translator may attempt to be. Just as the repetition of *Tamburlaine* part one as *Tamburlaine* part two cannot help but return something different, translation cannot help but alter that which it translates. Consequently, the belief that translation can bestow transcendental permanence on a text is illusory. Like the canon which can only give its texts the appearance of being outside history, translation cannot freeze time. Instead, translation serves as a reminder that transcendent, pre-Babelian communication is forever impossible. From the ruined foot of the Tower of Babel the notion of a transcendent text, whether it be achieved through translation or canonization, is exposed as a fallacy. It is this inevitability of transformation and transportation which *The Massacre at Paris* dramatizes and which possibly renders the play too problematic for the canon to accept.

Translating the Massacre: The Sources

According to the *Oxford English Dictionary* the word 'massacre' did not enter the English language until the Elizabethan era; it seems to have undergone a translational journey as a direct result of the Parisian slaughter of Saint Bartholomew's Day 1572.[52] The cultural transmission of the word 'massacre' from one linguistic community to another exemplifies the transpositional quality of translation, of the canon, and more particularly, of *The Massacre at Paris*: a play whose sources and whose narrative are preoccupied with notions of transportation and transformation. Translating an actual event into drama, *The Massacre at Paris* popularly narrates a story previously told in print by numerous other authors, most of them not English. Consequently, *The Massacre at Paris* cannot rely on suspense to engage its audience. Like the translator, the audience of *The Massacre at Paris* already knows what happens next.

According to John Bakeless the Bartholomew's Day massacre was 'the most fully reported [event] in history, up to that time'.[53] The events of the Parisian massacre seem to have permeated the international consciousness in a way only comparable to the psychological effect of the assassination of President Kennedy in the twentieth century. Even John Foxe's celebrated *Book of Martyrs* wearily refuses to rehash a story so often related elsewhere. Foxe maintains that 'because the true narration of this lamentable story is set forth in English at large, in a book by itself, and extant in print already, it shall the less need now to discourse that matter with any new repetition'.[54] Like the Guise's injunction in Marlowe's play to extend the Parisian slaughter from 'Retes to Dieppe, Mountsorrell unto Rouen' (vi.80),[55] the dissemination of the massacre continued long after the killing had stopped. In 'Reactions to the St. Bartholomew Massacres', Robert Kingdon notes that Catholic leaders responded to the slaughter by commissioning paintings, while Protestant leaders 'depended on verbal communication and turned to the printing industry'.[56] Determined to have their side of the story represented, the institutions of religious power conspicuously set the wheels of artistic propaganda in motion. A testimony to this impulse to tell tales, the editing history of François Hotman's biography of the massacre victim Admiral

Coligny reveals a clear bias towards a non-French readership. 'Published twice in Latin, in 1575, and then once in English and once in German, in 1576', *The Lyfe* was not translated into the author's native language, French, until the middle of the seventeenth century.[57] Far from an unhealthy preoccupation with their own suffering, the survivors of Saint Bartholomew's Day produced pamphlets designed to transport the massacre abroad where it might be unleashed to roam in search of sympathy, support and redress.

Stories of the massacre underwent constant re-presentation; 85 per cent of the total output of English writing on the contemporary state of France between 1561 and 1600 was comprised of translations of French texts.[58] Typical of this translational urge to transcribe, Jean de Serres's *The Three Partes of Commentaries ... of the Civill Warres of Fraunce* was published in three Latin versions from 1570 to 1573 and in one English edition in 1574.[59] Notable for its popularity, the tenth book of the *Commentaries* describes many of the events dramatized by the first six scenes of Marlowe's play. This tenth book is, however, not all that it seems. An addition with separate headings and in-dependent pagination, book ten is a reprint of François Hotman's *De Furoribus Gallicis*.[60] Already translated in 1573 as *A True and Plaine Report*, Hotman's Protestant account of the slaughter was thrice available to the Elizabethan reading public, in one guise or another.[61] Recapitulated again and again, the massacre was being carried away by time and translation until it soon took on the mantle of a myth.

As Marlovian scholarship amply proves, it is impossible to identify a single source for *The Massacre at Paris* from 'among the welter of narrative and polemical pamphlets which the bloody progress of French affairs from 1572 to 1589 called forth in both France and England'.[62] Inevitably reproducing a similar story every time, these pamphlets bred upon themselves. In the midst of such translational fecundity, *The Massacre at Paris* utilizes not only the more well-known Protestant pamphlets but also the Catholic League ones. Indeed, as Julia Briggs's timely 'Reconsideration' of Marlowe's play shows, the drama is far from 'a piece of blatant Protestant propaganda'.[63] Maintaining, moreover, 'that the whole section of the play centring on the murder of the Guise is actually treated, not from the Huguenot viewpoint at all, but from the League viewpoint',[64] Briggs makes a persuasive case for reappraising *The Massacre at Paris* as a sophisticated and complex drama. Involved in creating an economy between event, report and play, *The Massacre at Paris* must operate a system of transportative exchange. Marlowe's play must mediate between the transpositive demands of dramatization and the requirements of historical and textual fidelity.

Altering the running order of its sources, *The Massacre at Paris* highlights the temporal problems which blight translation's mission to make the past of one text the future of another. From the inclusion of Talaeus, who died ten years before the Parisian slaughter,[65] to the addition of a scene between Henry and the Duke of Guise prior to the king's assassination of his rival, the drama rearranges the events of the past. What is more, clearly indebted to Hotman's description of the Queen of Navarre's murder which tells how 'She was poysoned with a venomed smell of a pair of perfumed gloves, dressed by one Renat the kings apothicarie',[66] Marlowe's play post-dates the historical details of its source, transporting circumstances which occurred two months before the wedding of the queen's son, to his nuptial celebrations. Not simply a sequential compromise for the sake of dramatic effect, these adaptations to the timescale of history also expose the intercessions translation is forced to make with the past. Presuming that 'Marlowe worked too hurriedly and forgot his source',[67] Paul Kocher ignores the importance of these narrative deviations to an examination of the effects of time on translation. The very antithesis of forgetfulness, *The Massacre at Paris*'s source changes illustrate the translational difficulties contingent upon the transfer of information from a text written at one moment in one language, to a text translated at another in a different language. Translation's attempt to transport an event across the boundaries of time and language, with such equivalence that the original's recapitulation at a later date will be disguised, is inevitably doomed to failure. Recreating whatever it reproduces, translation changes its original. Conspicuously altering its own source texts, *The Massacre at Paris* draws attention to the act of transformation incumbent upon translation and upon the creation of the canon. An act, moreover, which is also evident in the many conversions, both religious and otherwise, which take place in the narrative of *The Massacre at Paris*.

Translating the Massacre: The Narrative

The Saint Bartholomew's Day massacre was characterized by conversion: the religious conversions of its participants and the physical conversions of its victims' bodies. Consequently, Marlowe's dramatization of the slaughter appropriately foregrounds notions of transformation. Implicated in the storm which ensued after the Reformation, the Saint Bartholomew's Day massacre was peopled by characters notorious for their spiritual conversions; Admiral Coligny, Petrus Ramus and the King of Navarre were notable apostates who had rejected Catholicism in favour of the new Protestant church. In Marlowe's retelling of history, transformation is everywhere apparent. Inverting the conventional structure of comedy which is meant to conclude with a wedding, Marlowe opens *The Massacre at Paris* with a marriage which is not the culmination of the action but rather its initiator; the wedding gives way to the massacre as celebration is replaced on stage by slaughter.[68] The transformation of mood wrought by the massacre's displacement of the wedding is underlined by the Guise's first soliloquy which is filled with images of conversion.

> If ever Hymen lour'd at marriage-rites,
> And had his altars deck'd with dusky lights;
> If ever sun stain'd heaven with bloody clouds,
> And made it look with terror on the world;
> If ever day were turn'd to ugly night,
> And night made semblance of the hue of hell;
> This day, this hour, this fatal night,
> Shall fully show the fury of them all.
> (ii.1–8)

Like Richard III's opening soliloquy in the play of the same name, the Guise's speech introduces a series of oxymoronic images.[69] Preparing to initiate the slaughter with the assassinations of the Queen of Navarre and the Admiral Coligny, the Guise imagines his enterprise as a reversal of nature. Turning light into dark, sunshine into blood, and day into night, the duke describes the perversity of the acts he is about to perpetrate, acts which will flout the natural order. However, the Guise is not content simply to invert convention. Instead he looks towards a process in which reversal is to be followed by yet further transformation. Hence day will turn into night, but then night will become like hell. Thus the Guise's speech introduces a transformational strategy the consequences of which are witnessed throughout the rest of the drama.

The Guise's images of conversion ultimately give way to acts of conversion: the transformation of living bodies into dead corpses in the ensuing massacre. This metamorphic process finds reinforcement in yet further verbal and visual expressions of conversion primarily focused on the religious symbol of the cross. The word 'cross' reverberates throughout *The Massacre at Paris*, from Catherine de Medici's first speech in which she maintains that the 'difference in religion' (i.15) of the newly-wed royals 'Might be a means to cross you in your love' (i.15–16), to the 'white crosses' (iv.30) worn by the Catholics during the massacre to signify not only their difference from the Protestants but also their moral rectitude. The apparently innocent image of the cross is consequently deconstructed by the post-Reformation world of the play as the symbol of Christ's suffering is distorted and perverted into a series of grotesque misrecognitions. The contradictions incumbent upon the image of the cross are most obviously realized at the murder of the Admiral Coligny. Discovered in bed, Coligny pleads with his attackers to be allowed to pray:

> *Adm.* O, let me pray before I die!
> *Gon.* Then pray unto our Lady; kiss this cross. [*Stabs him.*
> *Adm.* O God, forgive my sins!   [*Dies.*
> *Guise.* Gonzago, what, is he dead?
> (v.28–31)

Instructed to 'kiss this cross', the admiral is stabbed with Gonzago's dagger. A collision of diametrically-opposed images, the cross in the scene is meant to represent the crucifix of the rosary as well as the shape of the knife which eventually kills the admiral. The religious significance of the first meaning is therefore replaced by the deadly significance of the second. However, the image of the cross is even more protean than this contradiction implies, for the crucifix which Gonzago pretends to offer the admiral is spiritually as deadly as the dagger he receives; both endanger a Protestant. Indeed, as a Protestant convert, the Admiral has denounced the sanctity of Catholic symbols such as the cross. Hence Gonzago's instruction to 'kiss this cross', whether or not it means a crucifix or a dagger, effectively constitutes the same threat to the admiral's safety. *The Massacre at Paris*'s transformations therefore foreground the dislocation of meaning created by the Reformation. The Protestant victims of the massacre have turned their backs on the Catholic use of symbols and elaborate rituals to worship and consequently the cross can never again mean the same thing; the word itself and the shape it denotes divide the Catholic and the Protestant worlds.

In 'The Rites of Violence: Religious Riot in Sixteenth-Century France', Natalie Zemon Davis reveals that the atrocities carried out by religious crowds at this time were often executed in ways which transformed both the attackers and their victims. The religious rioters perpetrated crimes which imitated the punitive measures of their authorities. According to Davis, these acts of mimicry were not attempts to mock or to parody the establishment. Instead they were a means for the rioters to legitimize their illegal behaviour. Davis maintains that:

When the magistrate had not used his sword to defend the faith and the true church and to punish the idolators, then the crowd would do it for him. Thus, many religious disturbances begin with the ringing of the tocsin, as in a time of civic assembly or emergency. Some riots end with the marching of the religious 'wrongdoers' on the other side to jail.[70]

Aping officialdom, religious crowds sought to transform their victims into justifiably-punished criminals. Indeed, working towards this end, the victims were often dehumanized and their bodies transformed by the act of murder.[71] In *The Massacre at Paris* Marlowe dramatizes the transformational and ritualistic nature of religious violence at this time; the scenes of slaughter are even punctuated by the ringing of the tocsin.

Translating their unprovoked attacks on the Protestants into symbolic rites, the Guise faction repeatedly transfigure the corpses they create. Having overseen the murder of Admiral Coligny at the very beginning of the massacre, Anjou sends his body away to be dismembered and then dispatched to the gibbets on Mountfaucon:

Away with him! cut off his head and hands,
And send them for a present to the Pope;
And, when this just revenge is finished,
Unto Mount Faucon will we drag his corse;
And he, that living hated so the Cross,
Shall, being dead, be hang'd thereon in chains.
(v.43–8)

The admiral is doubly transformed by Anjou's instruction. Like the Duchess of Guise's pregnant body which is later imaged by her husband as a text without need of another man's commentary (xii.26), the admiral's flesh is turned into speaking pictures. Firstly, the admiral's severed head and hands are to be sent to the Pope to communicate not only his death but also his cause's impotence; the Protestants are left quite literally without a head or a leader and without the hands or the means to defend themselves. Secondly, what is left of the admiral's body is to be hung on one of the gibbets on Montfaucon where criminals were executed and their corpses allowed to decay. The admiral's body is consequently to be transformed from the body of a murder victim into the body of a criminal. However, it should be noted that Anjou's attempt to translate the admiral's corpse into an eloquent calling card somewhat backfires; by instructing that the admiral's body should be displayed on a cross, Anjou is inadvertently creating his enemy as a Christ-figure. In this way, the force of transformation unleashed by the massacre in the play is shown to be difficult to control. The audience of the play and the onlookers of the historical slaughter are at liberty to interpret the violence in unforeseen ways.

Despite Anjou's detailed instructions, Admiral Coligny's body significantly defies transformation. Far from becoming a fixed symbol of Catholic right, the admiral's corpse returns to the play three scenes later as the subject of a discussion about how best to dispose of a Protestant's corpse. Two men bring the admiral's body back on stage as they argue about what to do with it.

> *First Man.* Now sirrah, what shall we do with the Admiral?
> *Sec. Man.* Why, let us burn him for an heretic.
> *First Man.* O, no! his body will infect the fire, and the fire the air, and so
>   we shall be poisoned with him.
> *Sec. Man.* What shall we do, then?
> *First Man.* Let's throw him into the river.
> *Sec. Man.* O, 'twill corrupt the water, and the water the fish, and by the fish
>   ourselves, when we eat them!
> *First Man.* Then throw him into the ditch.
> *Sec. Man.* No, no. To decide all doubts, be ruled by me: let's hang him here
>   upon this tree. (viii.1–11)

Imagining the admiral's body transformed yet again, this time into noxious fumes and poisonous fish, the two men belie their fear that the dead admiral may turn into something beyond their control. The men are so frightened by the prospect of infection from the heretic's body that they dismiss the use of conventional means of religious purification, for example burning and immersion in water. Davis notes that:

> The religious significance of destruction by water or fire is clear enough. The rivers which receive so many Protestant corpses are not merely convenient mass graves, they are temporarily a kind of holy water, an essential feature of Catholic rites of exorcism. The fire which razes the house of a Protestant apothecary in Montpellier leaves behind it not the smell of death, of the heretic whom the crowd had hanged but of spices, lingering in the air for days, like incense.[72]

Clearly in the case of Admiral Coligny the normal rites of purification are not considered potent enough to prevent his body corrupting the Catholic population. Instead, the men decide to leave his corpse hanging on a tree. The admiral's hanging body may signify the failure of Anjou's intention to make the corpse symbolic. Equally, the stage image may also transform the admiral into a figure reminiscent of the disciple who betrayed Christ and then hanged himself – Judas. Whatever the admiral's body does signify at this point in the play, it is not a singular meaning. The admiral's body radically refuses to be transformed into a controllable symbol.

After the massacre Admiral Coligny and Petrus Ramus were named martyrs.[73] Marlowe's play therefore dramatizes a moment of historical transformation, a moment when Protestant martyrs were created. Seeking to establish a re-formed tradition of martyrs in opposition to the Catholic canon of saints, the Protestant survivors memorialized their dead in print. What is more, transforming the Catholic notion of canonization, Protestants such as John Foxe in his *Book of Martyrs* replaced 'the one-dimensional saints of the old tradition' with very human victims of persecution.[74] Warren Wooden explains that 'Foxe's martyrs are not plaster saints but flesh-and-blood humans, often wracked by doubts and fears. By reading accounts, often in the martyrs' own words, of how their faith in Christ conquered their fears of the fire without and the spiritual flaws within, the individual reader can fortify and prepare himself for the common end of all.'[75] Undergoing a final transformation, then, the bodies of the massacred were immortalized by being translated into texts, the texts of history and the texts of the theatre.

The Perpetuity of the Canon

Like the massacre's victims, texts are apparently immortalized by being taken into the canon and transformed. Such perpetuity is a prerequisite of canonization. A text must be characterized by survival to be available for the critical attentions of future generations. In *Exploding English*, Bernard Bergonzi claims that canonical texts 'from more remote periods' are usually chosen 'not because they are conspicuously excellent, but simply because they are there, having survived when much else perished'.[76] Bergonzi might argue, therefore, that Shakespeare's works have become a central part of the literary canon because they are easily available to future generations in the collected edition of the First Folio. Although this does not entirely account for Shakespeare's popularity, the relative completeness in which his works exist is certainly a factor in the continued performance and study of his plays. Survival is therefore not only the key criterion for a text's entry into the canon, it is also the quality which the canon retrospectively bestows upon a work. The canon takes texts which have survived from the past and gives them an appearance of transcendent and timeless durability. Survival is consequently an authorizing force which provides texts with an impression of innate value quite simply because they have persisted. Similar notions of survival and self-perpetuation are expressed in Marlowe's play as characters are transformed and recreate themselves as kings. The figure who most obviously exemplifies this process in *The Massacre at Paris* is Anjou, who is translated from murderer to king to murder victim as the French throne requires new successors to perpetuate it. In the play attention is focused on the difficulties of survival and succession as mothers murder sons and heirs are banished.

In *The Massacre at Paris*, survival is seriously jeopardized by the existence of a series of murderous figures, the most unnatural of which must surely be Catherine de Medici. Catherine is a maternal figure who ironically endangers the reproductive authority she is meant to consolidate. When she hears that her son, King Charles, has begun to regret the slaughter of the Protestants, Catherine exclaims:

> As I do live, so surely shall he die,
> And Henry then shall wear the diadem;
> And, if he grudge or cross his mother's will,
> I'll disinherit him and all the rest
> (viii.40–43)

Claiming the power of legitimation for herself, Catherine determines which of her children will survive and which will perish. When King Charles dies mysteriously only scenes later, the audience is left to wonder whether or not his death is as a direct result of his mother's words. Although the text refuses to clarify the cause of Charles's demise, it nevertheless tantalizes the audience with the possibility of Catherine's guilt. Following Henry's accession to his brother's throne, Catherine warns the Cardinal of Lorraine that if the new monarch interferes with her plans she will 'despatch him with his brother presently' (xi.64).

The survival of the French royal family is not only endangered by Catherine's murderous behaviour, but also by the exclusion of children from the court. The banishment of generative potency from the French royal family is marked by King Henry's homosexual and therefore reproductively barren relationship with Mugeroun. Henry's inability to produce an heir to succeed him is amply demonstrated when at the end of *The Massacre at Paris* he has to name Navarre as his successor. Similarly, the Duke of Guise's pregnant wife and unborn child are expelled from the court when it is discovered that the duchess has been having an affair with the king's lover, Mugeroun. Moreover, after the Duke of Guise's assassination, his son and heir is also exiled from the court. King Henry sends the child to prison to 'clip his wings' (xviii.124) in an open acknowledgement that as a potential successor to the throne he is a threat to the present incumbent. Consequently, survival is, paradoxically, more difficult for the Catholics in *The Massacre at Paris* than it is for the Protestants. For while Protestants like Admiral Coligny and Petrus Ramus achieve survival by becoming martyrs, by being 'canonized', the Catholic royal family radically fail to survive as they murder one another and exile the successors who might perpetuate their dynasty.

What is more, by showing that the French royal succession relies more on the survival of a candidate than on the rightfulness of his claim, *The Massacre at Paris* discloses the way in which institutions, like royalty and the canon, seek to naturalize their authority, to make their power appear essential when it is in fact artificial. The artificiality of the authority invested in powerful institutions is described by Edward Said in *Orientalism* when he notes that authority

> is formed, irradiated, disseminated; it is instrumental, it is persuasive; it has status, it establishes canons of taste and value; it is virtually indistinguishable from certain ideas it dignifies as true, and from traditions, perceptions, and judgments it forms, transmits, reproduces.[77]

Said points out that those institutions whose rightfulness has always been taken for granted are in fact constructed on insidious foundations of power. Indeed, if the authority of these institutions is questioned, it is revealed to be far from natural; the monarchy, like the canon, discloses under scrutiny its dependence not on an innate right but rather on the consent of its onlookers and participants. Similarly, the canon presents a particular politically-biased view of what constitutes literature that it proffers as organic, but which is actually no more authoritative than the current best-seller list. Thus because 'canons are complicit with power' they are able to perpetuate what are merely literary preferences as transcendent and incontestable pronouncements of value.[78]

The deceptive power structures which underpin the canon and the monarchy are examined in *The Massacre at Paris* by the fortunes of two contenders to the throne, the Duke of Guise and the King of Navarre. Despite their religious differences, the Duke of Guise and the King of Navarre are united not only by their appeal to the 'country's good' (xiii.11), but also by their common inhabitancy on the margins of the royal succession machine. Empowered more by political skill than genetic right, these characters highlight the legitimizing

myths on which all authority depends. Indeed, from his first soliloquy, the
Guise announces his determination to seize the French throne by exploiting
religious intolerance:

> I'll counterpoise a crown,
> Or with seditions weary all the world;
> For this, from Spain the stately Catholics
> Sends Indian gold to coin me French ecues;
> For this, have I a largess from the Pope,
> A pension, and a dispensation too;
> And by that privilege to work upon,
> My policy hath fram'd religion.
> (ii.58–65)

Assuming the vocabulary of Machiavelli, the Guise expresses his 'policy' or
intention to use religion as a justification for his actions. Thus, the Guise
unfurls the standard of Catholicism to fight beneath; religion is the means by
which the Guise legitimizes his otherwise illegitimate behaviour.

Unlike the Guise, Navarre does not reveal his political ambitions in the play.
Nevertheless, it is ultimately Navarre and not the Guise who succeeds to the
French throne at the end of *The Massacre at Paris*. Cleverly disguising his own
intentions, Navarre couches his royal aspirations in ostensibly innocent terms.
For instance, in the wake of King Charles's death, Navarre explains:

> opportunity may serve me fit
> To steal from France, and hie me to my home,
> For here's no safety in the realm for me:
> And now that Henry is call'd from Poland,
> It is my due, by just succession;
> And therefore, as speedily as I can perform,
> I'll muster up an army secretly,
> For fear that Guise, join'd with the king of Spain,
> Might seem to cross me in mine enterprise
> But God, that always doth defend the right,
> Will show his mercy, and preserve us still. (x.31–41)

This is an offensive speech expressed in defensive terms; Navarre claims that it
is his vulnerability rather than his ambition which induces him to raise an
army. Lashing together apparently contradictory groups of words, Navarre
uses Machiavellian terms such as 'opportunity', 'steal' and 'secretly' at the

same time he employs words of righteous anger such as 'just', 'defend' and 'right'. Navarre is thereby able to use cunning political means to achieve what he claims are moral ends. Unlike the Guise, Navarre manages to disguise his ambitious desires so that when he is eventually named Henry's successor he assumes the throne apparently effortlessly. It is this apparent effortlessness which makes Navarre's claim to the throne seem natural and legitimate. Like the canon, royalty in *The Massacre at Paris* relies on the naturalization of processes which are in actuality highly artificial and political. Monarchical power is consequently exposed as an elaborate confidence trick by Marlowe's play; succession occurs not as a result of right but as a result of survival and political skill. The gap between the apparently transcendent authorization of the king, and the actual political strategies which create him, is underlined at the end of *The Massacre at Paris* when historical events are utterly reversed. Dispensing with any pretence of historical accuracy, the play reveals that the maintenance of monarchical, canonical and theatrical power ultimately depends on retrospective myths created to accommodate the tastes of future nations, generations and audiences.

'Englishing' *The Massacre at Paris*

At the end of *The Massacre at Paris*, the play's narrative creates a succession of myths designed to please its English Protestant theatre audience. Employing myths of sameness which appeal to its audience's taste, the play exposes the ultimate transformation wrought by the canon and by other institutions of control: the transformation of the Other into the self. Carrying texts into itself, the canon transforms them to create a sense of commonality, to create the impression that all canonical works display the same features of persistence and of transcendental meaning. In a similar way, other powerful institutions convert and transform objects outside themselves to render their Otherness less problematic, effectively to make the Other like the self. At the end of *The Massacre at Paris*, this movement towards absolute cultural appropriation is rehearsed both by King Henry's pronouncements over the murdered body of his rival, the Duke of Guise, and, more finally, by his own dying words to his successor, Navarre. Just as Renaissance translators imaged the task of translation as a means to domesticate or 'English' a foreign text, Marlowe's play depicts events which pander to its English Protestant audience regardless of historical accuracy. According to Renaissance translators, a foreign text could be swallowed whole by the translator's own language and thereby converted into a domestic text. Indeed, in the dedication to his English translation of Castiglione's *The Book of the Courtier*, Thomas Hoby pictures the act of translation as the actual transformation of the foreign author into a fellow countryman. Hoby notes that having been translated into many other languages Castiglione has at last 'become an Englishman' in his edition.[79] Translating writer and text simultaneously, Hoby's translation underlines the absolute exchange which Renaissance translation was thought to offer; to paraphrase was not enough, the translator had to re-form his author as a compatriot, or more precisely, as himself. Consequently, texts written in foreign languages were not translated for their cultural difference, but rather for their ability to be made culturally similar.

The impulse to 'English' that which is not domestic is expressed in Marlowe's play when King Henry accuses his dead rival, the Guise, of a list of crimes against Elizabethan England. Henry maintains:

> This is the traitor that hath spent my gold
> In making foreign wars and civil broils.
> Did he not draw a sort of English priests
> From Douay to the seminary at Rheims,
> To hatch forth treason 'gainst their natural queen?
> Did he not cause the king of Spain's huge fleet
> To threaten England, and to menace me?
> Did he not injure Monsieur that's deceas'd? (xviii.100–107)

Alleging the Guise's responsibility for the Babington conspiracy of 1586, the Spanish Armada of 1588, and the death of Queen Elizabeth's suitor, the Duke d'Alençon, Henry seeks to justify the murder of his rival less to his attendant French courtiers than to his English theatre audience. Similarly, only a few scenes later when King Henry is murdered by a zealous friar, he dies saluting Queen Elizabeth and bidding Navarre to tell her that 'Henry dies her faithful friend' (xxi.107). Like Henry's condemnation of the Guise, his dying oath of allegiance to English Protestantism has no historical basis. As the play's original audience would probably have known, in reality, Henry's dying words were quite different. According to Julia Briggs, 'The dying King certainly announced Navarre his heir, but far from begging him to espouse the Protestant cause, he in fact urged him to convert to Catholicism, as the dispatches to Walsingham make clear'.[80] Thus the ending of *The Massacre at Paris* exposes the highly political effort to make the Other like the self, to create a myth of similitude which will please all involved.

However, the creation of a myth of sameness which underpins the concept of the canon, the usefulness of translation and the ending of Marlowe's play is eventually revealed to be untenable by *The Massacre at Paris*. The absolute cultural assimilation of the Other is shown to be impossible in Marlowe's play as it can only be achieved by extremely artificial means. The scenes depicting the deaths of the Duke of Guise and King Henry stand out in the play as moments of self-conscious myth-making which invite audience suspicion rather than acceptance. The impossibility of absolute cultural appropriation is, moreover, implied throughout the drama by the text's refusal to translate everything. Despite the play's examination of the forces of transportation, transformation and translation, the word '*tuez*' remains radically untranslatable in *The Massacre at Paris*. Shouted to initiate and to perpetuate the slaughter, the word '*tuez*' refuses to be assimilated into its English context. In the end *The Massacre at Paris* dwells not upon the successful assimilation of Otherness but instead upon the difficulties encountered by the transformation of the Other into the self, of a text into the canon, and of the French into the English. Consequently, Marlowe's play revises those notions of transcendental value and transformational order which have conventionally denied it entry into the institution of the canon and hence the annals of critical approbation.

Notes

1. Prologue, line 30. See chapter six on *The Jew of Malta*.
2. Kuriyama, C. B. (1980), p. 76.
3. The notion of 'badness' will be examined at length later in this chapter.
4. Collier, J. P. (1825), p. 244.
5. Collier, J. P. (1825), p. 244.
6. Nosworthy, J. M. (1945/46), p. 160.
7. Dabbs, T. (1991), p. 60.
8. Dabbs, T. (1991), p. 62.
9. Dabbs, T. (1991), pp. 64–5.
10. The resultant Marlowe, in such a reading, is a man rather like Shakespeare, who was of course also an actor. See my introduction, in which I argue that criticism's ongoing comparison of Marlowe with Shakespeare is typical of Marlovian scholarship in general.
11. Bakeless, J. (1942), p. 14.
12. Adams, J. Q. (1933/4), p. 446.
13. Croft, P. J. (1973), vol. 1, p. xiv.
14. Altick, R. D. (1960), p. 154.
15. Macherey, P. (1978), pp. 16–17.
16. Bennett, H. S., ed. (1931), p. 171.
17. Bennett, H. S., ed. (1931), p. 170.
18. Bennett, H. S., ed. (1931), p. 170.

19. Bennett, H. S., ed. (1931), p. 171.
20. Bennett, H. S., ed. (1931), p. 171.
21. Bennett, H. S., ed. (1931), p. 171.
22. Boas, F. S. (1940), p. 151.
23. Steane, J. B. (1964), p. 236.
24. Bakeless, J. (1942), p. 69.
25. Leech, C. (1986), p. 147.
26. Bennett, H. S., ed. (1931), p. 173.
27. Steane, J. B. (1964), p. 236.
28. Steane, J. B. (1964), p. 238.
29. Bennet, H. S., ed. (1931), p. 174.
30. Bennet, H. S., ed. (1931), p. 174.
31. Sanders, W. (1968), p. 23.
32. Sanders, W. (1968), p. 20.
33. Steane, J. B. (1964), p. 246.
34. anders, W. (1969), p. 21.
35. Bartels, E. (1993), p. 182.
36. Bennett, H. S., ed. (1931), p. 169.
37. As F. S. Boas explains in *A Biographical and Critical Study* (1940), pp. 167–8: 'After its first production by Henslowe at the 'Rose' in January 1593 it was revived at the same theatre on 19 June 1594, and had ten performances between that date and 25 September. A later revival took place in or soon after November 1598 when Henslowe on the 19th lent William Borne or Birde, who acted the Guise, twelve shillings that he might 'jmbrader his hatter', and on the 27th a further sum of twenty shillings that he might 'bye a payer of sylke stockens' in which to perform the part. It was evidently an expensive play to dress. When it was again revived in November 1601, three pounds were paid for 'stamell cllath' for a cloak, and other sums to the 'littell taylor Radford' for further materials and for work upon suits for the play. After final payment of his bill on 26 November, £7. 14s. 6d. had been laid out on costumes. About seven weeks afterwards, on 18 January 1602, the Admiral's Men bought the play, with two others, from Edward Alleyn for six pounds.'
38. Weil, J. (1977), p. 104.
39. Shepherd, S. (1986), p. 123.
40. Bartels, E. (1993), p. 112.
41. Guillory, J. (1993), p. 6.
42. Kermode, F. (1989), pp. 115–16.
43. Court, F. E. (1992), p. 167.
44. Kristeller, P. O. (1990), p. 3.
45. Mazzeo, J. A. (1967), p. 14.
46. Hoby, T. (1588), p. 3.
47. Hoby, T. (1588), p. 3.
48. Udall, N. (1548), preface, no pagination.
49. Winny, J. (1960), p. xiii.
50. Elsky, M. (1989), p. 81.
51. Kingdon, R. M. (1988), pp. 74–5.
52. Briggs, J. (1983), p. 268.
53. Bakeless, J. (1937), p. 19.

54. Foxe, J. (1877), vol. 8, p. 748.
55. All quotations from *The Massacre at Paris* are taken from H. S. Bennett's edition which forms one volume of a *Complete Works*. Published in a single volume with *The Jew of Malta*, this edition exhibits the canonical peripheralization of the play which is rarely printed independently in a modern spelling version.
56. Kingdon, R. (1974), p. 27.
57. Kingdon, R. (1988), p. 200.
58. Dickens, A. G. (1974), p. 54.
59. Bakeless, J. (1937), p. 21.
60. Dickens, A. G. (1974), p. 61.
61. Kocher, P. H. (1941), p. 350.
62. Kocher, P. H. (1947), p. 151.
63. Briggs, J. (1983), p. 263.
64. Briggs, J. (1983), p. 263.
65. Howell, W. S. (1956), p. 140.
66. Hotman, F. (1573), p. xxxv.
67. Kocher, P. (1947), p. 168.
68. Shakespeare adopts a similar structure in *Hamlet*, which begins with a wedding and ends in a funeral.
69. See, for example, the famous *Richard III* soliloquy, in which the 'summer' of the son of York has been turned to winter by Richard's discontent. Also note 'And all the clouds that lour'd upon our House/In the deep bosom of the ocean buried' (I.i.3–4), where one finds the same notion of looking disdainfully. Could this be a direct debt, or an indication to Shakespeare's audience that this is to be a political villain like the Guise?
70. Davis, N. Z. (1974), p. 213.
71. Davis, N. Z. (1974), p. 236.
72. Davis, N. Z. (1974), pp. 232–3.
73. The 1574 English translation of *The Logicke* describes Ramus on its title page as a 'martyr'.
74. Wooden, W. W. (1983), p. 47.
75. Wooden, W. W. (1983), p. 48.
76. Bergonzi, B. (1990), p. 81.
77. Said, E. (1979), pp. 19–20.
78. Kermode, F. (1989), p. 115.
79. Hoby, T. (1588), p. 2.
80. Briggs, J. (1983), p. 271.

Chapter 6

A Production of Kinds: Genre, *The Jew of Malta* and the Promise of Repetition

While *The Massacre at Paris* interrogates the transhistorical and tran-scendental assumptions which underpin the concept of the canon, *The Jew of Malta* considers another classificatory structure – genre. Consequently, both plays are concerned with those literary structures through and by which texts are conventionally read. In *The Massacre at Paris* the structure examined by the play is one which affects not only how a text is classified, but also, and more importantly, how a text is received; if a text is excluded from the canon it will rarely receive critical attention, and almost never critical approval. In *The Jew of Malta* the structure examined by the play is one which affects a text long before the point of its reception. *The Jew of Malta* considers the concept of genre which influences and informs a text both at the moment of its inception and again at the point of its reception. *The Jew of Malta* initiates its consideration of the concept of genre by classifying itself in the prologue and by then proceeding to complicate and to contradict this pronouncement throughout the rest of the play.

Introduced by the character Machevill, *The Jew of Malta* opens with a prologue which names the play's genre as tragedy. Machevill states:

> But wither am I bound, I come not, I
> To read a lecture here in Britanie,
> But to present the tragedy of a Jew,
> Who smiles to see how full his bags are crammed,
> Which money was not got without my means.
> (Prologue 28–32)[1]

Although a prologue is conventionally a device employed to communicate information directly and honestly to an audience, the prologue of *The Jew of Malta* raises a series of doubts about its speaker's integrity. Most obviously, the prologue is spoken by a character whose very probity is radically in question. The character of Machevill, or Make-Evil, embodies the popular perception of the political writer Niccolò Machiavelli, who was thought by Renaissance audiences to represent all that was untrustworthy and duplicitous in mankind. If the speaker of the prologue is living up to his reputation, his words are probably not truthful and hence his pronouncement that the play to be performed is 'the tragedy of a Jew' may not be accurate. Indeed, the statement may be deliberately misleading. What is more, the sentence which names the play's genre as tragedy is itself a lie. Despite Machevill's claim that he has not come to Britain to read a lecture, that is exactly what he has been doing for the previous twenty-seven lines of the prologue. Consequently, the play's genre is named by a notorious liar in a sentence which is itself an example of one of his lies. The classification of *The Jew of Malta* as a tragedy is therefore paradoxically made more uncertain by being stated; by naming the play as a tragedy within a specific dramatic context, *The Jew of Malta* introduces the possibility that its genre is open to redefinition depending upon when and by whom it is pronounced. Accentuating this uncertainty, the rest of the play fails to live up to the prescriptions of tragedy or for that matter of any established generic form. Inconsistencies of characterization, tone and plot combine to create a mishmash of styles which initiate but never consummate structural expectations.

The impression of generic uncertainty manufactured by *The Jew of Malta* has, not surprisingly, been a source of considerable concern for twentieth-century critics of the play. According to Howard Babb the play 'creates a realm of dramatic experience for which we have no name'.[2] Distorting the parameters of generic taxonomy which prove unable to contain it, Marlowe's play sets in motion critical anxieties which are aptly summarized by J. B. Steane's comment that 'There is a general feeling that this is a play of a distinctive character and an equally widespread difference of opinion as to what that character exactly is'.[3] The genre of *The Jew of Malta* seems to be problematic both at the point of its composition and at the moment of its reception. What is more, this uncertainty seems to be generated not simply by Marlowe's contradictory presentation of genre within the confines of *The Jew of Malta* but also by something inherently uncertain about the way in which literary forms are classified. It is this sense of the unknowable nature of genre which Umberto Eco's monastic thriller *The Name of the Rose* satirizes. In Eco's novel the motive and murder weapon in a series of clerical killings is Aristotle's treatise on comedy. Presumed since antiquity to be either fabulous or lost,[4] the sequel to *The Poetics* is retrieved in the novel only to be suppressed by the murderer. Believing that Aristotle's endorsement of the ridiculous in art will cause social disruption and even sacrilege, the murderer seeks to limit the work's transmission by impregnating the paper with lethal toxins. Each time a reader wets his eager fingers to turn its pages he is successively poisoned as the process of reading becomes simultaneously one of unwitting self-censorship. The investigator of the crime, Brother William, reconstructs the missing sequel to *The Poetics* through a series of clever deductions based on other books. It is this effort to fill the gap bequeathed by Aristotle's ostensible deferral of his discussion of comedy which typifies debates about genre. Indeed generic theories are often marked by a quest for definition and authority which constantly encounters loss and absence. The most extreme expression of this attempt to fill the generic gulf must surely be Lane Cooper's *An Aristotelian Theory of Comedy, with an Adaptation of the Poetics* which claims to revivify a text whose very existence is open to question. Reaching across the void of omission, genre criticism is characterized not only by a sense of loss, but also by an impulse towards recovery.

It is the compensatory nature of generic theory, that seems to be perpetually making amends for something missing, which coincides with inchoate issues surrounding Marlowe's *The Jew of Malta*. Even a brief examination of the play rapidly comes up against a series of fundamental historical and editorial questions to which there is no answer. Repeatedly involving the critic in a search for unknowable information, *The Jew of Malta* negotiates a network of absences. Entered in the Stationers' Register as early as 1594 by Nicholas Ling and Thomas Millington, 'The famouse tragedie of the Riche Jewe of Malta' did not appear in a published edition until 1633.[5] This gap of thirty-nine years between notification of the intention to print and the date of the first surviving copy epitomizes the impression that the play rests on irretrievable elements. Included in this inventory of absences are also the Jewish people and the works of Machiavelli, both of which were outlawed in Elizabethan society. Expelled by King Edward I in 1290,[6] there were legally no Jews in England until Oliver Cromwell readmitted them in 1650.[7] Similarly, Machiavelli's *Discourses* and *The Prince* were not printed in English until Dacre's editions of 1636 and 1640 respectively.[8] In this way, Marlowe's drama was created from the friction between the officially unavailable and the privately present. The uncertainty created by the unknowable historical elements of the play is therefore only compounded by the unclassifiable nature of the drama's genre. Indeed Marlovian criticism of the play has been largely preoccupied with the creation of theories to compensate for *The Jew of Malta*'s unrecognizable generic form. These theories seem to fall roughly into two critical camps; firstly, those which account for the play's generic incoherence by claiming that the text read today is the result of revision by a hand other than Marlowe's; secondly, those which account for inconsistencies in the structural form of the play by claiming that they represent Marlowe's attempt to create a new dramatic genre. These theories will be examined in detail before considering what the concept of genre actually entails.

The Problem with the Genre of *The Jew of Malta*: Revision?

According to John Bakeless, *The Jew of Malta* 'is not a great play, for it lacks almost, though not quite, all the ingredients of greatness ... for breaking squarely in two in the middle, it lacks even the saving virtue of unity.'[9] Bakeless goes on to claim that the text of *The Jew of Malta* which history has bequeathed scholarship in fact represents 'the great beginning of a play, or the remnant of a play that once was great.'[10] Bakeless characterizes the extant text of *The Jew of Malta* as a remnant or vestige of a lost Platonic whole, in much the same way as critics of *The Massacre at Paris* contend that it is a shortened version of an Ur-*Massacre* no longer available to scholarship. However, unlike the many critics of *The Massacre at Paris* cited in chapter five, who believe that even in its most complete form it was probably not a very good play, Bakeless maintains that *The Jew of Malta*'s dramatic inadequacies are the result of unwelcome interference by a playwright other than Marlowe who revised the work after its composition. Consequently, were *The Jew of Malta* to exist in its Marlovian entirety, Bakeless believes it would attain an artistic greatness which the extant edition can only gesture towards. Bakeless continues: 'There is no room for doubt that the first two acts are mainly Marlowe's. But who has been tampering with the rest? Who is the author of the extraordinary farrago that hustles the play to its ridiculous, though highly Elizabethan conclusion? No man knows.'[11] It is interesting to note here that although Bakeless recognizes the ending of *The Jew of Malta* as highly Elizabethan, he nevertheless contests that it is not by Marlowe, a highly Elizabethan playwright. This apparently wilful refusal to acknowledge the play as Marlowe's own seems to derive more from Bakeless's distaste at the nature of *The Jew of Malta*'s denouement than from any evidence of revision within the text itself. The length of time which elapsed between the play's first performance – it is mentioned by Henslowe as early as 1591 – and its publication in 1633 does not of necessity indicate that the subsequent edition was revised by a playwright other than Marlowe.[12] It was not uncommon for plays of the period to remain unpublished for many years. Moreover, Bakeless's use of the word 'farrago', which he repeats later in his discussion of the play,[13] consolidates the impression that it is the nature of the stage action which causes the critic discomfort rather than its authorial integrity.

Although Bakeless is unable to name the culprit in what he believes to be an act of textual desecration, subsequent critics have proved only too ready to point the finger of blame. D. J. Lake argues in 'Three Seventeenth-Century Revisions' that despite Thomas Heywood's involvement in the seventeenth-century revival of the text, it is Thomas Dekker's hand which appears in the play:

> To summarize, then, it would seem certain that the play has been revised, and perhaps the whole text copied out at some time in the period 1600–32, most probably by Dekker after 1604. We cannot rule out the presence of Heywood, but there is no linguistic evidence for it. It is just possible that Dekker made the revision at Heywood's request, or in collaboration with Heywood early in 1632 (Dekker died in August 1632). Whatever the circumstances, the fact of revision is now certain.[14]

Lake's certainty, however, is not universally shared by Marlovian critics. In his Revels edition of the play, N. W. Bawcutt persuasively argues that the 1633 quarto represents Marlowe's foul papers. The editor maintains that it is 'easier to see most of the confusions in the play as authorial mistakes and inconsistencies than as the blunders of a remarkably incompetent reviser'.[15] Moreover, Bawcutt dismisses the proposition that the play's publication, some forty years after its production, is evidence of revision. Instead, Bawcutt argues that if Shakespeare's manuscript of *The Comedy of Errors*, 'one of the most striking of Shakespeare's foul papers texts', did not appear in print until thirty years after it was probably written then why should not the quarto of *The Jew of Malta* also be derived from its author's own manuscript copy?[16] In a similar vein, J. C. Maxwell argues in 'How bad is the text of *The Jew of Malta*?' that criticism has 'been too ready to suspect the text simply on the ground of the lapse of more than forty years before publication'.[17] Maxwell goes on to point out '(a) that the doctrine of "continuous copy" is a figment of the editorial brain, and (b) that manuscripts, unlike apples, do not become corrupt simply by lying in a drawer'.[18] Maxwell's pointed comparison between apples and manuscripts finally unmasks the obstinacy on which theories of revision depend. By wilfully searching out signs of textual decay and deterioration where there need not be any, critics of *The Jew of Malta* who support the theory of revision only succeed in disclosing their own anxious inability to deal with a play which defies conventional notions of coherence and structural unity.

The Problem with the Genre of *The Jew of Malta*: A New Genre?

The assertion that a structurally-inconsistent text is not of necessity a corrupt one premises those theories which claim that in *The Jew of Malta* Marlowe endeavoured to create a new dramatic genre. By a method which seems to shut the stable door some time after the horse has bolted, criticism redraws the generic boundaries which would otherwise deny the play entry. Consequently, *The Jew of Malta* is retrospectively provided with the structural unity which it is conventionally thought to deny or even to deconstruct. In 'Marlowe as Experimental Dramatist' Edward Rocklin maintains that the play is the keynote in an innovative dramatic form: 'The brave sport of *The Jew of Malta* was thus a critical event in the emergence of the newer dramaturgy'.[19] The new dramatic form which the play is thought to inaugurate tends to be described by critics as a composite of subsidiary forms, a Frankensteinian blend of the illegitimate offspring of tragedy and comedy. *The Jew of Malta* therefore assumes a generic wholeness which ironically does not require structural coherence. In this vein, Clifford Leech concludes his discussion of the play by claiming that 'There is after all a sense of the tragic along with the dark comedy of it all.'[20] Marrying together a number of generic types which the drama fails to satisfy independently, criticism gives birth to a chimerical form in which inconsistency is a requirement rather than a flaw. As Thomas Cartelli notes:

> Instead of establishing a set of expectations which the rest of the play fails to fulfill, the opening scenes establish a pattern of discontinuity which disarms the audience of conventional expectations of logical development and accommodates it to the acquired freedom of the play's burlesque mode.[21]

The Jew of Malta's unwillingness to conform neatly to one category or another paradoxically gives it membership of, and access to, that most exclusive of clubs: the canon.

Rereading the drama as an expression of self-subverting generic forms, such as burlesque and farce, criticism seems simply to restate T. S. Eliot's influential pronouncement on the play that 'If one takes the *Jew of Malta* not as a tragedy or as a "tragedy of blood," but as a farce, the concluding act becomes intelligible … it is the farce of the old English humour, the terribly serious, even savage comic humour.'[22] Criticism reiterates traditional readings of the play which ultimately disclose scholarship's need to reconstruct the drama, be it the 1633 quarto or some lost Ur-manuscript, as a coherent generic whole. The theory of revision as well as the arguments for the play's reclassification consequently belie the futile hope that constant review will eventually rescind textual inconsistency. Like Brother William in *The Name of the Rose*, who invents Aristotle's missing treatise on comedy in his mind, Marlovian scholarship recreates *The Jew of Malta* as an authorially consistent and generically unproblematic play. This desire to refigure Marlowe's drama in ways which compensate for its generic incoherence directs attention to larger issues concerning the very nature and definition of genre. Moreover, this reassessment of genre acquires greater significance for Marlowe's play when it is remembered that *The Jew of Malta* was written at a time of great humanist activity, when classical literary precepts were being recovered and reapplied. It is at this moment, when the past was holding the present both captive and captivated, that *The Jew of Malta* was produced. Hence the very notion of genre requires consideration before examining its expression and complication within Marlowe's play.

Towards a Concept of Genre

In the *Anatomy of Criticism*, Northrop Frye notes that 'The very word "genre" sticks out in an English sentence as the unpronounceable and alien thing it is'.[23] Derived from the Latin *genus* or 'kind' and transferred wholesale from the French, the word 'genre' sets itself in relief from the rest of an English sentence. More familiar than Frye implies, however, the term's display of linguistic incongruity helps to convey its sense of paradigmatic uniqueness and individuality. Similarly, the italicization of 'genre', imprisoned within inverted commas or anchored by underlining, performs on paper the textual boundaries the expression designates. Despite, or perhaps because of, this rehearsal of meaning each time genre is written or spoken, the word actually defies attempts at comprehensive definition. For instance, the *Shorter Oxford English Dictionary* describes genre baldly as a 'kind; sort; style',[24] while M. H. Abrams explains in *A Glossary of Literary Terms* that it 'denotes a type or species of literature, or as we now often call it, a "literary form"'.[25] Supplying a pencil sketch where an oil-painted canvas would have been more appropriate, these definitions depict a structure without depth or shading. Inadequately representing a complex concept, the shortcomings of these accounts are, moreover, unrectifiable. Genre cannot be defined because it is itself a definition, a specific which connotes a greater significance. Dictionary descriptions of the term 'genre' can, therefore, only ever reveal the tip of an iceberg whose mass lies beneath the surface, beyond reductive analysis. The word genre indicates more than a kind or type of literature. The term implies an originary moment of genesis from which other creations are generated. Consequently, a genre looks back towards its own past which it resurrects again and again with each new elaboration of itself.

The generic compulsion to retrieve and to replicate coincides with the humanist agenda to rehabilitate texts from ancient times as models for contemporary works. The humanist recovery of these classical texts made generic models available to Elizabethan authors and thereby facilitated the imitation of ancient narrative and dramatic forms. The importance of this process for the creation of theories of genre in the Renaissance is noted by Rosalie Colie in *The Resources of Kind: Genre-Theory in the Renaissance*, when she explains:

> The texts in question were recovered from oblivion, published on the new-fangled presses, edited and quarreled over – and endlessly imitated. Why such models, and whence came their peculiar power? To be able to answer that question is to understand the Renaissance.[26]

The imaginative importance of the opportunity which the printing press offered to duplicate the past in standardized editions cannot be emphasized enough. It is this image of textual production and re-production, of the multiple act of creation from blank paper, which embodies the Renaissance artistic endeavour. Although contrary to the Romantic depiction of the Promethean poet, the image of the Elizabethan writer as a sort of human printing press does not detract from humanist literary achievement, but rather complicates it. By imagining the Renaissance artist as creator, craftsman and copyist, the image of the printing-press writer indicates the contradictory persona of the humanist author. Shackled to an infernal machine of his own making, the Renaissance artist had revivified the classics only to bind himself to them in an unending process of re-production.

The restoration of the ancient past as a pattern for future generations may be viewed in microcosm by the Renaissance revival of Aristotle's *Poetics*. In his translation of the treatise, W. Hamilton Fyfe maintains that *The Poetics*' 'modern life begins in Italy at the end of the fifteenth century. Since then it has been translated and edited and annotated in every century and in many languages, attaining at times the authority of a holy writ'.[27] The near divine authority of the *Poetics* depended for humanists not only upon its classical credentials, but also its provision of the raw materials for generic construction and reconstruction. Although Aristotle's work actually constitutes a tentative set of self-modifying literary guidelines, Renaissance artists deduced from these points creative rubrics which formed the basis of artistic endeavours for centuries. Of primary importance among these precepts are a concern for the historical and etymological origins of literature;[28] the establishment of a hierarchy of forms which posits tragedy above comedy because it is preoccupied with noble action;[29] the necessity of structural completion by creating a plot with a beginning, a middle and an end;[30] and finally, the requirement that art should only imitate reality within the confines of probability.[31]   Forged together, these principles produce a repeatable and consistent generic glass in which art can represent the world. What is more, this mirror does not simply reflect reality, it dictates it. The generic mirror presumes what reality can be and thereby prescribes its dimensions. The Renaissance generic frame was like Aristotle's assertion that poetry is 'something more philosophic and of graver import than history, since its statements are of the nature rather of universals, whereas those of history are singulars'.[32]

Universally applicable and transcendent, genre offers ways to categorize and to contain the world. For as Rosalie Colie maintains, genres are, much like the literary canons already discussed in the previous chapter, 'definitions of manageable boundaries, some large, some small, in which material can be treated and considered'.[33] The opportunity which genre promises, to convert reality into tractable gobbets of art, encouraged the rapid adoption of generic forms in Renaissance Europe. At a time when geographical and intellectual space appeared boundless, the setting of limits on reality must have proved a comforting way to accommodate the rapid pace of change. In his study of *Orientalism*, Edward Said notices the cultural tendency to reduce reality into manageable categories: 'One ought again to remember that all cultures impose corrections upon raw reality, changing it from free-floating objects into units of knowledge'.[34] The generic concentration and compartmentalization of knowledge within treatable frames is staged throughout *The Jew of Malta* as aphorisms, proverbs and maxims abound.

Infinite Riches or the Generic Compartmentalization of Knowledge

Unintentionally described by Barabas's phrase, 'Infinite riches in a little room' (I.i.37), the pithy sayings and truisms which preoccupy *The Jew of Malta* were first noticed in 1977 by Judith Weil in *Christopher Marlowe: Merlin's Prophet*. In her study, Weil draws attention to the play's deployment of numerous absolutes which form a succession of parabolic inversions. From Machevill's maxim-filled prologue to Barabas's advice to the Friar he is strangling to 'confess and be hanged' (IV.i. 146) and Pilia-Borza's assertion, '*Hodie tibi, cras mihi*' (IV.ii.17–19) or 'today your fortune, tomorrow mine', the characters consistently rely on anecdotal wisdom as a commentary on events, as a way to make the world of the play intelligible or perhaps simply tolerable.[35] In 'Marlowe and the Will to Absolute Play' Stephen Greenblatt touches on this phenomenon, declaring that 'Proverbs in *The Jew of Malta* are a kind of currency, the compressed ideological wealth of society, the money of the mind'.[36] Like genres, proverbs provide a communal code to experience, a universal key which all can employ.

By forming generalized connections, adages are able to tap into a system of shared transcendent knowledge which can comfort, protect from and even explain raw reality. This communality of 'truth' is demonstrated when Ithamore fetches for the nuns the poisoned porridge, which he brings on stage with a long ladle. Appealing to the audience's familiarity with the proverb 'he that eats with the devil had need of a long spoon' (III.iv.58–9), Ithamore raises a laugh which excludes and ridicules his master, Barabas, by identifying him with the Devil himself. However, the specificity of the joke detracts from the proverb's otherwise catholic currency. By rendering the saying in a particular dramatic context Ithamore only succeeds in making the Devil as threatening as a villainous Jew and the consequences of association with him merely comic. Thus, as soon as a truism is made individual and particular it is somehow robbed of its elemental 'truth'. For, as Greenblatt explains, 'the essence of proverbs is their anonymity'.[37] Hence a proverb can only remain valid as long as it also remains anchorless and unspecific. Flouting this rule, *The Jew of Malta* repeatedly subverts truisms by making them personal, specific, contingent and therefore controvertible. This process of complication through application does not only disrupt proverbs in *The Jew of Malta*, it also disrupts the broadest frame of cultural reference in the play – genre.

Like proverbs, which are also self-contained and iterable, genre does not travel well. Indeed, as genre is usually defined by its state of paradigmatic purity, it cannot help but be compromised at the same time as it is rendered useful. Like the 'class' traitor that it really is, genre betrays its origins, or at least its original, whenever it is exercised, whenever it is forced to become pragmatic, flexible and applicable. Primarily employed in two ways, genre operates as a taxonomic aid and as a means of communication. By the invocation and expression of these operations, *The Jew of Malta* examines the complexities of genre which attempts at definition sidestep. Each of these roles will be examined in turn.

Genre: A Pigeonhole?

A template beneath which literary texts may be placed for comparison, genre identifies recurrent structural patterns and thereby enables critics to categorize the works in which they appear. Although this description seems to imply that genre can achieve the highly accurate classification of literary texts, in practice this is not necessarily the case. Generic classification is often a complicated and problematic process as texts rarely comply utterly with the requirements of a particular genre. What is more, the classification of texts according to different genres relies upon the academy's agreement as to which characteristics are typical of which genres. Literary classification demands a level of critical consensus which is largely unachievable. As Paul Henradi notes in *Beyond Genre*: 'all works of literature are similar to each other in many ways and ... it depends entirely on the critic's point of view which similarities he should consider important enough for generic distinctions'.[38] The question of how to determine a common trait or recognizable mark of generic identity was taken up by Ludwig Wittgenstein in his *Philosophical Investigations*. Wittgenstein maintains that generic characteristics are best imagined in human terms as 'family resemblances', 'for the various resemblances between members of a family: build, features, colour of eyes, gait, temperament, etc. etc. overlap and criss-cross in the same way'.[39] Dispensing with the search for a set of definite features, the philosopher instead resolves the problem of distinguishing generic characteristics by identifying broad areas of familial similarity. However, as everyone knows, 'it's a wise man who knows his own father' and family resemblance is consequently an uncertain foundation on which to build a method of classification.

Complicating matters by introducing a theory of 'relative-ity' to the generic debate, Wittgenstein also engages with *The Jew of Malta*'s most fundamental concern – the sliding and seemingly arbitrary scale of difference by which humanity classifies itself. Penetrating to the play's very core, the issue of racial and financial diversity initiates and sustains the plot. It is Ferneze's ethnically inequitable tax which acts as a trigger for the play's events. Asked to contribute to the knights' economic rescue package, Barabas inquires, 'How, equally?' (I.ii.64), to which the Governor replies, 'No, Jew, like infidels' (I.ii.65). Establishing the parameters of discussion early on, the drama demonstrates the false categories men erect as an excuse to pilfer and to persecute. By viewing the Jews as a class apart, an inferior genre, Ferneze is able to justify their ruin. Similarly in the slave market scene humanity is categorized according to economic value. However, the financial classification of the slaves is openly ridiculed by Barabas in a process which deconstructs generic notions of absolute difference. Moving among the men with prices on their backs, Barabas quizzes the merchant as to their relative value, asking what makes one man more expensive than another:

BARABAS
Come then, here's the market-place; what's the price of this slave, two hundred crowns? Do the Turks weigh so much?
1 OFFICER
Sir, that's his price.
BARABAS
What, can he steal that you demand so much?
(II.iii.100–104)

Deliberately misconstruing the slave's price as his weight, Barabas makes a mockery of the Christians' application of financial distinctions to humanity. In a process which disturbs the relationship between money and mankind, the slave's price tag is revealed to be, like all labels, discretionary and arbitrary. Finally purchasing Ithamore from the soldiers, Barabas is told to 'mark him, sir, and take him hence' (II.iii.136). Placing a sign of ownership upon the man, Barabas rehearses the prologue's marking of the play's genre and in so doing underlines the point that naming does not necessarily indicate a fixed and determined identity. By naming the play's genre as tragedy and by naming Ithamore as his own, the play and the protagonist reveal the protean nature of classification which is open to alteration depending on when and by whom it is pronounced.

Genre: A Pigeon?

In *Kinds of Literature*, Alastair Fowler maintains that although many critics believe genre to be primarily useful as a tool of classification, in reality it 'is much less of a pigeonhole than a pigeon'.[40] Fowler goes on to explain that contrary to popular critical opinion, genre is less concerned with classification than 'with communication and interpretation'.[41] Fowler highlights here an alternative use of genre. Instead of being a pigeonhole or elaborate filing system for different literary forms, genre is more usefully considered, according to Fowler, as a carrier pigeon or communicator of meaningful messages. Arguing that by establishing repeatable structural forms genre creates specific expectations, which a writer can then fulfil or disappoint in ways which communicate meaning, Fowler introduces a theory of presumptive interpretation. Involving a simple binary method of reading in which a text either complies with or denies its generic model in significant ways, this use of genre can still not guarantee precision of meaning. For even if a text denies its stated generic form this does not necessarily provoke an unambiguous interpretation. The case of *The Jew of Malta*, whose subverted tragic form has produced critical confusion, amply attests to this point. Consequently, genre is not only an unsatisfactory taxonomic tool; it is also an equivocatory exegetical device.

The confusion induced by the thwarting of structural expectations is most obviously illustrated in the court-room scene at the beginning of *The Jew of Malta*. As Barabas is robbed of his wealth by Ferneze, the drama cites and recites different literary and biblical models each of which the narrative fails to satisfy. According to David Bevington in *From 'Mankind' to Marlowe*, the entire play should be read as a homiletic drama or generalized story about Man's spiritual journey. Bevington argues that 'The vicious and degenerated comedy in the later scenes is integral to the conception of the whole work as a homiletic intrigue'.[42] By reading the drama as an expression of the morality play genre, Bevington determines that the court-room scene should be interpreted as a test of Worldly Man's soul. However, even a brief consideration of the scene reveals that the structural models it recites produce complex and ambiguous significances which cannot be accounted for by recourse to the requirements of a single genre. The scene defies generic simplification. The court-room scene produces so many different readings that the play's protagonist becomes simultaneously identified with a number of contradictory archetypes from a variety of literary and biblical genres; during the course of the scene, Barabas is identified with Everyman, with the Jews who called for Christ's execution, with the thief released in Christ's place and even with Christ himself.

Structured around the reading of the knights' three Articles, the scene echoes Pontius Pilate's thrice-denied appeal to the Jews to release Jesus Christ (Luke 23: 18). Consequently, as Marlowe's Barabas rejects the Governor's successive decrees he is aligned with those biblical Jews who, rebuffing Pilate's attempts to liberate Jesus, chose instead to free a bandit named 'Barabbas' (John 18: 40). Confusing the operations of exegesis, the play posits Barabas in a doubly villainous role. Marlowe's Barabas is at once identified with those Jews who called for Christ to be crucified as well as the thief in whose place Christ died. What is more, the initial identifications invited by the court-room scene are further complicated when Ferneze justifies his treatment of Barabas in terms which recall the words of the Jewish Pharisee, Caiaphas. Ferneze tells Barabas that he has taken his wealth:

> To save the ruin of a multitude:
> And better one want for a common good,
> Than many perish for a private man
> (I.ii.100–102)

Ferneze's speech echoes Caiaphas's justification for betraying Christ to the Romans. As Judith Weil explains:

> Marlowe's allusion in this passage is one which an Elizabethan would almost certainly hear. Ferneze chooses words similar to those of the Jewish high-priest Caiaphas (John 11: 50) in order to 'justify' his treatment of Barabas: 'Nor yet do you consider that it is expedient for vs, that one man dye for the people, and that the whole nacion perish not'. He thereby aligns Barabas with Christ as victim and redeemer.[43]

Hence, Barabas is ultimately recreated in the scene as a Christ figure. His financial sacrifice is imagined as analogous to Christ's own physical sacrifice on the cross.

Ignoring the complex and contradictory significances of the scene, G. K. Hunter maintains in his influential article 'The Theology of Marlowe's *The Jew of Malta*' that 'the theological status of the Jew, typified by the name Barabas, was fixed and immutable'.[44] However, by constraining readings of Marlowe's play within the cement of biblical precedent, Hunter fails to notice that instead of being a point of interpretative clarity, the protagonist's name is in fact a site of ambiguity in *The Jew of Malta*. Named after the bandit who was freed in Jesus's place, Marlowe's Barabas should represent all that is loathsome to a Christian audience. However, Barabas's humorous complicity with the audience, coupled with his unfair treatment by the Christian characters in the play, creates him as an altogether more complex and less easily-defined character than Hunter would have critics believe. Indeed Barabas's moral ambivalence represents in miniature *The Jew of Malta*'s own generic indeterminacy, the play's refusal to live up to its named genre. Like the drama in which he appears, Barabas remains generically indefinable. He is the self-consuming centre of the play which eats away at the very possibility of absolute interpretation or absolute classification. Hence, even as a critical instrument of communication, genre proves unreliable. If genre is a carrier pigeon, it is one which comes home to roost in unpredictable and complicated ways. Indeed, the only thing which one can rely upon about genre in *The Jew of Malta* is that it will complicate those certainties for which it is popularly held to be valuable and worthwhile.

So What Is Genre Really Like?

Unable to classify or to communicate meaning in decisive ways, genre radically fails to fulfil its potential. By staging the shortcomings of conventional definitions of genre, *The Jew of Malta* reveals instead the concept's illusory nature. Ostensibly promising the clarification of literary forms and textual interpretations, genre in fact produces indeterminacy and equivocation. Genre is consequently shown to be a concept which cannot live up to its reputation, tantalizingly dangling the promise of an absolute order which it can never really deliver. It is this gap between the mythic and the actual uses of genre which demand the concept's redefinition. In her *Critical Idiom* study, Heather Dubrow offers a description of genre which is significantly different from conventional definitions. She maintains

> that genre invites yet another analogy from daily experience: the way a social institution, such as an established church or a legislative body functions. It is often possible to challenge such institutions, sometimes to overthrow them, but it is virtually impossible simply to exclude them from our lives. Because so many members of the culture do accept them, an attempt to ignore them acquires intensity and resonance.[45]

Dubrow points out here that like a social institution, genre may be challenged but never entirely destroyed because it possesses a certain cultural currency. The quality of persistence which Dubrow bestows upon genre becomes more intelligible when her analogy is taken to its logical conclusion. Like a legal institution, genre claims to establish a set of unimpeachable rules. However, also like a legal institution, genre's creation of these rules at the same time implies that they must ultimately be broken. A rule cannot exist without simultaneously bearing testimony to the possibility of its transgression. Consequently, legal institutions are created with an awareness of their own limitations and hence an in-built failure mechanism which allows them to persist; because the law anticipates its transgression, it has already compensated for the possibility of its failure and therefore cannot fail utterly. Similarly, genre establishes a set of rules which assume their eventual subversion. Genre can therefore only persist by at the same time expecting to be overthrown. The concept is consequently less involved with promising absolute order than with acknowledging the inevitability of exception, transgression and subversion.[46]

It is, moreover, this inevitability that preoccupies *The Jew of Malta* and which is rehearsed as numerous political and religious agreements are made, only to be broken. Opening with the knights' refusal to comply with the Turkish demand for tribute money and their subsequent flouting of the league with Selim-Calymath, the play stages statutory defiance. When Friar Barnardine uses Abigail's dying confession to blackmail her father, even canon law is broken in the drama. Friar Barnardine explains to the dying Abigail that he is legally not permitted to reveal her confession because:

> The canon law forbids it, and the priest
> That makes it known, being degraded first,
> Shall be condemned, and then sent to the fire.
> (III.vi.34–6)

However, transgressing the law he describes, Friar Barnardine does betray Abigail's confession. One of a number of law-breakers in *The Jew of Malta*, Friar Barnardine simply emulates the perfidiousness with which all human relations are regulated in the play, including Barabas's relationship with his daughter Abigail, and Mathias and Lodowick's friendship, both of which culminate in the ultimate illegal act of murder. All conventional codes of behaviour, all the absolutes which govern our lives, are found to be unsustainable in *The Jew of Malta*. Instead, what we are left with is the inevitability of transgression, exception and contamination. Consequently, degeneration is as much a characteristic of genre as are genesis, generation and regeneration.

This more complex post-structuralist description of genre finds expression in *The Jew of Malta*, a play which overturns biblical, social and literary absolutes to dwell upon notions of lawlessness, contamination and decomposition. Most obviously, the play is obsessed with images of disease. At the slave market Barabas tells the audience in an aside:

> I ha' the poison of the city for him,
> And the white leprosy.
> (II.iii.54–5)

Imagining Malta complete with its own poison, possibly the Ancona toxin recalled later (III.iv.69), and a leprous virus or plague, Barabas presents the world of the play as a place of contagion and pestilence. Polluted not only by illness, however, the island is also infected with a sexual corruption which spreads from the prostitute, Bella Mira, to the nuns and friars. Alluding to the consequences of the nuns' carnality, Barabas dwells upon pictures of increase, such as 'every year they swell, and yet they live' (IV.i.6), which marry together images of pregnancy with cancerous enlargement. This association of sex and sickness culminates in the mass poisoning of the nuns which dramatizes the ultimate act of degeneration – death.

In the past, critics of *The Jew of Malta* have been eager to attribute its plot inconsistencies and historical inaccuracies to the textual 'badness' of its quarto. However, this need not be the only explanation. Within a play which contemplates degeneration both literally and metaphorically, it is possible that these ruptures in logic are actually part of a network of structural incoherence which underlines the inevitability of generic exception, contamination and breakdown. For instance, one of the most contradictory narrative moments in the play occurs when Lodowick professes his love for Abigail, claiming 'Barabas, thou know'st I have loved thy daughter long' (II.iii.292), to which Barabas replies 'And so has she done you, even from a child' (II.iii.293). Apparently ignorant of Lodowick's statement to Mathias an act earlier that not only has he never seen Abigail before but he has never even heard of her (I.ii.393–406), Barabas collaborates with Lodowick in a textual falsification which pre-dates the love affair. Although this narrative inconsistency may be an intentional lie on Barabas's part, in order to emphasize Lodowick's improper haste in arranging his marriage to Abigail, the scene nevertheless remains a blunder of reason.[47] Alternatively, the plot inconsistency can be read as a deliberate debasement of the Aristotelian principle of plausibility, an enactment of the way in which genre inevitably unravels rather than maintains narrative structures.

Similarly, historical inaccuracies in the play need not be read as instances of hasty composition or deficient knowledge, but instead as expressions of generic deterioration and indeterminacy. For instance, when Martin Del Bosco attempts to persuade Ferneze to break his league with the Turks, he reminds the Governor of Malta how the citizens of Rhodes defied a similar Turkish invasion force. He explains:

> For when their hideous force invironed Rhodes,
> Small though the number was that kept the town,
> They fought it out, and not a man survived
> To bring the hapless news to Christendom.
> (II.ii.48–51)

Martin Del Bosco offers Ferneze the seige of Rhodes as an example of how far good Christians will go to withstand the Turkish threat. According to Martin Del Bosco, the citizens of Rhodes all sacrificed their lives resisting the infidel force. Indeed, Martin Del Bosco claims that so many Christians died at Rhodes there was no one left alive to bring the news to the surviving Christian nations. However, as Coburn Freer points out in 'Lies and Lying in *The Jew of Malta*', in reality the island of Rhodes was not destroyed by the Turks. In fact, the citizens of Rhodes surrendered to their Turkish invaders without loss of life.[48] Similarly, the description of the siege of Malta in the play lacks historical authenticity. In Marlowe's play the island falls to the Turks and Barabas is briefly made its governor before Ferneze seizes back control at the end of the drama. The less dramatic, although more accurate, outcome of the siege of Malta saw the infidel army simply give up and go home.[49]

The Jew of Malta is peppered with textual and historical inconsistencies which when read alongside the images of decay, deterioration and contamination in the play enact the very processes of genre, the inevitability of structural breakdown. What Marlowe's play discloses again and again is the inability of a genre to keep its paradigm free from contamination by other narrative structures. Consequently, the model of a genre is always compromised by its application. It is this circumstance that most radically contradicts conventional notions of genre which largely depend on the practicability of a pristine originary model. It is this model which enables criticism to classify literary forms accurately and to formulate interpretations of texts according to how far they comply with, or diverge from, certain structural expectations. However, the description of genre staged by *The Jew of Malta* and posited by post-structuralist theories obviously dispenses with this notion of para-digmatic purity. This dismissal of originary models has far-reaching consequences for those concepts of originality and imitation already discussed in the chapters on the two parts of *Tamburlaine* and *Dido, Queene of Carthage*. In the case of *The Jew of Malta*, revisions to the notion of the originary model are expressed in terms of a series of generic parodies, which will be considered next.

Questioning the Possibility of the Paradigm

The very idea of genre rests on the possibility of a pristine, transcendent paradigm. An originary model, the paradigm forms the template from which all subsequent theories of generic classification, communication and imitation are extrapolated. However, the paradigm depends on a notion of originality which is radically unsustainable. For the paradigm to be truly paradigmatic, it must be utterly and uncompromisingly original; it must be born of a specific moment before which there was nothing. The paradigm must come absolutely first or else it is simply a version or a derivation of another form and hence not completely immaculate and inviolable. The originary principle which underpins the notion of the paradigm is therefore unstable; it posits the possibility of an event happening outside of time in a place where there was never anything before. The paradigm is, therefore, a paradoxical entity. To be useful as a literary tool, it must be ahistorical, but to be possible as a concept, it cannot help but exist within time. In *Beyond Genre*, Paul Henradi poses the quandary on which the generic paradigm is based. Henradi ponders: 'How can I define tragedy (or any other genre) before I know on which works to base the definition, yet how can I know on which works to base the definition before I have defined tragedy?'[50] Henradi notes here that the notion of a pristine, ahistorical paradigm which encapsulates the originary moment when a genre's characteristics were created is not possible, because a tragedy could not be identified or described without there having been a form already in existence with the same features and name. In other words, a definition of genre cannot occur before works of literature have evolved to create and to distinguish the requirements of that structural form. The generic paradigm consequently falters in the space between the possibility of the spontaneous commencement of an artistic ideal and the evolutionary development of a literary tradition. Laying claim to a transcendent and isolated artistic uniqueness which it can never temporally defend, the originary model perpetuates a relentless search for that which came first which can only ever end in disappointment and failure.

The quest which genre inspires to locate the illusory co-ordinates of the originary paradigm may be noted in the work of those Marlovian scholars who attempt to freeze *The Jew of Malta* in the precedence of the past. In *The Reckoning*, Charles Nicholl maintains that Marlowe came by the idea for Barabas's poisoned porridge from Richard Baines's confession to the head of the Catholic Seminary at Rheims that he intended 'to "inject poison" into the college well, or the communal bath, and so take off the whole seminary in one fell swoop.'[51] In a similar vein, critics such as John Bakeless and N. W. Bawcutt have argued over the likelihood that Thomas Heywood added the sub-plot of the twice-murdered Friar (IV.i) when he came to revise the play.[52] Basing this hypothesis upon Heywood's use of the same device in his own drama, *The Captives*, which was performed in 1624, critics shift the burden of originality from one author to another, and the point of origination from one century to the next.[53] Despite criticism's desire to identify immaculate originary moments for the events of Marlowe's play, scholarship must eventually acknowledge that originality is always historically contingent and that no event can happen unequivocally first. As David Quint explains in *Origin and Originality*: 'For all the appearance it may lend the work of art of escaping the relativity of human history, originality is itself a relative quality.'[54]

Genre cannot stand apart from or above history, but always and in spite of its very nature, in relation to it. The inevitable friction which results from this collision of invention and convention is enacted in *The Jew of Malta*, a drama which seems to go out of its way to put new twists on old forms. Often accorded the status of a groundbreaking theatrical enterprise, the play is the subject of a heated critical debate about the originality of its presentation of Jewishness and Machiavellianism. Emphasizing that Marlowe 'did not merely borrow, but *created* stereotypes in his plays which later dramatists copied, developed from, or sometimes parodied',[55] John Bakeless typifies the critical perception of the play as the first step on a causeway of creativity which carried generic patterns forwards to inspire and be imitated by future generations. This appraisal of Marlowe's originality must, however, ignore those literary events which pre-date *The Jew of Malta*. Far from being the first Jew presented on the English stage, Barabas was actually a racial and character type with whom Elizabethan audiences would have been familiar. Printed as early as 1584, Robert Wilson's *The Three Ladies of London* contains a sympathetic portrait of a Jewish usurer named Gerontus. Forced to take a duplicitous merchant to court to regain a long-overdue loan, Gerontus eventually forgives the man his debt rather than force him to renounce his Christianity and thereby nullify their contract. Employing the Jew as a foil for Christian corruption, Wilson introduces a dramatic technique of religious satire which Marlowe adopts in his own play. Moreover, there is evidence to indicate that a secular Jew play existed even before Wilson's drama. Mentioned in Stephen Gosson's *The Schoole of Abuse* (1579) as an exemplary piece of theatre, the play is quite simply called *The Jew*. Gosson records 'The *Iew* and *Ptolome*, shown at the Bull, the one representing the greedinesse of worldly chusers, and bloody mindes of userers: the other very liuely descrybing how seditious estates, with their owne deuises, false friendes with their owne swoordes and rebellious commons in their owne snares are owerthrowne.'[56] Constructing a network of connections from greed to violence to the illumination of Christian vice, the theatrical idea of Jewishness in the secular drama of Marlowe's time was already established before *The Jew of Malta*.

Similarly, *The Jew of Malta*'s exploitation of political maxims commonly associated with the political writer Niccolò Machiavelli was neither unusual nor unique. Although never explicitly ascribed to the Italian counsellor, the *raisons d'être* of a number of Elizabethan stage villains coincides with the popular contemporary perception of Machiavellianism. Characters such as Lorenzo in Thomas Kyd's *Spanish Tragedy* (1587?), who murders his cousin and imprisons his sister, and Marlowe's own atheist tyrant, Tamburlaine, in the two plays of the same name (1587 and 1588?), display codes of behaviour which some critics maintain did not originate until *The Jew of Malta* half a decade later. What is more, the theatrical portrayal of Machiavellianism was only one of a series of influences generated by the civil servant's work. As N. W. Bawcutt argues in 'Machiavelli and Marlowe's *The Jew of Malta*': 'Sixteenth-century readers rarely saw Machiavelli in isolation; they tended to place him within existing traditions of thought, and what is more, to conflate and assimilate his ideas into those traditions.'[57] The reconstruction of Machiavelli on the Elizabethan stage was therefore only one in a knot of originary moments which bind *The Prince* to Innocent Gentillet's counter-attack and the principles of classical political philosophy. Machiavelli's thought, like Marlowe's artistry, was implicated in a number of 'firsts' which together cancel out the very possibility of locating a singular moment of originary creativity.

The inevitable failure of the generic paradigm to remain free from the corruption of earlier forms, of other texts, is examined in *The Jew of Malta* when the playwright self-consciously parodies one of his non-dramatic works. Paradoxically plagiarizing himself, Marlowe places the words of his lyric 'The

Passionate Shepherd to his Love' in the mouth of Ithamore, to distort and paraphrase. Ithamore tells his lover, Bellamira the prostitute:

> Content, but we will leave this paltry land,
> And sail from hence to Greece, to lovely Greece,
> I'll be thy Jason, thou my golden fleece;
> Where painted carpets o'er the meads are hurled,
> And Bacchus' vineyards over-spread the world:
> Where woods and forests go in goodly green,
> I'll be Adonis, thou shalt be Love's Queen.
> The meads, the orchards, and the primrose lanes,
> Instead of sedge and reed, bear sugar canes:
> Thou in those groves, by Dis above,
> Shalt live with me and be my love.
> (IV.ii.86–96)[58]

Within the course of the first three lines of the speech Ithamore dispenses with blank verse in order to adopt the same scheme of rhyming couplets as Marlowe's own lyric. This is, however, where the similarity between the two pieces of verse ceases. Transforming Marlowe's pastoral love-entreaty into an erotic epyllion, Ithamore disregards the delights of country living in favour of the exotic and counterfeit pleasures of the classical world. Rather than exploit the resources of nature in the creation of wool gowns and belts of straw like Marlowe's shepherd, Ithamore chooses 'Instead' to replace 'sedge and reed' with the excess of 'sugar canes'. Finally punctuating the fantasy by swearing to the fearful Roman god of the underworld, Dis, Ithamore creates a poem which stands in stark contrast to the swain's appeal to simplicity. Moreover, contextualizing the lyric in the action of the drama, Marlowe ironizes Ithamore's deployment of a sexually-persuasive poem in the courtship of a prostitute who has already been bought. By rendering a familiar form in a new way, Marlowe demonstrates not only the proliferation of so-called 'originals' which obliterate the concept of the originary paradigm, but also the inevitable artistic dialogue between different texts which imitation cannot help but initiate.

This dialogue of intertextuality significantly extends the intellectual borders of Marlowe's poem by juxtaposing it with other works. Consequently, just as Ithamore's verse is satirized by comparison with Marlowe's original, Marlowe's original is also affected by its re-contextualization in a process that questions the certainty with which Marlowe's lyric can be read. As Simon Shepherd maintains, Ithamore's parody asks 'questions about the status of his

[Marlowe's] own love lyric and its unspoken context'.[59] Opening the poem to interpretation, Marlowe's foregrounding of intertextuality must ultimately shoulder responsibility for the feverish poetic activity which his lyric excited. Answered directly in Sir Walter Ralegh's 'Nymph's Reply', 'The Passionate Shepherd' is also imitated, parodied and satirized in the anonymous 'Come live with me and be my dear', John Donne's 'The Bait' and J. Paulin's 'Love's Contentment'.[60] Unpicking the stitches of the originary paradigm, Marlowe enables the seams of his own lyric to expand and unfold outside the drama in a movement which confutes the generic principles of temporal isolationism and artistic individuality.

Crossing the Borders of Genre

Unable to locate a single, unitary moment of beginning, the generic paradigm is likewise unable to establish a point of absolute closure. Consequently, the borders of genre remain unpoliced and open to invasion. Illustrating this circumstance, *The Jew of Malta* dramatizes again and again the inability of genre to find an ending. For instance, in the first scene when Barabas is awaiting news of his argosy, the audience is encouraged to expect that the ship will be lost at sea and the Machiavellian Jew thereby punished. Manufacturing a sense of foreboding, the First Merchant tells Barabas that although he does not know what has happened to the argosy, he has heard his crew talk of her:

> They wondered how you durst with so much wealth
> Trust such a crazèd vessel, and so far.
> (I.i.81–2)

Barabas's concern for the fate of his argosy establishes a narrative expectation which the scene ultimately fails to fulfil. Indeed, a Second Merchant arrives moments later bringing news of the argosy's safe return laden with wealth. Barabas therefore confounds the divine judgement the play structurally gestures towards. An otherwise superfluous narrative moment, the exchange about the argosy serves to demonstrate the inability of genre to effect an expected ending and to create an anticipated outcome. Similarly, some time later in the play, when the Governor of Malta is told of Barabas's death, the audience is again tantalized with the expectation of an absolute conclusion. On hearing that the recently-arrested Barabas has died in gaol, Ferneze instructs his officers to throw the Jew's corpse out of the city walls.[61] Left on stage alone, however, the body stands up, not to receive the applause which conventionally mark the end of a play, but rather to reveal that the drama is not yet over. Commenting upon this moment in 'Renaissance Execution and Marlovian Elocution: The Drama of Death', Karen Cunningham notes that 'In these revivifications, Marlowe flaunts the possibility of fraudulent closure, of something amiss.'[62] The ending of the play which the protagonist's death usually signals is snatched away from the audience of *The Jew of Malta* in a moment which dramatically confuses theatrical convention. The actor playing Barabas gets to his feet in a movement which is at once a part of the play and an anticipation of the end of the play. For were it really the end of *The Jew of Malta*, the actor playing Barabas would, of course, rise from his character's death to receive the applause. In this instance, however, the actor rises from his death not because it is the end of the play but because his death has been a pretence both in theatrical as well as in narrative terms. The actor playing the Jew is therefore still in character; he is still Barabas and his play has still not reached its conclusion. The audience is consequently made to consider the difference between a real and a false ending. *The Jew of Malta* unravels the traditionally inviolable borders of genre to show the inevitable ruptures and flaws which allow art to transgress expectation and defy predictability.

In an endeavour to test the limits of genre, *The Jew of Malta* repeatedly stages the crossing over, through or beneath boundaries. Ranging from physical borderlines, such as the balcony Abigail throws the money bags over (II.i.46), and the 'dark entry' (III.iv.79) the nuns take the poisoned porridge through, 'Where they must neither see the messenger,/Nor make inquiry who hath sent it' (III.iv.80–81), to more metaphorical structures such as the family, the play dwells upon the violation of places which are meant to be sacrosanct. Rehearsing the penetration of supposedly inviolate structures, *The Jew of Malta* illustrates the unsustainability of the pristine generic paradigm. When Barabas rises on the other side of the city walls, he recovers in order to pass back across the divide and return to Malta once more; this time, however, Barabas is accompanied by an invasion force. Explaining to Calymath that he knows a way to enter the island fortress, Barabas says:

> Fear not, my lord, for here against the sluice,
> The rock is hollow, and of purpose digged,
> To make a passage for the running streams
> And common channels of the city.
> (V.i.87–90)

Conducting the Turks through the drains of the city, Barabas vitiates the city's isolation, inviting the enemy within. Literally passing through the boundaries of the island, Barabas demonstrates the inability of genre to remain closed. What is more, by infiltrating the city in this way, Barabas draws attention to the fundamental lie on which the island rests and on which the concept of genre falters: the lie of an immaculate state. At pains to generate the myth of its own purity, Malta's population is actually an ethnic melting-pot even before the Turks' invasion. Far from the bastion of Catholicism which the Knights of Saint John claim, the city is the halfway house of the world's aliens, an Ellis island writ large. However, unlike Ellis Island, no one is really an immigrant in Malta, because no one is a native. Instead, Malta is populated by different sections of humanity, by Jews, Turks, Spaniards, and Frenchmen, who are only distinguishable from one another by their access to and maintenance of the means of power. As Emily Bartels maintains, 'the play represents Malta itself as a place of difference – not in relation to some other, but within itself, and precisely because of its undefinable position outside.'[63] Failing to contain or to exclude the many contradictory and competing racial and ethnic factions in the play, Malta, like genre, is exposed as an essentially porous entity.

The permeability of genre, which renders it defenceless against pollution, is also staged familially throughout the play. It is worthwhile remembering here Wittgenstein's analogy between the common trait of generic taxonomy and familial resemblance. In a sequence of episodes which restate Hamlet's assertion, 'A little more than kin and less than kind', *The Jew of Malta* distorts the borders of the family group. For instance, Barabas's family is in a constant state of redefinition and reclassification. Upon discovering Abigail has returned to the nunnery Barabas adopts his slave and disinherits his daughter. As Barabas explains to his new son:

> for thy sake, whom I so dearly love,
> Now shalt thou see the death of Abigail,
> That thou mayst freely live to be my heir.
> (III.iv.61–3)

Casting aside his blood relative, Barabas embraces Ithamore into the family only to poison him later. Like the supposedly leaky body of the Jewish male, who was thought to menstruate,[64] the family group simultaneously admits and discharges its members by acts which redraw the lines of exclusion and inclusion. This challenge to ontological fullness culminates when Barabas is thrown out of the city walls and into another paradox.

As has been already explained, the resurrected 'corpse' of Barabas thwarts generic expectations of closure by crossing the physical and metaphorical borders which the play erects. More importantly, however, when Barabas gets to his feet 'outside' Malta he confuses the imaginative territories of theatrical space in a gesture which raises doubts about what is in and what is out. Thrown over the city's walls, Barabas is, dramatically speaking, on the outer edges of Maltese civilization. However, recovering himself on stage, it is clear to the audience that he remains within an enclosed structure – the very wooden 'O' which contains them also. Thus when Barabas exclaims ironically 'What, all alone?' (V.i.61), he is marking a dramatic double take; for in spite of his solitary presence on the stage he is not the only one inside the theatre's environs. Making much of this moment in relation to the sociological place of the Elizabethan stage outside London's city limits, Stephen Mullaney observes: 'in rising from his apparent double death, Barabas does transform the space he occupies; he translates it back into the theatrical space it has always been, now glimpsed at its recreative and nihilistic extreme.'[65] What is more, exposing that out is not always outside, but often and surprisingly within, *The Jew of Malta* complicates the parameters of the generic paradigm beyond rehabilitation. Indeed finally striking a deathblow against the critical assumption that genre is a pristine, timeless, unchanging and inviolable notion, the play re-presents the concept as a saggy mass of unravelling seams. Like Scrooge's Ghost of Christmas Present, then, the colossal and festive promise of genre must finally sweep aside its cloak to reveal the horror it conceals – the starvelings at its feet. If we look more closely, however, we can recognize these children – they are Prejudice and Fear and their family name is Stereotype.

Stereotypes

The human face of structures of classification, the stereotype replicates those paradigmatic principles which make genre both what it is, as well as what it can ultimately never be. Founded on certainties of difference which enable the classification of humanity within prescribed limits, the stereotype is the direct descendant of the same generic concerns which preoccupy *The Jew of Malta*. Coincidentally, the term 'stereotype' is derived from the vocabulary of the letterpress, which enabled classical genres to be widely transmitted and imitated during the Renaissance. A component of the printing-press image considered earlier, the stereotype is implicated ahistorically in the operations of artistic reproduction which confuse creativity and conventionality. In

Difference and Pathology, Sander L. Gilman explains that stereotyping was a method for casting multiple papier-mâché copies of a letter type from a reusable mould introduced in the late eighteenth century.[66] By the nineteenth century, Gilman explains, the phrase had become an abstraction.[67] Noting the importance of the term's etymology, Gilman continues: 'When, during the early twentieth century, social psychologists adopted *stereotype* to designate the images through which we categorize the world, they were perhaps more conscious than are we that "immutable structure" was essential to the meaning of the term they were appropriating.'[68] Consequently, like genre, the stereotype depends for its usefulness upon consistent reproduction: upon the duplication of a fixed set of imperatives in isolation from contextual complication.

In 'The Other Question ... The Stereotype and Colonial Discourse', Homi Bhabha elaborates upon Gilman's observations by underlining the paradox on which the stereotype rests:

> Fixity, as the sign of cultural/historical/racial difference in the discourse of colonialism, is a paradoxical mode of representation: it connotes a rigidity and an unchanging order as well as disorder, degeneracy and daemonic repetition. Likewise the stereotype, which is its major discursive strategy is a form of knowledge and identification that vacillates between what is always 'in place', already known, and something that must be anxiously repeated.[69]

According to Bhabha the stereotype is at once self-assured and self-doubting; it proffers an immutable form which it knows to be an impossibility in an ever-changing world. Indeed, as Bhabha explains, the stereotype 'is a simplification because it is an arrested, fixated form of representation that, in denying the play of difference ... constitutes a problem for the representation of the subject'.[70] The rejection of difference on which the stereotype is predicated proves insupportable, not only in relation to other forms, but also in relation to its own structure which can never be fixed and unitary. Jeremy Tambling points out the inevitability of the stereotype's mutability in 'Abigail's Party: "The Difference of Things"'. Tambling maintains that 'The Other is either potential Machiavel and capitalist or exploited figure ... the stranger in Elizabethan drama cannot be taken univocally: the figure frustrates clear lines of division.'[71] In spite of the ever-losing battle against diversity which the stereotype is forced to wage, it remains a much used form, especially in political propaganda. Perhaps this is because it offers, even if only for an instant, the Faustian promise to 'wall all Germany with brass', to re-present reality within man-made limits.

The stereotype is most often employed in colonial discourses as the site of justification; it is the place where inequality, injustice and invasion find exoneration. Explaining the political uses of the stereotype, Bhabha notes: 'The objective of colonial discourse is to construe the colonized as a population of degenerate types on the basis of racial origin, in order to justify conquest and to establish systems of administration and instruction.'[72] By reductively represent-ing the colonized as the opposite of Westerners, the colonizers can forgive themselves for treating them unfairly. However, to portray the colonized as the antithesis of the self, the stereotype must not only appear fixed and repeatable, it must in reality prove mutable enough to compensate for alterations in the subject's sense of its self. Extrapolated from those features which the self finds most incompatible with its own self-image, the Other must be constantly revised and reviewed to compensate for possible changes in selfhood. Gilman summarizes this process:

> Stereotypes are a crude set of mental representations of the world. They are palimpsests on which the initial bipolar representations are still vaguely legible. They perpetuate a needed sense of difference between the 'self' and the 'object', which becomes the 'Other'. Because there is no real line between self and the Other, an imaginary line must be drawn; and so that the illusion of an absolute difference between self and Other is never troubled, this line is as dynamic in its ability to alter itself as is the self.[73]

When the self's consciousness alters, the perception of the Other must also alter. In this way, the stereotype, like genre, reveals that there is nothing outside itself: that subject and object, or Other, are one and the same. Jeremy Tambling notes that the notion of the Other as extension of the self is staged in *The Jew of Malta* through the character of Barabas, who 'embodies, in terms of what he is taken to be, the features of the Christian society Christians most resent in themselves'.[74] Implicated in a mass psychological exorcism, the stereotype allowed Christian society to rid itself of its own demons by depositing them on the shoulders of the Jew. However, complicating and illuminating debates about the Other and the usefulness of the stereotype, Barabas self-consciously colonizes the techniques of colonial control to which he is subject.

One of the most controversial moments in the play, Barabas's 'I walk abroad a-nights' speech (II.iii.178–205), renders truth and falsehood indistinguishable. Offering a villainous example to his slave Ithamore, Barabas describes his exploits to date. Exploits, it must be remembered, which occur outside the realm of the play and therefore beyond the possibility of verification. Summoning up a catalogue of wrongdoing, Barabas records how he killed sick people while practising medicine in Italy, murdered soldiers under the pretence of war as an engineer and finally drove bankrupts to commit suicide while a usurer in Europe. Heaping stereotypical crime upon crime, Barabas creates a curriculum vitae which any Elizabethan Vice would be proud to call his own. Whether or not these crimes are based on fact remains irresolvable and ultimately irrelevant; true or false, disease, war and poverty are the endemic evils of Western society for which the Jew has been vilified for centuries. Thus, like Christ taking on the sins of the world at his crucifixion, Barabas notes every offence of which his race has been accused and assimilates them into one gargantuan figure, one great self-conscious stereotype to which no further monstrousness can be appended. Commenting on this scene, Simon Shepherd observes: 'The audience is not privileged to watch an ignorant alien unwittingly conforming to stereotype, but the fictional character looks back at them when he consciously performs a role they expect: the stereotype is thus not naturalised but acted.'[75]

The conscious adoption of the Jewish stereotype which Barabas rehearses above is simultaneously a gesture of defiance as well as an obeisance to conformity. Like locking one's own cell door, Barabas's assumption of the Jewish stereotype shows that he too can wield the key to Western colonialization, even if it must always be at the expense of his own freedom. Thus, despite Barabas's failure to emancipate the Jew from colonial discourse, his speech does succeed in destabilizing the terms of the debate. As Emily Bartels explains: 'The discrepancies within Barabas's representation of the Jew, like those within the text's, expose this identity as a fictional construct exploited as strategy and not offered as "truth".'[76] Disclosing the strategic nature of the stereotype, Barabas unfixes the techniques of colonial control to reveal that they are artificial, contingent and mutable. Thus, the means by which Europe contained the Other and identified itself are found to be arbitrary and limited. In the final scene of *The Jew of Malta* the play's consideration of structures of control culminates in the collapsing gallery which, like genre and the stereotype, embodies the promise of repetition, the tantalizing potential to do it all again.

The Promise of Repetition

Discovered in the stage direction of the 1633 edition '*with a hammer above, very busy*' (V.v), Barabas and the carpenters put the finishing touches to the collapsible gallery which has been set or framed to trap the Turkish general, Calymath. Erected for the sole purpose of imminent dismantling, the gallery emblematizes the self-defeating operations of genre – which is always fashioned with an in-built self-destruct button. What is more, like genre, the false balcony is a communal construction, edified by the consensual efforts of the carpenters who check off Barabas's list of requirements. Calling the work 'art indeed' (V.v.5), Barabas identifies his fellow helpers as artisans; they are the co-creators of his elaborate dramatic production. However, brought into use prematurely, the balcony betrays its creator when Ferneze cuts the cord and 'drops' Barabas through his own infernal mechanism. Revealed on stage in a cauldron below the gallery, Barabas's supposed fall illustrates the covert and fraudulent manner in which genre works; visibly no different, the balcony is not actually broken and Barabas does not really plummet into the boiling pot – he is found there. The processes of genre compensate for something missing, for an elemental authenticity which art can never supply.

In spite of his failure to execute the trick correctly and his own related downfall, Barabas remains vociferous to the end. Exposing his disruption of the drama's tragic form with his unrepentant list of grisly crimes, Barabas dies swearing, as his creator was reputed to have done only a year or so later.[77] However, even in the clutches of death and dramatic closure, the play transgresses generic boundaries. When Barabas finally emerges from the cauldron to receive his applause as an actor, not only is the play's lack of containment underlined, but also its re-productivity. The reusable balcony of the theatre and the 'undead' actor emulate genre's imitable structure which offers the seductive opportunity to do it all again. Like the printing press which kept churning out pristine editions of ancient and contemporary literature, Renaissance drama was itself held captivated, or perhaps, captive, by the possibility of repetition.

Notes

1. All references to *The Jew of Malta* are taken from T. W. Craik's New Mermaid edition (1966). London, A. & C. Black.
2. Babb, H. S. (1957), p. 94.
3. Steane, J. B. (1964), p. 166.
4. Aristotle states in *The Poetics* that: 'Reserving hexameter poetry and Comedy for consideration hereafter, let us proceed now to the discussion of Tragedy' (16) Although hexameter poetry is discussed in chapters twenty-three, twenty-four and twenty-six, comedy is either forgotten altogether, or treated elsewhere in some lost tract.

5. See Craik, T. W. (1966), p. viii. The 1594 entry in the Stationers' Register was probably a blocking device to prevent rival publishers claiming the play as their own. It is therefore unlikely that an edition was actually printed at this time of which there is no mention and no extant copies.

6. Cardozo, J. L. (1925), p.15.

7. Bakeless, J. (1942), vol. 1, p. 361.

8. Raab, F. (1964), p. 53.

9. Bakeless. J. (1942), vol. 1, p. 328.

10. Bakeless. J. (1942), vol. 1, p. 328.

11. Bakeless. J. (1942), vol. 1, p. 328.

12. Bawcutt, N. W., ed. (1978), p. 1.

13. Bakeless. J. (1942), vol. 1, p. 332.

14. Lake, D. J. (1983), p. 142.

15. Bawcutt, N. W., ed. (1978), p. 45.

16. Bawcutt, N. W., ed. (1978), p. 46.

17. Maxwell, J. C. (1953), p. 438.

18. Maxwell, J. C. (1953), p. 438.

19. Rocklin, E. (1988), p. 140.

20. Leech, C. (1986), p. 174.

21. Cartelli, T. (1988), p. 119.

22. Eliot, T. S. (1920), p. 92.

23. Frye, N. (1957), p. 13.

24. *The Shorter Oxford English Dictionary on Historical Principles,* 3rd edition, ed. C. T. Onions (1944), entry for 'genre'.

25. Abrams, M. H. (1981), p. 70.

26. Colie, R. L. (1973), p. 3.

27. Aristotle (1941), p. ix.

28. Aristotle (1941), pp. 7–8.

29. Aristotle (1941), p. 10.

30. Aristotle (1941), p. 21.

31. Aristotle (1941), p. 42, p. 78.

32. Aristotle (1941), p. 25.

33. Colie, R. L. (1973), p. 115.

34. Said, E. (1979), p. 67.

35. Other sayings include (I.i.192) 'Ego mihimet sum semper proximus' or 'I am my own dearest friend', from Terence's *Andria* (IV.i.12); see also (II.i.39) 'Bien para todos mi ganada no es' or 'I don't want to hand over the money I have gained to everybody', according to Bawcutt, N. W., ed. (1978) p. 100. See also (II.i.68) 'Hermoso placer de los dineros' which is Spanish for 'the beautiful pleasure of money'. Of course these phrases add to Barabas's exoticism as well as presenting the notion of genre in microcosm.

36. Greenblatt, S. (1980), p. 207.

37. Greenblatt, S. (1980), p. 208.

38. Henradi, P. (1972), p. 4.

39. Wittgenstein, L. (1953), 32e: 67.

40. Fowler, A. (1982), p. 37.

41. Fowler, A. (1982), p. 37.

42. Bevington, D. (1962), p. 219.
43. Weil, J. (1977), pp. 27–8.
44. Hunter, G. K. (1964), p. 216.
45. Dubrow, H. (1982), p. 3.
46. For a fuller exposition of poststructuralist theories of genre see Jacques Derrida's lecture 'The Law of Genre' in which he claims that the law of the law of genre is 'a principle of contamination, a law of impurity, a parasitical economy' (Derrida, J. [1992], p. 227); in other words, genres cannot help but mix with each other. They must inevitably become impure because their rule of exclusion must always be broken.
47. For a detailed consideration of the use of lies in the play see Coburn Freer's chapter, 'Lies and Lying in *The Jew of Malta*', in *'A Poet and filthy Play-maker': New Essays on Christopher Marlowe*, eds Kenneth Friedenreich, Roma Gill and Constance B. Kuriyama (1988). New York, AMS Press Inc., pp. 143–65
48. Freer, C. (1988), p. 146.
49. For a fuller examination of this historical inaccuracy see Craik, T. W., ed. (1966), p. ix, and Bakeless, J. (1942), vol. 1, p. 336.
50. Henradi, P. (1972), p. 2.
51. Nicholl, C. (1992), p. 124.
52. Bakeless, J. (1942), vol. 1, p. 357; Bawcutt, N. W., ed. (1978), p. 16.
53. Strangled by a jealous husband, Friar John's corpse is mistaken by his rival, Friar Richard and struck with a staff in *The Captives* (2430). Believing himself guilty of murder, Friar Richard tries to escape from the Abbey only to be pursued by Friar John's dead body in full armour, mounted on a horse. Terrified by his victim's apparent resilience, Friar Richard confesses to a crime he did not commit. The true murderer finally reveals himself complete with a pardon, saving the innocent Friar's life.
54. Quint, D. (1983), p. 5.
55. Bakeless, J. (1942), vol. 1, p. 19.
56. Chambers, E. K. (1923), vol. 4, p. 204.
57. Bawcutt, N. W. (1970), p. 23.
58. Compare Ithamore's version with Marlowe's own:

Come live with me, and be my love,
And we will all the pleasures prove
That valleys, groves, hills and fields,
Woods, or steepy mountain yields.

And we will sit upon the rocks,
Seeing the shepherds feed their flocks
By shallow rivers, to whose falls
Melodious birds sing madrigals.

And I will make thee beds of roses,
And a thousand fragrant posies,

A cap of flowers, and a kirtle,
Embroidered all with leaves of myrtle.

A gown made of the finest wool
Which from our pretty lambs we pull,
Fair linèd slippers for the cold,
With buckles of the purest gold.

A belt of straw and ivy-buds,
With coral clasps and amber studs,
And if these pleasures may thee move,
Come live with me, and be my love.

The shepherd swains shall dance and sing
For thy delight each May morning.
If these delights thy mind may move,
Then live with me, and be my love. (211)

From Stephen Orgel's edition of *Christopher Marlowe: The Complete Poems and Translations* [1971]. Harmondsworth: Penguin Books Ltd, 1971, p. 211.

59. Shepherd, S. (1986), p. 185.
60. Sir Walter Ralegh's 'The Nymph's Reply' appeared in *England's Helicon* (1600) following Marlowe's poem:

If all the world and love were young,
And truth in every shepherd's tongue,
These pretty pleasures might me move
To live with thee and be thy love.

But Time drives flocks from field to fold,
When rivers rage and rocks grow cold,
And Philomel becometh dumb;
The rest complains of cares to come.

The flowers do fade, and wanton fields
To wayward winter reckoning yields;
A honey tongue, a heart of gall
Is fancy's spring, but sorrow's fall.

Thy gowns, thy shoes, thy beds of roses,
Thy cap, thy kirtle, and thy posies,
Soon break, soon wither, soon forgotten,
In folly ripe, in reason rotten.

Thy belt of straw and ivy buds,
Thy coral clasps and amber studs,
All these in me no means can move
To come to thee and be thy love.

But could youth last and love still breed,
Had joys no date, nor age no need,
Then these delights my mind might move
To live with thee and be thy love.

(Quoted in Orgel, S, [1971], p. 212.)

This anonymous piece also appeared in *England's Helicon* following Ralegh's poem:

Come live with me and be my dear,
And we will revel all the year,
In plains and groves, on hills and dales,
Where fragrant air breeds sweetest gales.

There shall you have the beauteous pine,
The cedar and the spreading vine,
And all the woods to be a screen,
Lest Phoebus kiss my summer's queen.

The seat for your disport shall be
Over some river, in a tree,
Where silver sands and pebbles sing
Eternal ditties with the spring.

There shall you see the nymphs at play,
And how the satyrs spend the day,
The fishes gliding on the sands,
Offering their bellies to your hands.

The birds with heavenly tuned throats
Possess woods-echoes with sweet notes,
Which to your senses will impart
A music to inflame the heart.

Upon the bare and leafless oak
The ring-doves' wooings will provoke
A colder blood than you possess
To play with me and do no less.

In bowers of laurel trimly dight
We will outwear the silent night,
While Flora busy is to spread
Her richest treasure on our bed.

Ten thousand glow-worms shall attend,
And all their sparkling lights shall spend,
All to adorn and beautify
Your lodging with most majesty.

Then in mine arms will I enclose
Lilies' fair mixture with the rose,
Whose nice perfections in love's play
Shall tune me to the highest key.

Thus as we pass the welcome night
In sportful pleasures and delight,
The nimble fairies on the grounds
Shall dance and sing melodious sounds.

If these may serve for to entice
Your presence to love's paradise,
Then come with me and be my dear,
And we will straight begin the year.

(Quoted in Orgel, S. [1971], pp. 213–14.)

John Donne's 'The Bait' is included in *Songs and Sonnets* but presumably written around 1600:

Come live with me and be my love,
And we will some new pleasures prove,
Of golden sands and crystal brooks,
With silken lines and silver hooks.

There will the river whispering run,
Warmed by thine eyes more than the sun;
And there th'enamoured fish will stay,
Begging themselves they may betray.

When thou wilt swim in that live bath,
Each fish, which every channel hath,
Will amorously to thee swim,
Gladder to catch thee than thou him.

If thou to be so seen beest loth
By sun or moon, thou dark'nest both;
And if myself have leave to see
I need not their light, having thee.

Let other freeze with angling reeds,
And cut their legs with shells and weeds,
Or treacherously poor fish beset
With strangling snare, or windowy net:

Let coarse bold hands from slimy nest
The bedded fish in banks out-wrest,
Or curious traitors, sleave-silk flies
Bewitch poor fishes' wand'ring eyes.

For thee, thou need'st no such deceit,
For thou thyself art thine own bait;
That fish that is not catched thereby,
Alas, is wiser far than I.

(Quoted in Orgel, S. [1971], pp. 214–15.)

J. Paulin's 'Love's Contentment' is taken from MS.Harley 6918 (fol. 92), a miscellaneous collection of poems:

Come, my Clarinda, we'll consume
Our joys no more at this low rate;
More glorious titles let's assume
And love according to our state.

For if Contentment wears a crown
Which never tyrant could assail,
How many monarchs put we down
In our Utopian commonweal?

As princes rain down golden showers
On those in whom they take delight,
So in this happier court of ours,
Each is the other's favourite.

Our privacies no eye dwells near,
But unobservèd we embrace,
And no sleek courtier's pen is there
To set down either time or place.

No midnight fears disturb our bliss,
Unless a golden dream awake us,
For care we know not what it is,
Unless to please doth careful make us.

We fear no enemy's invasion,
Our counsel's wise and politic;
With timely force, if not persuasion,
We cool the homebred schismatic.

All discontent thus to remove
What monarch boasts but thou and I?
In this content we live and love,
And in this love resolve to die:

That when, our souls together fled,
One urn shall our mixed dust enshrine,
In golden letters may be read,
Here lie Content's late King and Queen.

(Quoted in Orgel, S. [1971], pp. 215–16.)

61. For possible examples of staging of this scene see J. L. Simmons's 'Elizabethan Stage Practice and Marlowe's *The Jew of Malta*' (1971), p. 96.
62. Cunningham, K. (1990), p. 218.
63. Bartels, E. (1993), p. 8.
64. James Shapiro explains in *Shakespeare and the Jews* (1992) that Christians commonly believed that male Jews menstruated. The 'foeder Judaicus' or foul smell of male menstruation was considered an indication of Jewish unnaturalness. Shapiro notes: 'The Jewish male body was, then, a leaky body, and as such a suspect one. Again and again the Jewish man was constructed as a creature of bodily fluids: spitting, stinking, menstruating, smearing faeces on Christian symbols, constantly falling in privies.' (p. 22). Of course, this Christian prejudice is also premised on the belief that Christ shed his own blood for the Jews who allowed him to be crucified. It is only appropriate then that Jewish males should be cursed with monthly bleeding.
65. Mullaney, S. (1988), p. 58.
66. Gilman, S. L. (1985), p. 15.
67. Gilman, S. L. (1985), p. 15.
68. Gilman, S. L. (1985), pp. 15–16.
69. Bhabha, H. K. (1983), p. 18.
70. Bhabha, H. K. (1983), p. 27.
71. Tambling, J. (1991), p. 99.
72. Bhabha, H. K. (1983), p. 23.
73. Gilman, S. L. (1985), p. 18.
74. Tambling, J. (1991), p. 102.
75. Shepherd, S. (1986), p. 175.
76. Bartels, E. (1993), p. 14.
77. Nicholl, C. (1992), p. 18.

Conclusion

Words Yet Remaining

Just as this study began by quoting the introductions of a number of works about Christopher Marlowe, it will end by reciting a number of conclusions to critical studies of the dramatist:

> There is no formal conclusion to this book, says he setting out on what looks remarkably like one.
>
> Too many issues remain insufficiently theorised, insufficiently researched, to be concluded. There are problems over the relationship between doubling and narrative, the gender status of boy performers, the discourse of star actors within the meaning of plays. There are problems over the definition and self-definition of the writer within and outside the players' company, the relationship between printing and performing, the selection of an 'authoritative' text for study.
>
> S. Shepherd, Marlowe and The Politics of Elizabethan Theatre, 1986, p. 208.

> We cannot judge him [Marlowe] with any finality, partly because great writers tend to exceed our grasp whatever we think to the contrary. Also because there are considerable gaps in our knowledge. We know just enough about his life to make us feel we know everything; and his works come to us sometimes in bad texts, almost certainly incomplete. He may indeed have written the anonymous works sometimes attributed to him. Whatever play it was in which '*Mars* did mate the Carthaginians' might have altered all our ideas about his development; the 'Marlo' which the conscientious Mr Fineaux of Dover learned by heart may have been all air and fire; and if he wrote a play with a 'mad Priest of the Sun' in it it may have been the best of all. Indeed if Marlowe were to see the extant body of work by which he is remembered, he might well wonder what all the fuss was about. And no doubt he would be very surprised by our answers.
>
> J. B. Steane, Marlowe: A Critical Study, 1964, pp. 361–2.

In a few short years Marlowe made a name for himself in the Renaissance theater, creating expectations that whatever else happened, his plays would bring spectacles of strangeness to center stage. And it must have been telling to see a dramatist with such a reputation choose a subject from English history and dramatize that subject in ways similar to what he had done with more exotic types. However it was perceived, the shift was certainly subversive, evidencing what makes each of his plays so important, both as a resisting voice to a dominant trend and as an indication of how that trend was manifest. For on Marlowe's stage there is no denial of the difference within – no denial that unspeakable acts are rendered unspeakable because of us not them, that we are 'to wonder at unlawful things' in order to see the supremacy of England and of the status quo, that the darkness of the dark continent as of the worlds beyond is 'ours' rather than 'theirs'.

E. C. Bartels, *Spectacles of Strangeness*, 1993, p. 75.

'That like I best which flies beyond my reach', cries the Duke of Guise in *The Massacre at Paris*, 'Though my downfall be the deepest hell!' Marlowe was a subjective writer who put much of himself into his heroes, and these lines are more appropriate to him than to the Guise. He began works on a great design which he could not complete. Intoxicated by the celestial vistas opened by the 'new philosophy', he attempted more than he, or anyone else, could achieve. Hence, the fragmentary, passionately intense, nature of his work, and the isolated scenes of unsurpassed lyricism, which he lacked the architectonic power to build into the great structures conceived by his imagination.

P. Henderson, *Christopher Marlowe*, 1952, p. 157.

All of these endings, with the exception of Emily Bartels's, paradoxically dwell upon the impossibility of ending. Simon Shepherd complains that there are too many outstanding issues concerning the conditions of the Elizabethan theatre even to attempt a formal conclusion. Similarly, J. B. Steane observes that finality is impossible in the case of Marlowe, not only because our knowledge of his works is incomplete, but also because as a dramatist he is too great to be encapsulated in a conclusion. Adopting a slightly different approach, Philip Henderson maintains that it is the dramatist and not the critic who is incapable of ending. He protests that Marlowe's dramatic designs are too ambitious and too philosophical to enable completion. Only Emily Bartels appears confident of providing the last word on the dramatist and ironically this is because the word itself is divided and fragmentary. Hence Bartels draws her study to its close with the conclusion that Marlowe's works are united by a common notion of selfhood as disunified.

Like these critics, I too find myself in need of a conclusion. However, unlike these critics, I do not want to claim that my difficulty in ending this study derives from a lack of information about the dramatist. As this study amply proves, there is more than enough written about or by the dramatist, Christopher Marlowe, to supply some final thoughts. Conclusion is consequently not problematic because of a paucity of information but rather because of the nature of the information available. In a study whose express aim is to re-examine the plays usually attributed to Christopher Marlowe, through post-structuralist theories of language which indicate the inevitability of multivalent texts and multiple interpretations, it would surely be inappropriate to draw unproblematically a series of conclusions about the drama. For when stable and determinate knowledge is found to be unattainable, the possibility of a concerted conclusion must also be illusory. Instead, the present ending will take its lead from Sara Munson Deats's epilogue in *Sex, Gender, and Desire in the Plays of Christopher Marlowe*. Deats notes:

> In *As You Like It*, Rosalind observes that, 'If it be true that a good wine needs no bush,/Tis true that a good play needs no epilogue.' This statement, I suggest, is equally relevant to a critical text like this one. However, after her disclaimer, Rosalind proceeds to compose an epilogue, and I will follow her example, while also remembering that 'brevity is the soul of wit.'[1]

Like Deats, who notes that a critical text needs no epilogue in the very moment of writing one, the present author also denies the necessity of an ending in the process of concluding the current work. In view of the study's methodology, which endlessly destabilizes the pronouncements of critical authorities, it would be not simply irresponsible but actually contradictory to draw the present work to an unproblematic revelatory climax. Refusing to compete in the teleological quest for the 'last word' on Marlowe, then, this study will not support a claim to interpretative primacy, nor tolerate a belief that the word can ever be final or unqualified. Instead of concluding, this conclusion will look forward to other post-structuralist studies of Renaissance works which will consider the very textuality of the texts under consideration. Hence the text I am now writing can only conclude by in turn offering itself up to the attentions of re-citation. Not a hands-up surrender, however, this obeisance to textuality is more a clawing gesture which pokes quotation marks in the air. The image this study finally proffers is, appropriately, the one with which it began; placing the fingers of criticism firmly around the Marlovian canon once more, inverted commas can be drawn which literally and theoretically mark the space for further debate.

Notes

1. Deats, S. M. (1997), p. 225.

Bibliography

Abrams, M. H. *A Glossary of Literary Terms*. 1981. London: Holt, Rinehart and Winston, 1941.

Adams, Joseph Q. 'The *Massacre at Paris* Leaf'. *The Library*, 4, 14 (1933–34): 447–69.

Allen, D. C. 'Marlowe's *Dido* and the Tradition'. *Essays on Shakespeare and Elizabethan Drama in Honour of Hardin Craig*. Ed. Richard Hosley. London: Routledge & Kegan Paul Ltd, 1963, pp. 55–68.

Altman, Joel B. *The Tudor Play of Mind: Rhetorical Inquiry and the Development of Elizabethan Drama*. London: University of California Press, 1978.

Altick, Richard D. *The Scholar Adventurers*. New York: The Macmillan Co., 1960.

Anglo, Sydney. 'Evident authority and authoritative evidence: The *Malleus Maleficarum*'. *The Damned Art: Essays in the Literature of Witchcraft*. Ed. Sydney Anglo. London: Routledge & Kegan Paul, 1977, pp. 1–31.

Aristotle. *Art of Poetry: A Greek View of Poetry and Drama*. Ed. W. Hamilton Fyfe. Oxford: Clarendon Press, 1940.

Axton, Marie. *The Queen's Two Bodies: Drama and the Elizabethan Succession*. London: Royal Historical Society, 1977.

Babb, Howard S. 'Policy in Marlowe's *The Jew of Malta*'. *English Literary History*, 2, 24 (1957): 85–94.

Bacon, Francis. 'The New Organon'. *A Selection of His Works*. Ed. Sidney Warhaft. London: Macmillan & Co. Ltd, 1965, pp. 326–92.

Bakeless, John. 'Christopher Marlowe and the Newsbooks'. *Journalism Quarterly*, 1, 14 (1937): 18–22.

_____. *The Tragicall History of Christopher Marlowe*. 2 vols. Cambridge, Massachusetts: Harvard University Press, 1942.

Bartels, Emily C. 'Malta, the Jew, and the Fictions of Difference: Colonialist Discourse in Marlowe's *The Jew of Malta*'. *English Literary Renaissance*, 1, 20 (1990): 1–16.

_____. *Spectacles of Strangeness: Imperialism, Alienation and Marlowe*. Philadelphia: University of Pennsylvania Press, 1993.

Barthes, Roland. *Roland Barthes by Roland Barthes*. Trans. Richard Howard. London: Macmillan, 1977.

_____. 'The Death of the Author'. *Modern Criticism and Theory: A Reader*. Ed. David Lodge. London: Longman, 1988, pp. 167–72.

Battenhouse, Roy W. *Marlowe's 'Tamburlaine': A Study in Renaissance Moral Philosophy*. 1964. Nashville: Vanderbilt University Press, 1941.

_____. 'Protestant Apologetics and the Subplot of *2 Tamburlaine*'. *English Literary Renaissance*, 3 (1973): 30–43.

Bawcutt, N. W. 'Machiavelli and Marlowe's *The Jew of Malta*.' *Renaissance Drama*, n.s., 3 (1970): 3–49.

_____, ed. *The Jew of Malta*. By Christopher Marlowe. The Revels Plays. Manchester: Manchester University Press, 1978.

Benaquist, Lawrence Michael. *The Tripartite Structure of Christopher Marlowe's Tamburlaine Plays and 'Edward II'*. Salzburg Studies in English Literature. Elizabethan and Renaissance Studies, 43. Salzburg: Institut für Englische Sprache und Literatur, 1975.

Bennett, H. S., ed. *The Jew of Malta and The Massacre at Paris*. By Christopher Marlowe. London: Methuen & Co. Ltd, 1931.

Bennington, Geoff. 'Demanding History'. *Post-Structuralism and the Question of History*. Eds. Derek Attridge, Geoff Bennington and Robert Young. Cambridge: Cambridge University Press, 1987, pp. 15–29.

Berek, Peter. '*Tamburlaine*'s Weak Sons: Imitation as Interpretation before 1593'. *Renaissance Drama*, n.s., 13 (1982): 55–82.

Bergonzi, Bernard. *Exploding English: Criticism, Theory, Culture*. Oxford: Clarendon Press, 1990.

Bevington, David M. *From 'Mankind' to Marlowe: Growth of Structure in the Popular Drama of Tudor England*. London: Oxford University Press, 1962.

Bevington, David and Eric Rasmussen, eds. *Doctor Faustus: A- and B-texts (1604, 1616)*. By Christopher Marlowe. The Revels Plays. Manchester: Manchester University Press, 1993.

Bhabha, Homi K. 'The Other Question ... The Stereotype and Colonial Discourse.' *Screen*, 4, 24 (1983): 18–36.

Bloom, Harold. *The Anxiety of Influence: A Theory of Poetry*. New York: Oxford University Press, 1973.

Boas, Frederick S. *Christopher Marlowe: A Biographical and Critical Study*. Oxford: Clarendon Press, 1940.

Bowers, Fredson, ed. *The Complete Works of Christopher Marlowe*. By Christopher Marlowe. 2 vols. Cambridge: Cambridge University Press, 1973.

Bredbeck, Gregory W. *Sodomy and Interpretation: Marlowe to Milton*. London: Cornell University Press, 1991.

Brennan, Michael. *Literary Patronage in the English Renaissance: The Pembroke Family*. London: Routledge, 1988.

Briggs, Julia. 'Marlowe's *Massacre at Paris*: A Reconsideration'. *The Review of English Studies*, n.s., 34 (1983): 257–78.

Briggs, W. D., ed. *Edward II*. By Christopher Marlowe. London: David Nutt, 1914.

Burgess, Anthony. *A Dead Man in Deptford*. London: Vintage, 1993.

Campbell, Lily B., ed. *The Mirror for Magistrates*. Cambridge: Cambridge University Press, 1938.

Cardozo, J. L. *The Contemporary Jew in the Elizabethan Drama*. Amsterdam: H. J. Paris, 1925.

Cartelli, Thomas. 'Endless Play: The False Starts of Marlowe's *Jew of Malta*'. *'A Poet and a filthy Play-maker': New Essays on Christopher Marlowe*. Eds Kenneth Friedenreich, Roma Gill and Constance B. Kuriyama. New York: AMS Press Inc., 1988, pp. 117–28.

Chambers, E. K. *The Elizabethan Stage*. 4 vols. Oxford: Clarendon Press, 1923.

Charlton, H. B. and R. D. Waller, eds. *Edward II*. By Christopher Marlowe. London: Methuen & Co. Ltd, 1930.

Collier, John Payne., ed. *A Select Collection of Old Plays*. 12 vols. London: Septimus Prowett, 1825, vol. 8.

_____. *The History of English Dramatic Poetry to the Time of Shakespeare and Annals of the Stage to the Restoration*. 3 vols. London: John Murray, 1831, vol. 3.

Collinson, Patrick. 'The Monarchical Republic of Queen Elizabeth I'. *Bulletin of the John Rylands University Library of Manchester*, 69 (1987): 394–424.

Colie, Rosalie L. *The Resources of Kind: Genre-Theory in the Renaissance*. Ed. Barbara K. Lewalski. London: California University Press, 1973.

Connor, Steven. *Samuel Beckett: Repetition, Theory and Text*. Oxford: Basil Blackwell Ltd, 1988.

Cook, Albert. *History/Writing*. Cambridge: Cambridge University Press, 1988.

Cooper, Lane. *An Aristotelian Theory of Comedy, with an Adaptation of the Poetics*. New York: Howarth, 1922.

Court, Franklin E. *Institutionalizing English Literature: The Culture and Politics of Literary Study 1750–1900*. Stanford, California: Stanford University Press, 1992.

Craik, T. W., ed. *The Jew of Malta*. By Christopher Marlowe. New Mermaids. London: A & C Black, 1966.

Croft, P. J. *Autograph Poetry in the English Language*. 2 vols. London: Cassell, 1973.

Culler, Jonathan. *On Deconstruction: Theory and Criticism after Structuralism*. London: Routledge & Kegan Paul, 1983.

Cunningham, J. S., ed. *Tamburlaine the Great*. By Christopher Marlowe. Revels Plays. Manchester: Manchester University Press, 1981.

Cunningham, Karen. 'Renaissance Execution and Marlovian Elocution: The Drama of Death'. *Proceedings of the Modern Languages Association*, 2, 105 (1990): 209–22.

Cutts, J. P. 'The Ultimate Source of Tamburlaine's White, Red, Black and Death?' *Notes and Queries*, 203 (1985): 146–7.

Dabbs, Thomas. *Reforming Marlowe: The Nineteenth-Century Canonization of a Renaissance Dramatist*. London: Associated University Presses, 1991.

Davis, Natalie Zemon. 'The Rites of Violence: Religious Riot in Sixteenth-Century France'. *The Massacre of St. Bartholomew: Reappraisals and Documents*. Ed. Alfred Soman. The Hague: Martinus Nijhoff, 1974, pp. 203–42.

Deats, Sara Munson. *Sex, Gender, and Desire in the Plays of Christopher Marlowe*. London: Associated University Presses, 1997.

Derrida, Jacques. 'Différance'. *Speech and Phenomena: And Other Essays on Husserl's Theory of Signs*. Trans. David B. Allison. Evanston: Northwestern University Press, 1973, pp. 129–60.

_____. *Of Grammatology*. Trans. Gayatri Chakravorty Spivak. London: The Johns Hopkins University Press, 1974.

_____. 'Freud and the Scene of Writing'. *Writing and Difference*. Trans. Alan Bass. London: Routledge & Kegan Paul Ltd, 1978, pp. 196–231.

_____. 'The Law of Genre'. *Acts of Literature*. Ed. and Trans. Derek Attridge. London: Routledge, 1992, pp. 221–52.

De Serres, Jean. *The Three Partes of Commentaries ... of the Civill Warres of France 1572*. Trans. Thomas Timme. 1574.

Dickens, A. G. 'The Elizabethans and St. Bartholomew'. *The Massacre of St. Bartholomew: Reappraisals and Documents*. Ed. Alfred Soman. The Hague: Martinus Nijhoff, 1974, pp. 52–70.

Dubrow, Heather. *Genre*. The Critical Idiom. London: Methuen & Co. Ltd, 1982.

Dupré, Louis. *Passage to Modernity: An Essay in the Hermeneutics of Nature and Culture*. London: Yale University Press, 1993.

Dutton, Richard. 'Marlowe and Shakespeare: Censorship and Construction'. *The Yearbook of English Studies*, 23 (1993): 1–29.

Eagleton, Terry. *Literary Theory: An Introduction*. Oxford: Basil Blackwell, 1983.

Eco, Umberto. *The Name of the Rose*. Trans. William Weaver. London: Pan Books Ltd, 1984.

Eisenstein, Elizabeth L. *The Printing Press as an Agent of Change: Communications and Cultural Transformations in Early-Modern Europe*. 2 vols. Cambridge: Cambridge University Press, 1979.

Eliot, T. S. *The Sacred Wood: Essays on Poetry and Criticism*. London: Methuen & Co. Ltd, 1920.

Elsky, Martin. *Authorizing Words: Speech, Writing, and Print in the English Renaissance*. London: Cornell University Press, 1989.

Foucault, Michel. 'What is an Author?' *Textual Strategies: Perspectives in Post-Structuralist Criticism*. Ed. Josue V. Harari. London: Methuen & Co. Ltd, 1980, pp. 141–60.

Fowler, Alastair. *Kinds of Literature: An Introduction to the Theory of Genres and Modes*. Oxford: Clarendon Press, 1982.

Foxe, John. *The Acts and Monuments*. Revised Rev. Josiah Pratt. 4th edn. 8 vols. London: The Religious Tract Society, 1877.

Freer, Coburn. 'Lies and Lying in *The Jew of Malta*'. *'A Poet and a filthy Play-maker': New Essays on Christopher Marlowe*. Ed. Kenneth Friedenreich, Roma Gill and Constance B. Kuriyama. New York: AMS Press Inc., 1988, pp. 143–65.

Friedenreich, Kenneth. 'Marlowe Criticism and *On the Origin of Species*'. *Christopher Marlowe: An Annotated Bibliography of Criticism Since 1950*. London: The Scarecrow Press Inc., 1979, pp. 1–17.

Friedenreich, Kenneth, Roma Gill, and Constance B. Kuriyama, eds. *'A Poet and a filthy Play-maker': New Essays on Christopher Marlowe*. New York: AMS Press Inc., 1988.

Frye, Northrop. *Anatomy of Criticism: Four Essays*. Princeton: Princeton University Press, 1957.

Gaskell, Ian. '*2 Tamburlaine*: Marlowe's "War against the Gods"'. *English Studies in Canada*, 2, 11 (1985): 178–92.

Gatti, Hilary. *The Renaissance Drama of Knowledge: Giordano Bruno in England*. London: Routledge, 1989.

Geckle, George L., ed. *Tamburlaine and Edward II: Text and Performance*. Basingstoke: Macmillan Education Ltd, 1988.

Gentillet, Innocent. *A Discourse upon the Means of Wel Governing and Maintaining in good Peace, A Kingdome, or other Principalitie ... Against Nicholas Machiavelli the Florentine*. Trans. Simon Patericke. 1602.

Gibbons, Brian. '"Unstable Proteus": *The Tragedy of Dido Queen of Carthage*'. *Christopher Marlowe*. Ed. Brian Morris. Mermaid Critical Commentaries. London: Ernest Benn Ltd, 1968, pp. 25–46.

Gill, Roma, ed. 'Dido Queene of Carthage'. *The Complete Works of Christopher Marlowe: The Translations*. By Christopher Marlowe. Oxford: Clarendon Press, 1987, vol. 1, pp. 113–74.

_____, ed. *Doctor Faustus*. By Christopher Marlowe. Oxford: Clarendon Press, 1990.

Gilman, Sander L. *Difference and Pathology: Stereotypes of Sexuality, Race, and Madness*. London: Cornell University Press, 1985.

Goldschmidt, E. P. *Gothic and Renaissance Bookbindings*. 2 vols. London: Ernest Benn Ltd, 1928, vol. 1.

Goulart, Simon. *Mémoires de l'estat de France*. 3 vols. 1576.

Grantley, Darryll, and Peter Roberts, eds. *Christopher Marlowe and English Renaissance Culture*. Aldershot: Scolar Press, 1996.

Greg, W. W., ed. *Marlowe's Doctor Faustus 1604–1616*. By Christopher Marlowe. Oxford: Clarendon Press, 1950.

Greenblatt, Stephen. 'Marlowe and the Will to Absolute Play'. *Renaissance Self-Fashioning: From More to Shakespeare*. London: University of Chicago Press, 1980, pp. 193–221.

Greene, Thomas M. *The Light in Troy: Imitation and Discovery in Renaissance Poetry*. London: Yale University Press, 1982.

Guillory, John. *Cultural Capital: The Problem of Literary Canon Formation*. London: University of Chicago Press, 1993.

Gurr, Andrew. *Playgoing in Shakespeare's London*. Cambridge: Cambridge University Press, 1987.

Guy, John. *Tudor England*. Oxford: Oxford University Press, 1988.

Guy-Bray, Stephen. 'Homophobia and the Depoliticizing of *Edward II*'. *English Studies in Canada*, 2, 17 (1991): 125–33.

Hamilton, Donna B. *Shakespeare and the Politics of Protestant England*. London: Harvester Wheatsheaf, 1992.

Harper, J. W., ed. *Tamburlaine*. By Christopher Marlowe. New Mermaids. 1984. London: A. & C. Black Publishers Ltd, 1971.

Hattaway, Michael. 'The Theology of Marlowe's *Doctor Faustus*'. *Renaissance Drama*, n.s., 3 (1970): 51–78.

_____. *Elizabethan Popular Theatre: Plays in Performance*. London: Routledge & Kegan Paul, 1982.

Healy, Thomas. *New Latitudes: Theory and English Renaissance Literature*. London: Edward Arnold, 1992.

_____. *Christopher Marlowe*. Plymouth: Northcote House Publishers Ltd, 1994.

Henderson, Philip. *Christopher Marlowe*. 1974. Brighton: The Harvester Press Ltd, 1952.

Henradi, Paul. *Beyond Genre: New Directions in Literary Classification*. London: Cornell University Press, 1972.

Heywood, Thomas. *The Captives*. Ed. Arthur Brown. The Malone Society Reprints. Oxford: Oxford University Press, 1953.

Hillebrand, Harold Newcomb. 'The Child Actor: A Chapter in Elizabethan Stage History'. *University of Illinois Studies in Language and Literature*, 1, 11 (1926): 1–356.

Hilton, Della. *Who Was Kit Marlowe?: The Story of the Poet and Playwright*. London: Weidenfeld & Nicolson, 1977.

Hoby, Thomas, trans. *The Courtier of Count Baldesar Castilio*. 1588.

Holinshed, Raphael. *The Laste Volume of the Chronicles of England, Scotlande, and Irelande*. London: Lucas, 1577.

Hopkins, Lisa. '"Lear, Lear, Lear!": Marlowe, Shakespeare, and the Third'. *The Upstart Crow*, 16 (1996): 108–23.

Hotman, François. *A True and Plaine Report of the Furious Outrages of France*. 1573.

Howell, Wilbur Samuel. *Logic and Rhetoric in England, 1500–1700*. Princeton, New Jersey: Princeton University Press, 1956.

Hunter, G. K. *John Lyly: The Humanist as Courtier*. London: Routledge & Kegan Paul, 1962.

_____. 'The Theology of Marlowe's *The Jew of Malta*'. *Journal of the Warburg & Courtauld Institutes*, 27 (1964): 211–40.

Ive, Paul. *The Practise of Fortification*. 1589.

Jardine, Lisa and Anthony Grafton. '"Studied for Action": How Gabriel Harvey Read his Livy'. *Past and Present*, 129 (1990): 30–78.

Jump, John D., ed. *Doctor Faustus*. By Christopher Marlowe. Revels Plays. 1990. Manchester: Manchester University Press, 1962.

_____, ed. *Tamburlaine the Great Parts I and II*. By Christopher Marlowe. London: Edward Arnold, 1967.

Keefer, Michael H., ed. *Doctor Faustus: A 1604-Version Edition*. By Christopher Marlowe. Ontario: Broadview Press Ltd, 1991.

Kelly, Henry Angsar. *Divine Providence in the England of Shakespeare's Histories*. London: Oxford University Press, 1970.

Kelsall, Malcolm. *Christopher Marlowe*. Leiden: E. J. Brill, 1981.

Kermode, Frank. *History and Value: The Clarendon Lectures and the Northcliffe Lectures 1987*. Oxford: Clarendon Press, 1989.

Kingdon, Robert M. *Myths about the St. Bartholomew's Day Massacres 1572–1576*. Cambridge, Massachusetts: Harvard University Press, 1988.

_____. 'Reactions to the St. Bartholomew Massacres in Geneva and Rome'. *The Massacre of St. Bartholomew: Reappraisals and Documents*. Ed. Alfred Soman. The Hague: Martinus Nijhoff, 1974, pp. 25–39.

Kocher, Paul H. 'François Hotman and Marlowe's *The Massacre at Paris*'. *Proceedings of the Modern Languages Association*, 1, 56 (1941): 349–68.

_____. *Christopher Marlowe: A Study of his Thought, Learning, and Character*. Chapel Hill: University of North Carolina Press, 1946.

_____. 'Contemporary Pamphlet Backgrounds for Marlowe's *The Massacre at Paris*'. *Modern Language Quarterly*, 2, 8 (1947): 151–73.

Kristeller, Paul Oskar. *Renaissance Thought and the Arts: Collected Essays*. Princeton: Princeton University Press, 1990.

Kronick, Joseph. 'Emerson and the Question of Reading/Writing'. *Genre*, 3, 14 (1981): 363–81.

Kuriyama, Constance Brown. *Hammer or Anvil: Psychological Patterns in Christopher Marlowe's Plays*. New Brunswick, New Jersey: Rutgers University Press, 1980.

Kyd, Thomas. *The Spanish Tragedy*. Ed. J. R. Mulryne. New Mermaids. London: A. & C. Black, 1970.

Lake, D. J. 'Three Seventeenth-Century Revisions: *Thomas of Woodstock*, *The Jew of Malta*, and *Faustus B*'. *Notes and Queries*, n.s., 2, 30 (1983): 133–43.

Larner, Christina. *Witchcraft and Religion: The Politics of Popular Belief*. Ed. Alan Macfarlane. Oxford: Basil Blackwell, 1984.

Leech, Clifford. *Christopher Marlowe: Poet for the Stage*. Ed. Anne Lancashire. New York: AMS Press Inc., 1986.

LePage, Peter V. 'The Search for Godhead in Marlowe's *Tamburlaine*'. *College English*, 8, 26 May 1965: 604–9.

Levin, Harry. *Christopher Marlowe: The Overreacher*. London: Faber & Faber Ltd, 1961.

Logeman, H., ed. *The English Faust Book of 1592*. Trans. P. F. Gent. Amsterdam: Schroder, 1900.

Lom, Herbert. *Enter a Spy: The Double Life of Christopher Marlowe*. London: Merlin Press, 1978.

Lydgate, John. *Lydgate's Troy Book A.D. 1412–1430*. Ed. Henry Bergen. London: Kegan Paul, Trench, Trubner & Co. Ltd, 1906.

Macherey, Pierre. *A Theory of Literary Production*. Trans. Geoffrey Wall. London: Routledge & Kegan Paul, 1978.

Machiavelli, Niccolò. *The Discourses*. Ed. Bernard Crick. Trans. Leslie J. Walker. Harmondsworth: Penguin Books Ltd, 1970.

_____. *The Prince*. Ed. Peter Bondanella. Trans. Peter Bondanella and Mark Musa. Oxford: Oxford University Press, 1984.

Maclure, Millar, ed. *Marlowe: The Critical Heritage 1588–1896*. London: Routledge & Kegan Paul, 1979.

Maguire, Liam. *Icarus Flying: The Tragical Story of Christopher Marlowe*. Surrey: Ormond Books, 1993.

Mallon, Thomas. *Stolen Words: Forays into the Origins and Ravages of Plagiarism*. New York: Ticknor & Fields, 1989.

Marcus, Leah S. 'Textual Indeterminacy and Ideological Difference: The Case of *Dr Faustus*'. *Renaissance Drama*, n.s., 2 (1989): 1–29.

Marlowe, Christopher. *The Tragedie of Dido Queene of Carthage*. 1594.

_____. *The Massacre at Paris*. Ed. W. W. Greg. Malone Society Reprints. Oxford: Oxford University Press, 1928.

Martin, Richard A. 'Marlowe's *Tamburlaine* and the language of Romance.' *Proceedings of the Modern Languages Association*, 2, 93 (1978): 248–64.

_____. 'Fate, Seneca, and Marlowe's *Dido Queen of Carthage*'. *Renaissance Drama*, n.s., 11 (1980): 45–66.

Maxwell, J. C. 'How bad is the text of *The Jew of Malta*?' *Modern Language Review*, 48 (1953): 435–8.

Mazzeo, Joseph Anthony. *Renaissance and Revolution: The Remaking of European Thought*. London: Martin Secker and Warburg Ltd, 1967.

McGann, Jerome J. *A Critique of Modern Textual Criticism*. London: Chicago University Press, 1983.

McMurtrie, Douglas C. *The Book: The Story of Printing and Bookmaking*. London: Oxford University Press, 1943.

Meltzer, Françoise. *Hot Property: The Stakes and Claims of Literary Originality.* London: University of Chicago Press, 1994.

Merchant, W. M., ed. *Edward II.* By Christopher Marlowe. New Mermaid. London: A. & C. Black, 1967.

Metzidakis, Stamos. *Repetition and Semiotics: Interpreting Prose Poems.* Birmingham, Alabama: Summa Publications Inc, 1986.

Montaigne, Michel de. 'On Repenting'. *Montaigne's Essays.* Trans. Michael A. Screech. Harmondsworth: Penguin, 1991.

Muir, Kenneth. 'Marlowe and Shakespeare.' *'A Poet and a filthy Playmaker': New Essays on Christopher Marlowe.* Ed. Kenneth Friedenreich, Roma Gill and Constance B. Kuriyama. New York: AMS Press Inc., 1988, pp. 1–12.

Mullaney, Steven. *The Place of the Stage: License, Play and Power in Renaissance England.* London: Chicago University Press, 1988.

Murray, John Tucker. *English Dramatic Companies: 1558–1642.* 2 vols. London: Constable & Company Ltd, 1910.

Nashe, Thomas. 'Summer's Last Will and Testament'. *The Unfortunate Traveller: and Other Works.* Ed. J. B. Steane. 1987. London: Penguin Books Ltd, 1972, pp. 146–207.

Nicholl, Charles. *The Reckoning: The Murder of Christopher Marlowe.* London: Jonathan Cape, 1992.

Norris, Christopher. *Derrida.* Modern Masters. London, Hammersmith: Fontana Press, 1987.

Nosworthy, J. M. 'The Marlowe Manuscript'. *The Library*, 4, 26 (1945–46): 158–71.

Oliver, H. J., ed. *Dido Queen of Carthage and The Massacre at Paris.* By Christopher Marlowe. Revels Plays. London: Methuen & Co. Ltd, 1968.

O'Neill, Judith, ed. *Critics on Marlowe.* London: George Allen & Unwin Ltd, 1969.

Orgel, Stephen, ed. *The Complete Poems and Translations.* By Christopher Marlowe. Harmondsworth: Penguin Books Ltd, 1971.

Ormerod, David and Christopher Wortham, eds. *Doctor Faustus: The A-Text.* By Christopher Marlowe. Nedlands: Western Australia University Press, 1985.

Palmer, Philip Mason and Robert Pattison More, eds. *The Sources of the Faust Tradition: From Simon Magus to Lessing.* New York: Oxford University Press, 1936.

Parkes, M. B. *Pause and Effect: An Introduction to the History of Punctuation in the West.* Aldershot: Scolar Press, 1992.

Perlina, Nina. *Varieties of Poetic Utterance: Quotation in the Brothers Karamazov.* London: University Press of America, 1985.

Plato. *The Republic.* Trans. Richard W. Sterling and William C. Scott. London: W. W. Norton & Co., 1985.

Proser, Matthew N. '*Dido Queen of Carthage* and the Evolution of Marlowe's Dramatic Style'. *'A Poet and a filthy Play-maker': New Essays on Christopher Marlowe.* Ed. Kenneth Friedenreich, Roma Gill and Constance B. Kuriyama. New York: AMS Press Inc., 1988, pp. 83–97.

Quint, David. *Origin and Originality in Renaissance Literature: Versions of the Source.* London: Yale University Press, 1983.

Raab, Felix. *The English Face of Machiavelli: A Changing Interpretation 1500–1700.* London: Routledge & Kegan Paul, 1964.

Ramus, Peter. *The Logike.* 1574.

Ribner, Irving. *The English History Play in the Age of Shakespeare*. London: Oxford University Press, 1957.

Richards, Susan. 'Marlowe's *Tamburlaine II*: A Drama of Death'. *Modern Language Quarterly*, 26 (1965): 375–87.

Rocklin, Edward L. 'Marlowe as Experimental Dramatist: The Role of the Audience in *The Jew of Malta*'. *'A Poet and a filthy Play-maker': New Essays on Christopher Marlowe*. Eds. Kenneth Friedenreich, Roma Gill and Constance B. Kuriyama. New York: AMS Press Inc., 1988, pp. 129–42.

Rowse, A. L. *Christopher Marlowe: A Biography*. 1981. London: Macmillan Press Ltd, 1964.

Said, Edward W. *Orientalism*. New York: Vintage Books, 1979.

Sales, Roger. *Christopher Marlowe*. English Dramatists. Basingstoke: Macmillan Education Ltd, 1991.

Sanders, Wilbur. *The Dramatist and the Received Idea: Studies in the Plays of Marlowe and Shakespeare*. Cambridge: Cambridge University Press, 1968.

Sartiliot, Claudette. *Citation and Modernity: Derrida, Joyce, and Brecht*. London: University of Oklahoma Press, 1993.

Schumaker, Wayne. *The Occult Sciences in the Renaissance: A Study in Intellectual Patterns*. London: California University Press, 1972.

Scot, Reginald. *The Discoverie of Witchcraft (1584)*. Ed. Rev. Montague Summers. Great Britain: John Rodker, 1930.

Shakespeare, William. *Richard III*. Ed. Antony Hammond. The Arden Shakespeare. London: Methuen, 1981.

———. 'The Tragedy of Hamlet, Prince of Denmark'. *The Complete Works*. Ed. Stanley Wells and Gary Taylor. Oxford: Clarendon Press, 1988.

Shapiro, James. *Shakespeare and the Jews*. The Parkes Lecture. Southampton: Southampton University Press, 1992.

Shapiro, Michael. *The Children of the Revels: The Boy Companies of Shakespeare's Time and their Plays*. New York: Columbia University Press, 1977.

Shepherd, Simon. *Marlowe and the Politics of Elizabethan Theatre*. Brighton: Harvester Press Ltd, 1986.

The Shorter Oxford English Dictionary on Historical Principles. 3rd edn. Ed. C. T. Onions. Oxford: Clarendon Press, 1944.

Sidney, Philip. *A Defence of Poetry*. Ed. Jan Van Dorsten. Oxford: Oxford University Press, 1966.

Simmons, J. L. 'Elizabethan Stage Practice and Marlowe's *The Jew of Malta*'. *Renaissance Drama*, n.s., 4 (1971): 93–104.

Smeed, J. W. *Faust in Literature*. London: Oxford University Press, 1975.

Smith, Mary Elizabeth. *'Love Kindling Fire': A Study of Christopher Marlowe's The Tragedy of Dido Queen of Carthage*. Salzburg Studies in English Literature. Elizabethan & Renaissance Studies, 63. Salzburg: Institut für Englische Sprache und Literatur, 1977.

Sprenger, James and Henry Kramer. *Malleus Maleficarum (1484)*. Trans, Rev. Montague Summers. Great Britain: John Rodker, 1928.

Steane, J. B. *Marlowe: A Critical Study*. Cambridge: Cambridge University Press, 1964.

Stow, John. *A Summarie of Englyshe Chronicles*. 1565.

_____. *A Summarie of the Chronicles of England*. 1575.

_____. *A Summarie of the Chronicles of England*. 1590.

Summers, Claude J. *Christopher Marlowe and the Politics of Power*. Salzburg Studies in English Literature. Elizabethan and Renaissance Studies, 22. Salzburg: Institut für Englische Sprache und Literatur, 1974.

Tambling, Jeremy. 'Abigail's Party: "The Difference of Things" in *The Jew of Malta*'. *Another Country: Feminist Perspectives on Renaissance Drama*. Ed. Dorothea Kehler and Susan Baker. London: The Scarecrow Press Inc., 1991, pp. 95–112.

Thomas, Vivien and William Tydeman, ed. *Christopher Marlowe: The Plays and their Sources*. London: Routledge, 1994.

Thurn, David H. 'Sovereignty, Disorder and Fetishism in Marlowe's *Edward II*'. *Renaissance Drama*, n.s., 21 (1990): 115–41.

Tucker Brooke, C. F., ed. *The Life of Marlowe and The Tragedy of Dido Queen of Carthage*. By Christopher Marlowe. London: Methuen & Co. Ltd, 1930.

Tyler, Sharon. 'Bedfellows Make Strange Politics: Christopher Marlowe's *Edward II*'. *Drama, Sex and Politics*. Ed. James Redmond. Themes in Drama, 7. Cambridge: Cambridge University Press, 1985, pp. 55–68.

Udall, Nicholas, trans. *The Paraphrase of Erasmus upon the Newe Testamente*. 1548.

Urry, William. *Christopher Marlowe and Canterbury*. London: Faber & Faber, 1988.

Virgil. *Aeneid*. Ed. and trans., H. Rushton Fairclough. London and Cambridge, Massachusetts: Loeb, 1974.

Warren, Michael J. 'The Old Man and the Text'. *English Literary Renaissance*, 2, 2 (1981): 111–47.

Weil, Judith. *Christopher Marlowe: Merlin's Prophet*. Cambridge: Cambridge University Press, 1977.

Wells, Stanley and Gary Taylor, eds. 'To the Great Variety of Readers'. By John Heminges and Henry Condell. *The Complete Works*. By William Shakespeare. Oxford: Clarendon Press, 1988.

Whelan, Peter. *The School of Night*. London: Warner Chappell Plays, 1992.

Wilson, Richard. *Will Power:Essays on Shakespearean Authority*. New York: Harvester Wheatsheaf, 1993.

Wilson, Robert. *The Three Ladies of London 1584*. Malone Society Reprints. Oxford: Oxford University Press, 1911.

Winny, James, ed. *Elizabethan Prose Translation*. Cambridge: Cambridge University Press, 1960.

Wittgenstein, Ludwig. *Philosophical Investigations*. Trans. G. E. M. Anscombe. Oxford: Basil Blackwell, 1953.

Wooden, Warren W. 'Childermass Ceremonies in Late Medieval England: The Literary Legacy'. *Fifteenth-Century Studies*, 4 (1981): 195–205.

_____. *John Foxe*. Boston: Twayne Publishers, 1983.

Wraight, A. D. and Virginia F. Stern. *In Search of Christopher Marlowe: A Pictorial Biography*. 1993. Chichester: Adam Hart (Publishers) Ltd, 1965.

Wyler, S. 'Marlowe's Technique of Communicating with his Audience, as Seen in his *Tamburlaine* Part I'. *English Studies*, 4, 48 (1967): 306–16.

Young, Edward. *Conjectures on Original Composition.* Ed. Edith J. Morley. Manchester: Manchester University Press, 1918.
Zunder, William. *Elizabethan Marlowe.* Cottingham: Unity Press Ltd, 1994.

Index

Printed and bound by CPI Group (UK) Ltd, Croydon, CR0 4YY

01/05/2025

01858342-0016